A HIKING GUIDE TO THE NATIONAL PARKS & HISTORIC SITES OF NEWFOUNDLAND

A HIKING GUIDE TO

THE NATIONAL PARKS & HISTORIC SITES OF

NEWFOUNDLAND

BARBARA MARYNIAK

GOOSE LANE

Published by Goose Lane Editions with the assistance of the
Canada Council, 1994.

Cover photograph by Jamie Steeves, "James Callaghan Trail,"
courtesy of the Canadian Parks Service.
Back cover photograph by Dayle Cammaert.
Book design by Brenda Berry.
Maps provided by Cold Ocean Design Associates.

Printed and bound in Canada by Gagné Printing.

10 9 8 7 6 5 4 3

Canadian Cataloguing in Publication Data

Maryniak, Barbara, 1954-
  A hiking guide to the national parks and historic sites
  of Newfoundland
  Includes bibliographical references and index.
  ISBN 0-86492-150-0

1. Trails — Newfoundland — Guidebooks.
2. Hiking — Newfoundland — Guidebooks.
3. Newfoundland — Guidebooks. I. Title

GV199.44.C22N56 1994 &96.5'1'09718 C94-950065-8

Goose Lane Editions
469 King Street
Fredericton, New Brunswick
Canada E3B 1E5

This book is dedicated to the people of Newfoundland, and to all of those who helped write it.

CONTENTS

PREFACE

When my family and I moved to St. John's from England in 1989, one of the things we most looked forward to was getting out and seeing Newfoundland — experiencing the space and emptiness, breathing the fresh, clean air and hiking in the National Parks. We thought we would find lots of books about hiking to help us choose our trails, but much to our chagrin we found very little, and what we did find was often confusing.

I started gathering bits and pieces of information about the parks and making my own notes. I collected anything I could lay my hands on about their history, flora and fauna, and trails. Given my notoriously bad memory, I wanted to have everything in one place, easily accessible and preferably in my pocket. The idea of a book was a natural progression.

Support from my family, friends and even strangers drove me on. They were especially kind after my manuscript, disks, copies, backups, notes, references and names were lost in a dramatic house fire three weeks before my submission deadline in December 1992. Three years of work was lost amongst the charred remains, not to mention the house and everything in it. It is thanks to Goose Lane Editions and their special support that the book was rewritten. They gave hope and sent kind words and warming packages at a very difficult time.

Almost exactly a year has passed and the manuscript has risen out of the smouldering ashes. The park superintendents and their staffs sent me information once again (unfortunately much of it is without names or sources and is therefore not included in the bibliography), and the book has once more taken shape. I must thank the park staff members who were lumbered with rereading the clumsy preliminary drafts. I hope I have been sensitive to their comments.

When all seemed doom and gloom and the maps' future became uncertain, Cold Ocean Design Associates in St. John's stepped in to save the day. I am extremely grateful for their long hours of hard work.

I have racked my appalling memory and searched through the library computers, shelves and archives to find all the references I used. I have been successful with some but others have eluded me, lost by the fire forever. Nevertheless, I would like to acknowledge those unknown sources.

As for the hikers, I have to thank all my friends and family who either volunteered or were cajoled into walking and rewalking all the trails with me as I mumbled into my dictaphone, took photos and made notes. Some are friends and neighbours in Newfoundland, others came on holiday from England or Belgium to find themselves dragged out on the trails, still others made special trips from England or across the island to accompany and support me. I thank them all.

Last, but not least, a special word of thanks needs to go to my long-suffering husband for his sturdy shoulder and unwavering belief in me. Not to mention the "computer technical support," without which I would have been lost, and the cordon bleu catering services (both in the field and at home), without which I and our two daughters would have gone hungry.

This book has followed a long and arduous path on its way to the book stores. It may be my name on the cover, but it is thanks to the combined effort of many people that it finally got there. Thank you all.

BM 1993

INTRODUCTION

A rocky island fortress projecting out of the cold Atlantic Ocean off the east coast of Canada, Newfoundland is the youngest province in the family of Confederation, and yet the oldest part of the country to be inhabited by Europeans. For 500 years its way of life has been governed by the fishery, and although it is a harsh land (erroneously reputed as enshrouded in fog the whole year round), a rugged beauty possesses this island of rock with its endless forests of thin scraggly trees, countless bogs and mile upon mile of coves, inlets and bays. The people speak with a delightful accent somewhere between a rich Irish brogue and a mainland North American drawl, and the island is featured in books with such forbidding titles as *This Marvellous, Terrible Place* and *Come Near At Your Peril*, but then turns up next to Bahrain in *Island gods — Exploring the World's Most Exotic Islands*. The island of Newfoundland is a place of bizarre and wonderful dichotomies.

What is this place they call the "New Founde Land"? Why does it stir such strong emotions in those who live there? Why did Joey Smallwood (one-time premier of the province) reject the notion of an "ex-Newfoundlander," professing passionately that "once a Newfoundlander, always a Newfoundlander"? Why if you are not born on the island, will you never be considered a true Newfoundlander? Why do so many "Come From Aways" (or CFAs, which is the local expression for outsiders who live on the island) leave after a few years of battling hori-

Map 1: NEWFOUNDLAND OVERVIEW

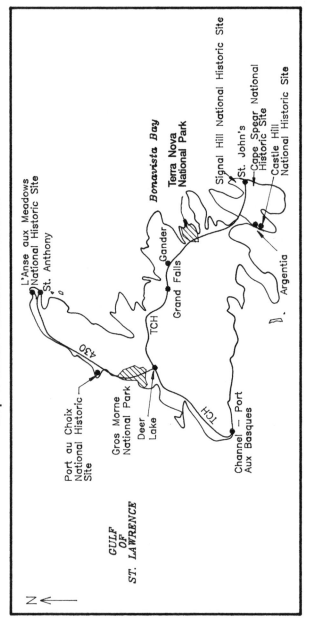

L'Anse aux Meadows National Historic Site

St. Anthony

Port au Choix National Historic Site

Gros Morne National Park

Deer Lake

430

TCH

GULF OF ST. LAWRENCE

N ←

Channel — Port Aux Basques

TCH

Grand Falls

Gander

Bonavista Bay

Terra Nova National Park

Argentia

Signal Hill National Historic Site

St. John's

Cape Spear National Historic Site

Castle Hill National Historic Site

zontal rains and refreezing snows? Why do so many Newfoundlanders leave in search of jobs, yet find themselves unable to cut the umbilical cord to the island?

From the first day that I arrived in St. John's, the island has intrigued me. St. John's looks like part of Canada, albeit a poorer, less-sophisticated part. The people look the same, the same supermarket and drug chains are found there: McDonald's, A & W and Burger King reign supreme, as do the K Marts and Zellers. Yes, the pace is slower, the paintwork is chipping and the potholes are notorious. There is a unemployment rate of a little more than 20% (this is the official figure, but recent calculations by the *Evening Telegram,* which include all the people who have even stopped looking for work, puts the figure closer to 63%). Newfoundland is a "have not" region, its future uncertain, but it is quite identifiable as Canada. And yet, as I look closer, the narrow streets of downtown St. John's, the clusters of colourful houses on exposed rocky headlands, the tiny harbours with their piles of lobster pots, the songs of sealing and fishing begin to invade my pores. Newfoundland changes you. It is Canada, but it is different, very different. There is no place quite like it. It is a "distinct society" just as much as Quebec is. The longer I live here, the more obvious this becomes.

Newfoundlanders are tough, hardy people with a heritage of struggling and surviving. For hundreds of years they have lived in tiny outports that cling to inhospitable headlands and fished seas that are as ruthless as they have been fruitful. In many ways their lives have not changed much over the years. Their strong sense of identity, the loyalty they have to their communities, their values and standards (which are refreshingly old-fashioned) and the way of life, have created a people who are fiercely independent. Will the way of life survive is the question on everyone's lips. With the fishery in tatters, and 35,000 fishermen unable to work because of the cod moratorium announced in 1992, the doubts and fears are very real.

Newfoundland has two National Parks — Gros Morne and Terra Nova — and five National Historic Sites — L'Anse aux Meadows, Port au Choix, Castle Hill, Cape Spear and Signal Hill. The two National Parks are as different from one another as hills are from valleys, but both encompass some of Newfoundland's finest scenery. Terra Nova contains a gentle landscape of rolling hills covered in coniferous trees backed by deep inlets of still, blue waters. Thirty percent of the park is covered by water, with three tongues of seawater punching into the land and hundreds of ponds dotting the forests, bogs and fens. Bird life flourishes around the estuaries and tidal salt marshes. Eagles are common and tern colonies are protected from marauding gulls. The weather is milder along this more sheltered coastline of Bonavista Bay, the winds feel gentler and the sun stronger. The trails are not strenuous and the campgrounds are full of families with children.

Gros Morne is wild, rugged and untamed. The scenery is as dramatic as it is varied, harsh and bleak in some parts, domestic and pastoral in others. A long coastline of desolate cobble beaches littered with driftwood and debris bears witness to the vicious nature of the sea that borders its western boundary. Majestic fjords cut vertical clefts into the stark plateaus of the Long Range Mountains, and ancient peridotite rocks tinge the Tablelands to a warm orange-red hue. Some trails are very strenuous, clambering steeply to vantages overlooking deep, landlocked fjords, others are gentle walks around tranquil ponds where beavers swim in the shadows of dusk. Alongside the families and senior citizens who rarely venture into the depths of the park are the dedicated backpackers looking for a wilderness experience and a challenge. Apart from their physical beauty, wildlife, natural history, geology and recreational attractions, both Gros Morne and Terra Nova have a rich and colourful human history which is often described in the interpretive programmes and exhibits scattered throughout the parks.

In contrast to the National Parks, the five National Historic Sites (called Parks until recently) were established for their historical interest and importance rather than for the natural beauty of their locations. It just so happens that each sits in a marvellous setting of its own. By the very nature of these sites, recreational activities are not their primary focus. However, the trails that do exist are fundamental in capturing the importance and atmosphere of each location. It may seem a long way to drive to the tip of the Northern Peninsula to see the Viking village at L'Anse aux Meadows, but you will not be disappointed by either the drive or the site. So it is with all the sites. They are worth hunting out.

How to Use the Book: The object of this book is to get readers to discover the gems in Newfoundland's rocky crown. Undoubtedly, the best way to do this is to explore the parks and sites themselves. I hope the book encourages you to do so.

The book has been organized so that each park has its own introduction (for the historic sites the introduction is primarily historical) at the end of which there is a brief section entitled How to Get There that features information on driving times and distances. This is followed by a longer section called Useful Information offering a variety of information on accommodations, shopping, hours of opening, telephone numbers, etc. Each park or site has an overall map showing the trails, and Gros Morne and Terra Nova have additional maps of trails. Each trail has its own section, including a quick reference at the beginning giving time/distance, difficulty, trail condition, a short summary, how to get to the start of the trail and a detailed trail log with times against which to pace yourself. Some trails pass through the sites of abandoned settlements, mills or shipyards, others pass the homes of moose, lynx or beavers, still others cross ancient rocks thrust up from the earth's mantle. Wherever I have found an interesting aspect to a trail, I have included a section at the end called Background Notes. I do not profess to be a historian, botanist or natural history expert, only an interested layperson, and my premise has been that if I am interested in something, perhaps you will be, too. For those who are interested in the island's history, geography or flora and fauna, there is a bibliography at the back of the book. Bookshops and craft shops on the island usually have a good selection of books on Newfoundlandia. Any prices given in the book are just an indication of costs for your convenience, but these should always be checked. The same applies to schedules and opening hours, which may change.

Trails at a Glance: For those not interested in detailed trail directions, those wanting to choose a trail to fill a specific time slot, those wanting to know what trails are good for children or those just wanting a quick note about the trail, the respective Trails at a Glance tables that precede each of the three sections of trails should be useful. Time, distance, level of difficulty and a short description of each trail are noted here in table form for quick reference. Five additional fishing trails are added to the end of the

Terra Nova table. These are signposted from the Trans-Canada Highway as hiking trails but they are only for anglers walking to ponds. They are in poor condition and since hikers are not encouraged to walk them, they are not covered in the trail descriptions.

Times and Distances: Both Gros Morne and Terra Nova provide some trail literature and maps. However, please note that there are discrepancies between the park distances and times and those I have recorded. I have timed myself walking on all the trails, so I know how long the hikes took me. I consider myself an average walker with strong hikers overtaking me with ease and weaker ones plodding behind me, so I believe my times are a good base from which to pace yourself. As for distances, although it is interesting to know how far you have walked, it is more important to know how long it will take you to walk the trail. With this in mind, the trail directions emphasize times, not distances. Distances have been given out of interest and were recorded on a pedometer, but by virtue of this instrument's limitations I accept that these can only be considered approximate. Road distances were taken from a car odometer, but, as with the trail distances, there are definite discrepancies between what I have recorded, what the official distances are and what you find on the road signs. I have stuck to what I recorded.

Spellings: Spellings of place names have been taken primarily from park data, supplemented by the *Gazetteer of Canada: Newfoundland,* the Newfoundland and Labrador Official Highway Map and topographical maps. However, there are constant discrepancies. If there are two completely different names for the same place, I have given both names (e.g., in Gros

LEGEND OF MAP SYMBOLS

	Warden's Cabin
	Picnic Area
	Campground
	Sewage Dumping Area
	Lookout
	Summit
	Bridge
?	Visitor Centre
	Fishing Pond
C	Cemetery
	Lighthouse
N ↑	North
P	Parking
■	Fishing Premises
	Boat Tour
	Main trails
	Other trails
	Road
	Brook
●	Community

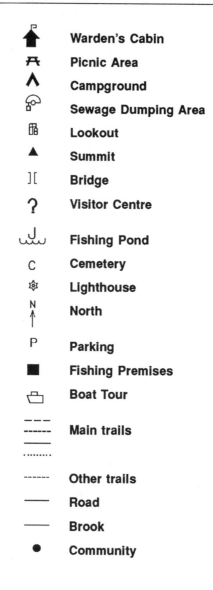

Morne the Stanford River is now the Slants River).
Place names in the possessive case were particularly
troublesome (e.g., in Terra Nova, Salton's Brook is
often spelt Saltons Brook, Buckley's Cove becomes
Buckley or Buckleys Cove and Minchins Cove sometimes has the apostrophe and other times it doesn't).
I have cut through this Gordian knot of apostrophes
by simply eliminating them all (e.g., Buckleys will
only appear spelt that way). St. John's is, of course,
an exception to the rule.

Trail Maps: The trail maps are only included for the
hiker to get a feel of the trail's location and are not
designed to be used in place of the trail directions.
The legend on page 18 gives the definition for map
symbols. Those wanting greater detail and accuracy
should purchase the topographical maps available
from Gros Morne and Terra Nova National Parks. I recommend carrying these at all times especially when
walking unmaintained and unmarked trails.

Notes on Hiking in Newfoundland: This book is designed for all abilities and ambitions; however, the
more experienced are unlikely to need much of
the basic information. **All the trails are day hikes.**
Although there are several longer hikes in Gros
Morne, they are not covered here. Information about
them can be obtained from the Visitor Centre or
from Gros Morne Adventure Guides in Rocky Harbour (see Gros Morne Useful Information, page 32).
In Terra Nova it is also possible to backpack the
Outport trail and rest overnight in the primitive
campsites along the way, or to stop at campsites
along the canoe route through Dunphys Pond. Information can also be obtained from the Visitor
Centres. All backpackers should register with park
staff before venturing into the back country.

Whenever going on a hike, be prepared. If you wanted two words to describe the Newfoundland weather, they would be "unpredictable" and "blustery." Even if it is warm and sunny, take some wind protection with you — you are likely to need it around the next bend or on the next hilltop. The best way to dress is in layers, and always carry a rain-jacket. I also recommend pants rather than shorts — it rarely gets that hot anyway.

Footwear is always a problem when walking in Newfoundland. Many of the trails have good, packed surfaces, but equally many do not. Some trails in Terra Nova cross bogs, are not in very good condition and are quite wet. Rubber boots are awkward to walk in and make hiking tiring. Personally, I do not like them, but for some trails they are a must. Lightweight hiking boots are definitely the best choice except for the very wettest of trails. With a comfortable pair that have a good sole and ankle support, you can walk twice as far as with the wrong footwear. Sneakers are adequate on many trails if you don't have hiking boots, but be prepared for tired feet.

There are a few trails in Gros Morne (notably Winter House Brook Canyon and North Rim) which rise to plateaus where there are no marked trails. You will hear different opinions about what you need to bring with you if you go on these trails. The fundamental thing to remember, as mentioned above, is that the weather is unpredictable. The sun may be shining when you start in the morning, but before you know it you could be engulfed in mist with visibility down to a minimum. Where there is no marked trail and you have to navigate by landmarks, reduced visibility can be daunting and dangerous. Even experienced hikers have been caught out by freak snow storms in July, so once more, be prepared. For these hikes I recommend taking along emergency supplies of food and water, extra layers of clothing, matches in a waterproof container, a compass, a topographical map, a reflective foil blanket and windproof clothes. Also remember to take garbage bags on all hikes for the removal of anything you take in. These trails have been identified in the trail directions and are amongst the best ones in the park. They are usually very strenuous — another reason to chose a clear day — because after all that effort it is a great disappointment to see a wall of mist when you know there is a spectacular view of a landlocked fjord or coastline just beyond.

Another tip is to always take along some insect repellent, as what starts as a leisurely walk to a cascading waterfall can become a nightmare with blackflies and mosquitoes. However, the level of interference varies according to year, weather, time of day, etc. For example, the first time I walked the Bakers Brook Falls trail in Gros Morne, I mistakenly brought a picnic to have at the bench overlooking the falls. Even the dog did not know where to hide from the attacking critters. The following year I deliberately left my picnic behind — much to my chagrin, for there was not a blackfly in sight (and it was exactly the same time of year).

Although they are often awkward and heavy, you will definitely regret it if you do not bring your camera and binoculars.

When to Go and What to Expect of the Weather: When standing on a headland watching icebergs drifting by, sitting on a boat watching a humpback whale surfacing mere feet from starboard, or coming across a caribou silhouetted against the setting sun (having already passed a black bear and young

moose calf along the same trail), then Newfoundland is truly an "island god." But when the wind
blows horizontal rain or snow into your face, when
you wade through giant puddles of newly thawed
snow knowing they will become an ice rink fit for
the St. John's Maple Leafs by morning, when you
stand scraping ice off your windshield or battling
with the frozen car lock as the wind cuts through to
your very bones, then, yes, it is a "terrible place."

If you visit the parks in the summer months, which
is when most people travel, you will not see this
winter fury. However, you must still come adequately
prepared. To echo the sentiments of Newfoundland
writer Patrick O'Flaherty, if you want a pretty little
island you should go to PEI, not Newfoundland.
This is true for more than the obvious reasons. If you
come looking for constant shorts weather, you will
be disappointed. More likely, one day may be shorts
weather and the next longjohns weather. If you are
lucky you will have shorts weather exclusively, but
equally so you could have only longjohns weather.
We're back to the old adage "be prepared." If you
aren't prepared for all contingencies, you could ruin
your holiday; if you are prepared, you'll love it.

Summer comes late on the island. Mid-June is the
start of the summer season, but it can still be quite
cool with nature only just awakening. In St. John's
the leaves on the trees don't fully open until mid-
June, although inland this is usually earlier. It is also
the month when you are most likely to still see the
magnificent icebergs which drift past the island's
shore from April till early July. Sometime during
June there is a two-week foggy season that heralds
the arrival of the capelin, little fish whose life cycle
includes spawning on rocky beaches around the
island, being collected for use in the kitchen, as
compost in the garden and as an aphrodisiac for the

Japanese. By July the weather is warming up, but most years the icebergs are drifting south or more likely melting. Whale watching is highly productive at this time, but blackflies become a nuisance in low-lying, sheltered places. August usually has the best weather, but it is also the most popular month (having said that, except for Labour Day weekend, the parks are rarely full and even then, except for a few select places, "crowded" is not a term that needs to be used). September is my favourite month for hiking. Fall is lovely in Newfoundland. It is usually warm and sunny, and the colours of the turning autumn leaves add a mellow contrast to the harsh and rugged headlands. However, Labour Day (first weekend in September) is the official end of the season, and some facilities will be closed or running on off-season hours (see Useful Information for each park). If this does not bother you, then I recommend this time of the year. By November the first snows may be falling, but there is nothing stopping you from taking a hike on a bright, sunny, wintry day. Just be sensible where you go. And of course there is cross-country skiing (for which Gros Morne and Terra Nova are open).

No matter when you choose to visit the parks, the invisible magnets will draw you in, bathing your eyes in the unspoilt beauty of the wilderness, recharging your batteries with tranquillity, immersing you in scenery and soothing away the tensions and stresses of modern life. And just when you think you cannot take any more, you round a corner . . . and there is yet another golden sunset, blue fjord or rugged headland to tempt you on. Once you make that first visit, it will haunt you for the rest of your days.

JAMES CALLAGHAN TRAIL:
Ten Mile Pond from the top of Gros Morne. BM

GROS MORNE NATIONAL PARK

Rugged and unspoilt, wild and untamed, Gros Morne National Park is a place of untold beauty distinguished by its geology. The foremost jewel of Newfoundland's rocky, windswept crown, it is a land that is as varied as it is beautiful.

Established in 1973, Gros Morne National Park catapulted into international recognition in 1987 when it was added to UNESCO's list of World Heritage Sites. Today it sits on an international podium alongside Banff, Jasper, Yoho and Kootenay National Parks (in the Canadian Rockies), as well as the Pyramids of Egypt and Australia's Great Barrier Reef. Lying halfway up the west coast of Newfoundland, the park covers 1,805 sq km (700 sq mi). It is 650 km (390 mi) from St. John's, 625 km (375 mi) from the ferry terminal in Argentia (summer only) and 300 km (180 mi) from the ferry terminal at Channel-Port aux Basques. The park straddles the southern end of the Viking Trail (Route 430), which runs north from Deer Lake, through the park for 86 km (52 mi), up the Northern Peninsula to St. Anthony, across the Strait of Belle Isle to Labrador and ends in Red Bay.

At the park's southern entrance in Wiltondale, a 50 km (30 mi) spur (Route 431) runs west around Bonne Bay and ends in Trout River. It is in this southernmost portion that the Tablelands are found. These are the ancient rocks that were instrumental in the addition of Gros Morne to UNESCO's list. Thrust up from the earth's mantle by forces that moved continental plates, the peridotite rock has turned golden by exposure to the atmosphere. Only a few plant species can overcome the lack of nutrients and high levels of toxicity and survive the arctic conditions and fearsome winds. Birches, tamaracks and junipers grow prostrate along the ground, their thin, wiry trunks extending horizontally in an effort to survive. Harebells, campions and other arctic flowers cling to sparse pockets of soil, and the pitcher plant, Newfoundland's provincial flower, thrives by collecting insects in its carnivorous bucket. The wide valley and plateau better evoke the deserts of Nevada than a park in Newfoundland.

The dramatic scenery of Gros Morne continues with fjords that a particularly enthusiastic reporter for *The Globe and Mail* described as "unsurpassed by fjord grandeur anywhere in Norway or New Zealand." Although Gros Morne's fjords are somewhat shorter than these famous counterparts, the massive, vertical wedges cloven out of the grey rock are nevertheless spectacular. Bare walls of grey rock plummet hundreds of metres to valleys and landlocked ponds. Thin waterfalls from plateau ponds cascade gracefully and evaporate into mist. Hard and rugged, silent and still, these penetrating chasms mark the plateaus like ragged scars.

One fjord — technically the only true fjord as the others are now cut off from the sea — is different. Called Bonne Bay, it harbours a gentle domesticity. Open to the Gulf of St. Lawrence, its arms spill back between forested hills like floodwater through a valley. Once a seaway for boats carrying pitprops (wooden baulks used as mine shaft supports) and lumber to the markets of Scotland and England, today its stillness is marked only by scattered fishing and recreational boats and the seasonal ferry boat pottering between Norris Point and Woody Point (hopefully the ferry will continue to run — its future was undecided at the time of writing).

On the misty plateaus above the fjords, caribou roam in herds, and arctic hare and rock ptarmigan live camouflaged against the tundra vegetation. Low, dense, twisted spruce and fir form impenetrable bands across the plateau. This is tuckamore (called krumholz in the Alps), and it is found all over blustery Newfoundland. These densely growing trees, usually spruces, are moulded and shaped into contorted forms by the ferocious winds that sweep the Long Range Mountains. Situated at the northern end of the Appalachian chain, the Long Range Mountains date back 1,250 million years and are the backbone of Newfoundland. At 806 metres, Gros Morne Mountain is the highest peak in the park and the second highest peak in Newfoundland. The James Callaghan trail climbs to its summit, where it is met by the sea of rocks (or felsenmeer) that give the mountain its distinctive grey, bald appearance.

Away from the mountains, caribou and mist, another world exists in Gros Morne. From the grey slopes of the mountains an extensive peat bog or fen extends over the coastal lowlands. The bogs provide an ecosystem for plants that thrive under wet conditions. Sphagnum mosses absorb water like sponges. Bakeapples, a Newfoundland delicacy, grow profusely. So does the pink flowering sheep laurel and the strange, leathery pitcher plant. Moose graze on the grasses and aquatic plants that grow in the numerous ponds.

The lowlands end on terraces above windswept cobble beaches littered with bleached logs and battered lobster pots. Here lie the victims of powerful storms that have been known to dash coastal steamers against the rocks like matchsticks. Behind the beaches, impenetrable miniature forests of tucka-more bend against the ruthless winds. Terns swooping into the water to catch fish, humpback whales spout-ing offshore and minke whales gracefully arching through the cold Gulf waters — all draw visitors onto boat trips. Along this rock-strewn coastline, two long, sandy beaches backed by dunes are an unexpected find.

Clustered around the coastal terraces is the human history of Gros Morne. About 4,500 years ago, the Maritime Archaic Indians reached this area and settled in coastal camps from which they fished and hunted. The reason for their disappearance is unknown, but it coincides with the arrival of the Groswater and later the Dorset Eskimos, both of the Paleo Eskimo tradition. As with the Maritime Archaic Indians, these hunters and gatherers were depend-ant on marine resources. They came south from Labrador about 2,700 years ago and remained until their disappearance 1,500 years later. Within the park only small seasonal camps have been excavated, and much evidence has been washed away by the sea. However, further up the Northern Peninsula at Port au Choix, archaeologists have excavated an ex-tensive site containing burial grounds of the Maritime Archaic Indians and dwellings of both Groswater and Dorset Eskimos.

Europeans began appearing along the west coast of Newfoundland in the 15th century, but settlers did not arrive at Bonne Bay until the 1800s, with other communities following later. Fishing was the mainstay of the families that lived along the wind-swept coast. Cut off from the outside world except for boats and a cart track/winter mail road running along the beaches and terraces, these families led isolated lives. Some communities thrived as fishing centres, whereas the prosperity of those around

Bonne Bay depended largely on logging, trading, fur trapping and farming.

Along the battered shoreline, weatherworn sheds and cabins still dot the beaches. They are shabby and look abandoned but for the stacks of lobster pots piled neatly against them and the boats pulled up onto the cobbles outside. Some days men sit in the doorways repairing nets, while children play around their feet. On others they paint the upturned boats they built with their own hands or fix the nets and lobster pots. Much of the time the premises stand empty and the men are gone, but the store sheds, remnants of trails, tiny cemeteries, lighthouses and grassy clearings tell the human story of a way of life.

With the withdrawal of logging operations, the decline in the trading and collapse of the fishery, many people living around the park have turned to it and to tourism for employment. A spirit of entrepreneurship is developing and leading to a renewal in the region's economic prospects. Visitor accommodation is slowly increasing in the form of cabins, hospitality homes and a motel in Cow Head. There are not many restaurants, but those that have opened serve delicious home-cooked foods such as cod tongues, lobster, fish and chips, bakeapple cheesecake and blueberry pie. During the long winter months women knit and stitch, and there are several craft shops with stocks of guernsey sweaters, crocheted decorations, Newfoundland souvenirs and home-baked goods for sale to visitors.

The park's Visitor Centre is just off Route 430 outside Rocky Harbour. It is a must for information about the interpretive programmes, for the slide shows about the park and for the latest copy of the park information booklet, called *Tuckamore*. Maps, including a trail map, and some books can be purchased at the centre, and staff are helpful about park activities. Those wishing to backpack must first register at the centre, and those wishing to fish need to purchase licences.

There are five main campgrounds in the park, plus others for backpackers in more remote areas. Berry Hill, outside Rocky Harbour, is the largest and most centrally located. Green Point and Trout River lack hot showers and flush toilets. Both amenities are available at Lomond, Shallow Bay and Berry Hill, with the latter two also boasting sewage dumps. For those not camping, lodgings can be found in the enclave communities. Most of these are listed in the Newfoundland and Labrador Department of Tourism Travel Guide (see Gros Morne Useful Information, page 32), or information can be obtained from the park staff.

There is plenty for everyone to do in the park. Several picturesque picnic areas overlook Bonne Bay and the Gulf of St. Lawrence. Some of these have boat launches. At Lobster Cove Head there is an exhibit of human history, and at Broom Point there is another about fishing. There are numerous interpretive boards about the human and natural history of the area scattered throughout the park, and the remains of the ill-fated steamer SS *Ethie* lie on the beach by Martins Point as a reminder of the sea's unpredictable viciousness. Outside Rocky Harbour there is a recreation complex with a 25-metre indoor pool, shallow bay and hot tub. At Shallow Bay, Lomond and Trout River there is unsupervised swimming. Power boats are allowed on Trout River Pond and Bonne Bay, but canoeing and kayaking should be done only after consultation with park staff or in the company of Gros Morne Adventure Guides (see Gros Morne Useful Information, page 32).

Tour boats take tourists up the landlocked fjords of Western Brook Pond and Trout River Pond and are an excellent and easy way to see the gorges. Allow 35-45 minutes for the easy walk to the tour along Western Brook Pond. A few private companies run boat tours around the Gulf of St. Lawrence and Bonne Bay; information is available from the Visitor Centre. Intrusion on the landscape has been kept to a minimum while opening the park to visitors. It is still a very natural place, and there is no better way to see it than on your own two feet. There are over 200 km (120 mi) of hiking trails in the park, and they vary from strolls along the beach to strenuous climbs to elevated plateaus to walks around ponds and along coastal meadows. (There are also several backpacking routes across the Long Range Mountains, but they have not been included in this book. Information can be obtained from the Visitor Centre.) Each trail shows different features of the park, and all the trails are constantly being upgraded and new ones added. Whatever your walking level, take the time to leave the road, the vantage points and the exhibits, and go into Gros Morne. You can't expect to see it all in a few days, but you may just get close enough to feel its pulse and plan a longer trip for another year.

How to Get There:
- Take the Trans-Canada Highway towards Deer Lake and turn onto Route 430 (Viking Trail).
- Continue for approximately 29 km (17 mi) to Wiltondale.
- For the northern part of the park — the Visitor Centre (33 km/20 mi), Rocky Harbour (36 km/22 mi), Cow Head (81 km/49 mi) and the northern exit of the park (86 km/52 mi) — continue straight along Route 430.
- For the southern part of the park — Woody Point (22 km/13 mi) and Trout River (40 km/24mi) —

turn left onto Route 431. After 10 km (6 mi) pass into the park and continue through the communities around Bonne Bay to a sharp left-hand bend immediately before Woody Point. Take the bend and continue to Trout River.

Useful Information:

Gros Morne National Park
PO Box 130, Rocky Harbour,
Newfoundland, AOK 4NO. Tel: (709) 458-2417.

When to Go: Although the park's summer season is from approximately mid-June to Labour Day, hiking can begin by late May. However, at this time of the year there may still be snow in sheltered places, and the James Callaghan trail up Gros Morne Mountain remains closed until around late June. Newfoundland's summer comes late, so June and early July can still be cool. August and especially September are the best times to go. October has beautiful fall colours but is cooler. Hiking can continue into November if there is not too much snow, although by then the weather can be cold and wet. Even in the summer mitts and hats can be necessary, and by October they and windproof outerwear are a must.

Visitor Centre: The park's Visitor Centre is located outside Rocky Harbour just off Route 430. Summer season: end of the third week in June to Labour Day (first weekend in September), open daily 09:00-22:00. Shoulder season: April to the end of the third week in June, and Labour Day to the end of October, open daily 09:00-16:00. Winter months: open daily 09:00-16:00 (with possible periods of closure). At the centre pick up a copy of *Tuckamore* (the park's information pamphlet), a park map and information about the interpretive programme. Maps, some books, slides and a video can be purchased, and exhibits and slide shows viewed.

Vehicle Permit: At the time of writing no vehicle permits were required; however, they are to be introduced in the summer of 1994, so check with the Visitor Centre (at the time of writing prices were not available).

Park Campgrounds: There are five campgrounds in the park. No reservations are accepted except for group camping at Berry Hill. None of the campgrounds have electrical, water or sewage hook-ups and there are no phones or laundromats. 1993 prices (including GST) were as follows:

	1 Night	4 Nights	7 Nights
BERRY HILL	$11.25	$33.75	$56.25
SHALLOW BAY	$8.75	$26.25	$43.75
LOMOND	$8.75	$26.25	$43.75
TROUT RIVER	$7.25	$21.75	$36.75
GREEN POINT	$7.25	$21.75	$36.75

There are also several primitive campgrounds throughout the park and across the Long Range Mountains. There is no charge for these, but all campers must register at the Visitor Centre before backpacking to them. They all have pit toilets and picnic tables, and some have tent platforms and barbecue pits. The campground seasons are as follows:

BERRY HILL: open from early June to Canadian Thanksgiving (mid-October).

GREEN POINT: open year round, but water is shut off during the snow season and except for a small parking area by Route 430, the access road is not ploughed.

SHALLOW BAY: open from the end of the third week in June to Labour Day.

LOMOND: open from the end of the third week in June to Labour Day.

TROUT RIVER: open from the end of the third week in June to Labour Day.

Private Campgrounds: There is one private campground in Rocky Harbour. It operates from around May 20 to September 30 and has both semi-serviced (electrical and water, no sewage) and unserviced sites, hot showers, flush toilets, a dumping station and a convenience store. Juniper Campground: (709) 458-2917, on Route 230 (Pond Road) in Rocky Harbour.

Accommodation: There are no park cabins, but private accommodation in the form of cabins, hospitality homes and a small motel can be found in Wiltondale, Rocky Harbour, Norris Point, Cow Head, Woody Point and Trout River, all outside the park boundary. Listings can be found in the Newfoundland and Labrador Travel Guide available from the Department of Tourism, 1-800-563-6353 or (709) 729-2830, or ask at the Visitor Centre.

Interpretive Programme: The park runs an excellent interpretive programme, so drop in at the Visitor Centre for the latest schedule. The programme includes evening events at the Visitor Centre, guided walks, a children's programme, and campfires at Lobster Cove Head. Events carry on regardless of bad weather.

Lobster Cove Head Lighthouse Exhibit: Summer season: end of the third week in June to Labour Day, open daily 10:00-20:00. Shoulder season: first three weeks in June, and Labour Day to the end of September, open daily 10:00-18:00. This exhibit in the old lighthouse is about the coastline and its inhabitants from 4,000 years ago to the present day. One room has been restored to its original appearance and there is a video about the park.

Broom Point Fishing Premises Exhibit: Summer season: end of the third week in June to one week past Labour Day, open daily 10:00-18:00. Restored fisherman's shed and summer cabin. Two retired fishermen are interpreters at the exhibit and add information, flavour and texture to the visit.

Wiltondale Pioneer Village: Located just before the southern entrance of the park at Wiltondale, this is a cluster of buildings representing life in the area in the 1920s. These include a log barn, church, schoolhouse, house and general store. Showers and a laundromat, and a tea room and craft shop are also available. The village is organized by the Bonne Bay Development Association, (709) 453-2470. Season: early June to the end of September, open daily 09:00-20:00. There is a small entrance charge.

Boat Tours: Boat tours are a good way to see the park. The tours on Western Brook Pond and Trout River Pond are narrated cruises and are very educational.

WESTERN BROOK POND: 2 hr 30 min. Reservations and information are available from the Ocean View Motel in Rocky Harbour, (709) 458-2730. Schedule: June 21 to Labour Day, 10:00, 13:00 and 16:00 daily. Shoulder season: June 1 to June 20, and Labour Day to the end of September,

13:00 daily. 1993 prices (inc. GST) are around $23.00 adult, $6.00 child 8-16, under 7 no charge. There is a 35-minute walk (slower walkers need to count 45 minutes) from the parking lot to the boat launch where new facilities are currently under construction. These include toilets, ticket sales counter, chalet with deck, exhibits and a picnic area, and are due for completion in 1994.

TROUT RIVER POND: 2 hr 30 min. Reservations and information, (709) 451-2101. Schedule: mid-June to September 15, 09:30, 13:00 and 16:00. 1993 prices (inc. GST) around $21.40 adult, $11.77 child 11-16, under 11 no charge, seniors $16.05.

I'SE DA BYE TOURS: Norris Point: 2 hours except Sunday when they are 3-4 hours. Reservations and information from Ocean View Motel in Rocky Harbour, (709) 458-2730. Schedule: June 1 to September 30, Monday to Saturday, 13:00. Sunday special (features live entertainment and music), 14:00. 1993 prices (inc. GST) around $23.00 adult, $6.00 child 8-16, under 7 no charge.

There are also some boat tours at Bakers Brook and St. Pauls Inlet run by local fishermen. Ask at the Visitor Centre for more information.

Wharves and Boat Launches: Boat launches are situated at Lomond campground, Mill Brook picnic area and Trout River day-use area, and there are municipal launches at Winter House Brook and Norris Point.

Canoeing: Contact the Visitor Centre for more information, or see Adventure Guides below.

Swimming: A 25-metre indoor pool, shallow bay and hot tub are in the recreation complex on Route

430 between Rocky Harbour and the Berry Hill campground. Summer season: mid-June to Labour Day. Schedules and prices are available at the Visitor Centre.

Fishing: A specific National Parks fishing licence is required in all National Parks in Canada. There are also bag limits for all species and total bans on some. For up-to-date information and licences, contact the Visitor Centre.

Bonne Bay Ferry: The 30-minute ferry crossing from Woody Point to Norris Point is a very enjoyable way to get across Bonne Bay. However, at the time of writing the ferry's future was uncertain, so visitors should contact the Visitor Centre for up-to-date information, schedule and prices.

Adventure Guides: Gros Morne Adventure Guides, Rocky Harbour, (709) 686-2241, contact Sue Rendell or Bob Hicks. They can organize hiking, kayaking and canoeing trips to the Long Range Mountains and other less-accessible parts of the park of one day or of four days to two weeks. They also have mountain bike rentals, but check with the park where cycling is allowed.

Places to Eat: Fast-food outlets have not arrived in the communities of Gros Morne, but there are some excellent family-run establishments that are worth a visit. Ask at the Visitor Centre.

Groceries: Although there are some small convenience stores and general stores in the communities, it is easier to stock up with the basics before coming. In the summer months some craft shops sell home-baked goods which are worth trying, and in Rocky Harbour there is a fruit and vegetable stall (summer only). Also ask about buying fresh fish and lobsters (when in season). Deer Lake has a supermarket and some other stores.

Laundromats: At the time of writing there were laundromats at Wiltondale Pioneer Village, Gros Morne Crafts and Laundromat (Rocky Harbour) and Shallow Bay Motel and Cabins (Cow Head). Only the latter operates year round.

Banks: Banking is not easy in the park, so it is best to bring what you need with you. There is a Bank of Montreal in Rocky Harbour, but it does not have cash machines and will not cash personal cheques (cash advance on Mastercard only). Travelling south, Deer Lake has a cash stop and bank; going north, Port au Choix has a bank.

Propane: The only place within the park where propane is available for motor homes is at Hiscock's grocery, opposite the Esso gas station in Norris Point. The alternative to Hiscock's is either Deer Lake or Port au Choix.

Sewage Dumping Stations: Berry Hill campground outside Rocky Harbour has a dumping station open from early June to mid-October, as does Shallow Bay campground near Cow Head. Juniper campground in Rocky Harbour (a private campground open May 20 to September 30) has a dump for its customers. Along Route 431, between Wiltondale and the park entrance, Lomond River Lodge Trailer Park (a private campground open May to September) has a dump.

Medical Clinics and Hospitals: There are medical clinics in Trout River, Woody Point and Cow Head, and Norris Point has a small hospital (Bonne Bay Hospital).

RCMP: Rocky Harbour, (709) 458-2222 or 458-2055.

Newfoundland and Labrador Department of Tourism: 1-800-563-6353.

Bonne Bay Development Association: (709) 453-2470.

Map 2: GROS MORNE NATIONAL PARK

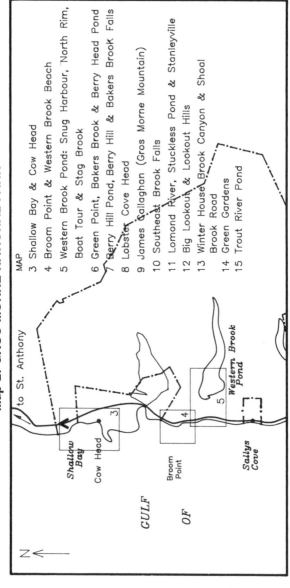

MAP

3 Shallow Bay & Cow Head

4 Broom Point & Western Brook Beach

5 Western Brook Pond: Snug Harbour, North Rim, Boat Tour & Stag Brook

6 Green Point, Bakers Brook & Berry Head Pond

7 Berry Hill Pond, Berry Hill & Bakers Brook Falls

8 Lobster Cove Head

9 James Callaghan (Gros Morne Mountain)

10 Southeast Brook Falls

11 Lomond River, Stuckless Pond & Stanleyville

12 Big Lookout & Lookout Hills

13 Winter House Brook Canyon & Shoal Brook Road

14 Green Gardens

15 Trout River Pond

to St. Anthony

GULF

OF

Shallow Bay

Cow Head

Broom Point

Western Brook Pond

Sallys Cove

N ←

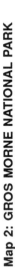

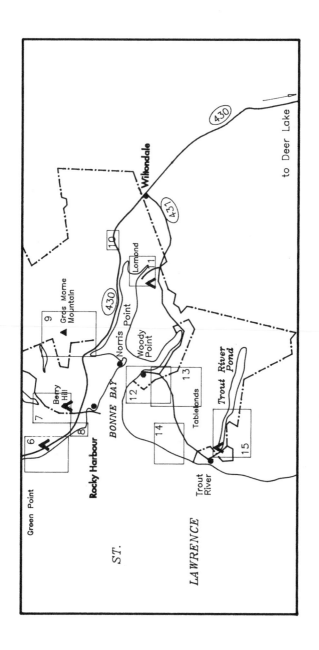

GROS MORNE NATIONAL PARK   41

GROS MORNE - Trails at a Glance

Name	Time* hr:min	Distance* (approx)	Difficulty
Shallow Bay (map 3)	0:45	3 km (1.8 mi)	easy
Detour 1	0:05	250 m/yd	easy
Detour 2	0:03	200 m/yd	easy
Cow Head (map 3)	0:45	3.25 km (2 mi) loop	moderate
Broom Point (map 4)	1:30	5.5 km (3.3 mi) loop	easy
Detour	0:15	750 m/yd loop	easy
Western Brook Beach (map 4)	1:05	4.25 km (2.6 mi) loop	easy
Western Brook Pond			
Boat Tour (map 5)	0:35	3 km (1.8 mi)	easy
Stag Brook (map 5)	1:00	4.5 km (2.7 mi)	easy
Snug Harbour (map 5)	1:45	7.6 km (4.6 mi)	moderate
North Rim Ascent (map 5)	4:30	12.5 km (7.5 mi)	very strenuous
Green Point (map 6)	1:10	5.25 km (3.2 mi)	easy
Bakers Brook (map 6)	0:40	3 km (1.8 mi)	easy
Berry Head Pond (map 6)	0:35	2 km (1.2 mi) loop	easy
Berry Hill Pond (map 7)	0:30	1.8 km (1.1 mi) loop	easy
Berry Hill (map 7)	0:25	1.3 km (.8 mi) loop	strenuous
Bakers Brook Falls (map 7)	1:15	4.8 km (2.9 mi)	easy

Name	Time* hr:min	Distance* (approx)	Difficulty
Lobster Cove Head (map 8)	0:50	2.75 (1.7 mi) loop	easy
James Callaghan (map 9)	5:15	18 km (10.8 mi) loop	very strenuous
Southeast Brook Falls (map 10)	0.05	500 m/yd	easy
Lomond River (map 11)	1:10	4.75 km (2.9 mi)	moderate
Stuckless Pond (map 11)	2:40	10 km (6 mi) loop	moderate
Stanleyville (map 11)	0:40	2 km (1.2 mi)	moderate
Lookout Hills (map 12)	1:40	5.75 km (3.5 mi)	moderate
Big Lookout (map 12)	2:50	6.5 km (3.9 mi)	very strenuous
Tablelands Shoal Brook Road (map 13)	1:20	5.4 km (3.2 mi)	moderate (strenuous rtn.)
Winter House Brook Canyon (map 13)	3:25	9.25 km (5.6 mi) loop	very strenuous
Green Gardens Trail 1 (map 14)	1:10	4.5 km (2.7 mi)	strenuous
Trail 2 (map 14)	5:30	15.5 km (9.3 mi) loop	very strenuous
Trout River Pond (map 15)	1:45	7.0 km (4.2 mi)	moderate

*unless stated otherwise times and distances are one way
Note: Backpacking in the Long Range Mountains is not covered in this book. For more information contact the Visitor Centre or Gros Morne Adventure Guides (see Gros Morne Useful Information, page 37).

Map 3: SHALLOW BAY & COW HEAD

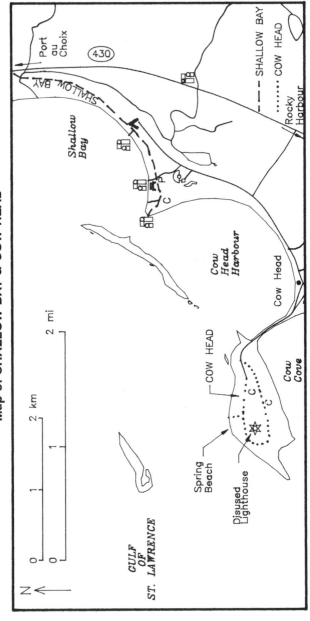

SHALLOW BAY
(map 3)

DETOUR 1: parking lot to cemetery:
Time: 5 min
Distance: 250 m/yd one way

DETOUR 2: parking lot to telescope platform/beach:
Time: 3 min
Distance: 200 m/yd one way

TRAIL: parking lot to campground/beach:

Time: 15 min	**Difficulty:** easy;
Distance: 1 km	good for children
(.6 mi) one way	**Condition:** maintained

TRAIL (cont): campground/beach to end of trail:

Time: 30 min	**Difficulty:** easy;
Distance: 2 km	good for children
(1.2 mi) one way	**Condition:** maintained

Summary of Trail:

Starting at the picnic area behind the sandy beach and large grassed area, two short detours lead to a tern-viewing platform and cemetery, and the trail follows the old mail road through the dense coastal forests. At Shallow Bay campground a short spur gives access to the sandy beach and another viewing platform. At this point, those wishing a shorter walk can double back along the beach, whereas those wanting a longer walk can continue north through dense forests. The trail crosses Slants River (also known as Stanford River) and ends in a small gravel clearing by Route 430.

How to Get There:
- Take route 430 north from Rocky Harbour.
- After about 41 km (25 mi) pass the road on the left to Cow Head.
- After a further 2.5 km (1.5 mi) turn left for Shallow Bay and Cow Head.
- Continue for 1.3 km (.8 mi) and at the junction turn right onto the gravel road to Shallow Bay campground.
- After 1.2 km (.7 mi) pass the dumping station and take the next road left to the picnic area.
- Continue for 400 m/yd to the parking area.

Trail Directions:
Detour 1: parking lot to cemetery:
Facing the sea from the parking lot, turn left. Follow the gravel path/cart track through the grasses and wildflowers to the tiny, fenced cemetery in the trees.

5 min Pass to the right of the cemetery enclosure and continue to the wooden viewing platform and interpretive board overlooking Cow Head Harbour and Peninsula. Return to the parking area.

Detour 2: parking lot to telescope platform:
From the parking lot, take the path across the playing field towards the sea.

3 min At the viewing platform overlooking the beach and islands there is a telescope and interpretive boards about dunes and terns. Watch for the terns (called stearin in Newfoundland). They have pointed, swallowlike tails and a sharp angle in their wings and can be seen swooping and diving for fish. If terns are frightened off their nests, gulls will eat their eggs and chicks, so please do not disturb nesting birds. Dunes are a rare find in Newfoundland, and since trampling destroys the marram grasses that stabilize the sands, please do not walk on the dunes. Return to the parking lot.

Trail: parking lot to end of trail (via campground):
Facing the sea from the parking lot, turn right along the gravel path into the woods. Pass the clearings brimming with buttercups, flag iris, tiny, white, star-shaped stitchwort and blue-tufted vetch. Originally, these clearings contained houses and gardens; today, only a lone bench stands on the edge of one.

13 min Pass Shallow Bay campground on the right (access from the campground to the trail is opposite site 16, right of site 19 and by the playground).

15 min With the playground on the right, turn left along the short spur to the beach and viewing platform. This is the place to watch the sunsets over the Gulf of St. Lawrence. If you are short of time, you can return from the platform to the picnic area via the beach; otherwise, go back to the trail and continue north through the forest.

20 min Ignore the small track on the right.

25 min Pass alongside the sand dunes on the left.

30 min The path bends to the right, passes through two small hollows and emerges onto a disused gravel road, where you turn left. Sand dunes covered in marram grass creep across the road from the left, wildflowers grow in the banks on the right and birds sing cheerfully.

40 min Cross the wooden pedestrian bridge over Slants River (also known as Stanford River).

45 min Pass under the power lines and arrive at the gravel clearing off Route 430.

Background Notes:
Today Shallow Bay is a favourite spot for vacationers coming to enjoy the safe, sandy beach. Only the

more discerning who notice the cemetery hidden in the trees might wonder why it is so far from a community. Look a little further and you will find other signs that people once lived here, for this is the site of the abandoned community of Belldowns Point. The belt of crooked trees behind the dunes no longer shelters clapboard homes and sheds, vegetable gardens, woodpiles and lobster pots from harsh winter gales. There is no sign of the colourful houses with shining stoves, handmade furniture and hooked mats, and if it were not for the neat little cemetery, you would not know the community ever existed. The women who knitted the fishermen's distinctive guernsey sweaters have died or moved away. The men who painted the dories, built the lobster traps and fished in the bay are names on gravestones.

COW HEAD
(map 3)

Time: 45 min
Distance: 3.25 km (2 mi) loop
Difficulty: moderate; good for children

Condition: not maintained; can be wet

Summary of Trail:

The lighthouse trail begins from the abandoned community on the Cow Head peninsula and passes through meadows and dense forest along the lighthouse path. From the miniature red and white lighthouse, it scrambles up to Big Hill. From this highest point the trail crosses a large meadow of wildflowers and then returns to the wharf through the outskirts of the deserted village. A short detour turns off the main trail before the lighthouse and leads to a beach of fascinating configurations created by the movement of continental plates.

How to Get There:
- Take Route 430 north from Rocky Harbour.
- After about 41 km (25 mi) turn left for Cow Head.
- Continue for 3.5 km (2.1 mi) and on the second sharp right bend, turn left (no signpost) before the red fire hydrant. If you pass the post office on the right, you have gone too far.
- Continue for 1.5 km (.9 mi) over the causeway, enter the old village, continue to the wharf (where the paved road ends) and park. Please park carefully so as not to obstruct the fishermen.

Trail Directions:
From the wharf, walk back along the paved road to the sharp left bend and turn right onto the cart track. Walk up the hill and take the right fork towards the distant radio mast. Pass the few derelict houses and, before you reach the Roman Catholic cemetery on the left, take the grassy fork on the right into the meadows. A few gardens still remain, but most are abandoned and have become patches of grasses and wildflowers.

3 min Sign to the Lighthouse on the left.

5 min Sign for the Lighthouse Path. Grassy cart track enters the dense coastal forest.

10 min Ignore the paths that lead to the small clearings with barbecue pits and pit toilet. At the fork, take the left path. (The right path is signposted to Spring/Beach, where the solidified jumble of limestone has been dumped on the beach in a storm of petrified waves. In between the thick limestone beds, pools of green water stand in the depressions formed by darker, thinner beds of shale. Notice where you come out onto the beach as the path is easy to miss on the way back.)

12 min Staying with the main path, take the left fork uphill (right fork also leads to the beach) and pass the piles of metal garbage discarded from the lighthouse on the cliffs on the left.

15 min At the next fork, take the path on the left up the hill to the miniature lighthouse. (The old path continues straight and is reputed to end on the beach at the far end of the peninsula; however, it rapidly degenerates into a very wet bog and is lost.)

16 min The lighthouse is barely 12 feet high and is red, white and rusty, with an iron ladder onto a tiny viewing platform. It's a perfect little gem, but be careful of the nearby cliff face. Scramble up the rocks to the right of the structure, take the rough path past the faded sign to Big Hill, and then follow the orange arrows on the rocks and trees. Ignore all turnings.

22 min Now you are at the highest rock outcrop at the edge of a very large meadow where settlers' ponies and sheep used to graze. Enjoy the views and watch the fishermen chugging towards the harbour with a veil of squawking gulls behind them. Head across the meadow of wildflowers in the direction of the beacon (no path), and look for a small, orange survey ribbon tied to a branch on a tree at the edge of the meadow (about halfway between the beacon and the power post). Pass to the right of it and continue straight through the trees in the direction of the beacon until you reach the tie ropes of the power post.

57 min Another orange survey ribbon (on the tie rope) marks the short, steep scramble down to a small grassy clearing. Once in the clearing, continue towards the beacon enclosure.

1 h Pass with the enclosure on your left, and then turn left onto a very overgrown cart track. This short track ends at a gravel road. Turn right (left returns to the wharf) and pass the back of the Roman Catholic cemetery.

1 h 7 min Pass the new cemetery on the right.

1 h 10 min At the paved road from the causeway, turn left and continue between the derelict houses and sheds.

1 h 15 min Arrive back at the wharf.

Background Notes:

Look at a map of Newfoundland and you will see hundreds of intriguing and poignant place names such as Hearts Desire, Hearts Content, Ragged Harbour, Doting Cove and Little Hearts Ease. Then there's Doctors Harbour, Admirals Cove, Tickle Harbour, Castors River, Badgers Quay and Black Duck Cove, each named by someone for some reason. Who were Sally of Sallys Cove and Daniel of Daniels Harbour, and were there ever flowers at Flowers Cove? And what of Cow Head. Where did that name come from? The search for answers leads to many theories. Was Cow Head Peninsula named by French fishermen after a colony of walrus they called sea cows, or is it that the peninsula resembles a cow's head? There are probably as many theories as families living in the community. Whatever the true reason, the peninsula of Cow Head has as rich a past as its distinctive name might suggest.

If you have a moment on your way back from the peninsula, pop into the tiny Tête de Vache Museum in the Fire Department. See the round, handsewn wreath in memory of 91-year-old Rosa Vincent and other knickknacks and artefacts dating back to the first English settlers of the 1830s.

Long before Captain James Cook surveyed the

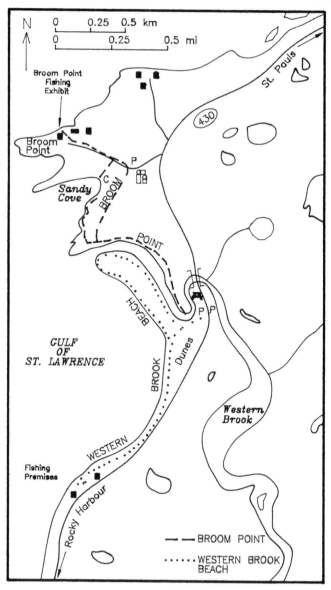

Map 4: BROOM POINT & WESTERN BROOK BEACH

N

0   0.25   0.5 km
0   0.25   0.5 mi

Broom Point
Fishing
Exhibit

Broom
Point

Sandy
Cove

P

430

St. Pauls

GULF
OF
ST. LAWRENCE

Western
Brook

Fishing
Premises

Rocky Harbour

— — BROOM POINT
· · · · · WESTERN BROOK
        BEACH

Cow Head area in 1768 it had been inhabited by man. Traces of habitations suggest it was used by Paleo Eskimos 2,000 years ago and possibly by the Maritime Archaic Indians before them.

BROOM POINT
(map 4)

DETOUR: Sandy Cove and Fishing Exhibit
Time: 15 min
Distance: 750 m/yd one way

TRAIL: path to Western Brook and then along beach

Time: 1 hr 30 min	**Condition:** 500 m/yd
Distance: 5.5 km	of maintained, packed
(3.3 mi) loop	gravel path; otherwise
Difficulty: easy;	cobble and sand beaches
good for children	

Summary of Trail:
After visiting the fishing exhibit, turn off to the tiny cemetery at Sandy Cove before walking along the short coastal trail. The maintained first part runs from the parking area to a meadow terrace overlooking the mouth of Western Brook. At this point the brook meanders around a large sandbar and into the sea, and by continuing south alongside it the walk can be extended for a further kilometre. After returning to the maintained trail, a divergence northwards leads to an interesting cobble beach.

How to Get There:
- Take route 430 north from Rocky Harbour.

- After 30 km (18 mi) pass Western Brook picnic area on the left.
- After a further 1.3 km (.8 mi) turn left for Broom Point Fishing Exhibit.
- Continue along the dirt road for 600 m/yd (pass the telescope on the left), and take the right fork into the parking lot (left fork continues on to the fishing premises, but there is only parking for the cemetery closer to the exhibit).

Trail Directions:
Detour: Sandy Cove and Fishing Exhibit:

From the parking lot, walk down the gravel road towards the sea and the fishing exhibit.

2 min After 100 m/yd, turn left by the gravel parking lot and the sign for Broom Point, and follow the grassy path.

4 min Come out onto Sandy Cove where a tiny cemetery of white crosses sits on the slope looking out to sea — a simple statement on the harsh lives led along this coast. Out of 22 graves, only two belong to adults; the rest are children and babies.

10 min Return to the gravel road and turn left.

15 min At the fishing exhibit explore the tackle store piled high with lines, traps, nets, boats and other fishing paraphernalia. Talk to the interpreters about the life of the Mudges and other fishermen. They will explain how herring were caught as bait for lobster, how the lobster and cod traps were made and how fish were gutted, split, salted and laid on the rocks to dry. After seeing the store, go and visit the tiny cabin where the three brothers and their wives lived during the summer fishing season. Look through the photographs from their family album. On the way back to the parking lot, take a detour to the tiny sheltered clearing (on the left before the barrier) where the three Mudge women had their vegetable garden. Travelling up and down the coastline you can see clusters of sheds and stores just like this one. They look deserted but the way of life lingers on, and many are still used by fishermen over the summer months.

Trail: Western Brook and Beaches:

Take the path signposted Western Brook opposite the parking lot (on the right of the toilets). Cut through the thick tuckamore where crackerberries, twin-flowers and mosses grow alongside the path.

1 min Pass the bench that overlooks Sandy Cove and the cemetery on the right. The path burrows through the tuckamore, emerges into a clearing of large, dry trunks and tall cow parsnips, and then continues through a glade of young spruce and fir trees.

6 min The trail leaves the shelter of trees and crosses a grassy coastal meadow of wildflowers. Contorted tuckamore grows on the dunes on the left. It survives the harsh conditions by forming dense matted crowns against the wind.

7 min The maintained path ends overlooking the mouth of Western Brook and the large sandbar of Western Brook Beach which cannot be reached from this side. If the tide is low, take the steps down to the beach and continue for a kilometre along the sand and boulders until the beach ends. Marram grass grows on the dunes behind the beach, and overhead the terns and gulls squawk at the fish in the brook.

20 min The beach ends at the bend in the brook, so turn back and return to the steps.

35 min Back at the top of the steps, turn left and

walk around the edge of the meadow (there is no path). At a convenient point, scramble down to the beach and head north towards the cliffs.

40 min Walk around the base of the cliffs and look at the patterned beach cobbles. Please remember that you are not allowed to remove anything from the park.

50 min The cliffs become steep, so turn back (Sandy Cove looks very close but the last few metres on the rocks are very dangerous). Return to the maintained path and walk back to the parking lot.

1 hr 5 min Back at the parking lot.

Background Notes:

By 1808 Broom Point was an established summer fishing community where several families ran a successful fishery. The shacks, cabins and flakes were passed from father to son, generation after generation, but by the time the park was established in the 1970s only two families retained their premises and fished from the point. Of these two the Rumbolts still fish there today, but the Mudges have moved away. In 1990 the park restored the Mudge brothers' cabin and store and opened them as an exhibit depicting the traditional way of life of fishermen in the 1960s.

WESTERN BROOK BEACH
(map 4)

Time: 1 hr 5 min
Distance: 4.25 km (2.6 mi)
Difficulty: easy loop; good for children

Condition: 250 m/yd of maintained path, then sandy beach

Summary of Trail:

The trail along one of Newfoundland's rare white sand beaches begins by the Western Brook picnic area, a pleasant grassed clearing sheltered from sea breezes by dunes. It passes through trees along the sandy banks of Western Brook as it cuts a short, meandering path through the dunes. The brook is a scheduled salmon river, but it has been closed to fishing for a couple of years. Once through the dunes, the beach is wide and open. There is a sandbar to the north, and gulls and terns hover overhead. Swimming is not recommended because of the dangerous undertow.

How to Get There:

- Take Route 430 north from Rocky Harbour.
- After 25 km (15 mi) pass the parking lot for Western Brook Pond and the boat tour on the right.
- Continue for a further 5 km (3.1 mi) and, before the bridge over Western Brook, turn left into the Western Brook Beach picnic area.

Trail Directions:

From the parking lot, take the path signposted Shoreline. In the distance the Long Range Mountains form a backdrop to the coastal plain; in the foreground the brook meanders round the marram grass and tuckamore-covered dunes. Please keep off the dunes as foot traffic damages the marram grass that stabilizes the sand.

2 min Bank of steps down into the trees. Sign, Dangerous Undertow. Swimming not recommended. The path skirts round the edge of the sand dunes.

5 min Emerge onto the beach and continue north on the sandbar alongside the brook.

15 min The brook flows into the sea around the end of the sandbar. Continue around and walk back along the ocean side of the beach.

30 min Pass the path back to the parking area on the edge of the dunes.

45 min At the fishing premises (this cluster of cabins and sheds should not to be confused with those at Broom Point which are a reconstruction referred to as a Fishing Exhibit) the dunes and wide sandy beach end. Turn around and return to the parking lot. The water may look calm, but in the autumn powerful storms lash this coast. A retired fisherman who still occasionally fishes from this spot once left his boat moored by the breakwater. After half an hour he returned because a storm had picked up and he was concerned about his boat. By this time the sea was so violent that he found the boat smashed up on the shelf where the sheds and cabins stand.

1 hr 5 min Back at the parking lot.

Background Notes:

The Atlantic salmon is found on both sides of the Atlantic Ocean, but it is no longer the plentiful species it used to be. Overfishing, pollution, hydroelectric developments, the destruction of spawning grounds by logging, indiscriminate fishing and increased codtrap interception have all contributed to the decline of salmon stocks since the 1960s. As a result, in 1992 Newfoundland closed its commercial salmon fishery to allow the stocks to recover and introduced more stringent regulations for recreational salmon fishing. Western Brook and its tributaries have been closed indefinitely to preserve a representative sample for study and interpretation.

WESTERN BROOK POND
(map 5)

TRAIL 1: Boat Tour
Time: 35 min
Distance: 3 km
(1.8 mi) one way
Difficulty: easy;
good for children

Condition: maintained;
boardwalk and gravel
path

TRAIL 2: Stag Brook
Time: 1 hr
Distance: 4.5 km
(2.7 mi) one way
Difficulty: easy; good
for older children

Condition: first part as
trail 1, then boardwalk
and gravel path

TRAIL 3: Snug Harbour
Time: 1 hr 45 min
Distance: 7.6 km
(4.6 mi) one way
Difficulty: moderate;
good for older children

Condition: first part as
trail 1, then woodland
path with some roots
and muddy patches;
1 km (.6 mi) along coarse
sand beach

TRAIL 4: North Rim Ascent
Time: 4 hr 30 min
Distance: 12.5 km
(7.5 mi) one way
Difficulty: very
strenuous; not suitable
for children

Condition: first part as
trail 3, then unmaintained
primitive path; very steep
and rough

Summary of Trails:
Western Brook lies in one of several massive landlocked fjords that are characteristic of Gros Morne

Map 5: WESTERN BROOK POND: BOAT TOUR, SNUG HARBOUR, NORTH RIM & STAG BROOK

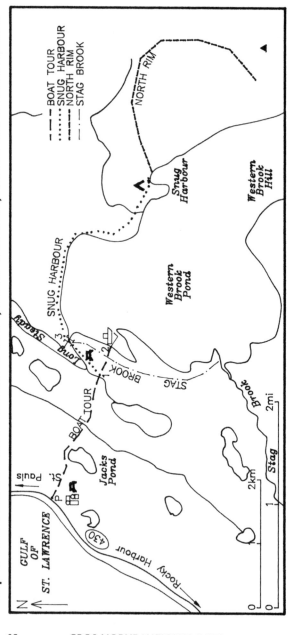

National Park. The Boat Tour trail consists of an easy walk from the parking lot across a coastal plain to the boat terminal wharf (see page 35 for details). Ground-level views of the gorge can also be enjoyed along two trails around the western end of the pond where it spills out onto the lowlands. Here the Stag Brook trail runs well back from the pond through low spruce forests south of the boat terminal. It is a pleasant walk, commanding views of the gorge throughout, and it can be easily taken before or after the boat trip.

The Snug Harbour trail around the north shore of the pond is a longer alternative. It passes through boreal forests through which only isolated glimpses of the gorge are caught. However, a later section along a sandy beach is open, giving views across the pond to the boat terminal and lowlands. The trail ends on the beach at Snug Harbour, where the dark gorge looms formidably.

The North Rim trail continues from Snug Harbour up the north flank, along the North Rim and to the back of the gorge. Although this is a back-packing route, the first part can be walked by day hikers, but it is a long and strenuous hike which should not be undertaken lightly. The North Rim ascent should not be attempted in poor weather as landmarks are necessary for bearings. Emergency supplies should be brought along, as well as a compass and a map. In the space of 4 km (2.4 mi) the trail ascends over 600 m/yd along a very rough path, and once above the treeline the route across the arctic/alpine landscape is unmarked and difficult to follow. The view is exhilarating.

How To Get There:
- Take Route 430 north from Rocky Harbour.
- After 25 km (15 mi) turn right into the parking area for Western Brook Pond and the boat tour.

Trail Directions:
Trail 1: Boat Tour

From the parking lot, follow the signs for the Boat Tour. Take the new boardwalk around the island of shrubs (right leads to small clearings with picnic tables, left to toilets) and take a look through the telescope on the large viewing platform. Next, turn left for the boat tour and continue over the coastal lowlands on the boardwalk and gravel path. Under water until 10,000 years ago, today the lowlands constitute a peat bog harbouring numerous species of bog plants including irises, sheep laurel, wild roses, bog cottons, pitcher plants, sphagnum mosses and wild orchids. Blueberries, partridge-berries and bakeapples (also known as cloudberries) are tough survivors of harsh winters, but tamaracks, spruces and firs have become stunted and deformed. Moose thrive under the harsh conditions, grazing around the ponds and feeding on twigs.

5 min The boardwalk skirts the left bank of Jacks Pond. On still days the water mirrors the distant gorge and on windy days the spray from the pond drenches the boardwalk.

15 min Pass the bench on the right.

23 min Pass a second bench on the right.

25 min Junction (1 on map) and signpost to Snug Harbour, left, and Boat Tour, straight. There is no sign for the North Rim (left) or Stag Brook (straight).

30 min Pass a third bench.

32 min Junction (2 on map) and signpost to Western Brook Pond, straight, Stag Brook, right. Left connects to the seasonal bridge (3 on map) along the Snug Harbour trail, but it is not signposted (15 min/800 m/yd one way).

35 min Arrive at the pond and boat terminal wharf. Toilets, ticket sales counter, chalet with deck, exhibits and picnic area were all under construction at time of writing, so directions here may be different.

Trail 2: Stag Brook
Take trail 1 as far as junction 2.

32 min At junction 2, turn right for Stag Brook and take the gravel path through the low spruce and fir forest. The pond will be approximately 250 m/yd to the left.

34 min The path narrows and continues over boardwalks and packed gravel with some small muddy patches. Views of the gorge rise above the low spruces and alders, their twisted and contorted trunks evidence of the strong winds and freezing temperatures. Marsh grasses grow in boggy areas.

50 min Take the steps down; the path then bends and continues immediately behind the shoreline. Contorted birches, firs and spruces grow on either side.

52 min Climb the steps up the small hillock and down the other side and follow the series of small boardwalks. The path may be wet in parts.

55 min Pass the signpost to the pit toilets and turn left down the steps to the narrow sandy beach where a small brook trickles into the pond.

Trail 3: Snug Harbour
Take trail 1 as far as junction 1.

25 min At junction 1, turn left for Snug Harbour and continue along the gravel path through the boreal forest. Pass Long Steady behind the trees on the left. This is a quiet backwater of Western Brook where ducks can be observed. At the far end of the pond the path bears right over a small ridge.

40 min At junction 3 a large seasonal bridge crosses Western Brook and a second path returns towards the boat terminal. Signpost to Western Brook Pond, right, and Stag Brook, right, but there is no sign for the Snug Harbour trail, which continues over the bridge. On the other side follow the packed earth path meandering through the spruce, fir and birch forest. Look for moose spoor and signs of bear. The trail is largely level with some muddy patches, roots and a few short boardwalks; glimpses of the pond and the dark flanks of the gorge flicker through the trees on the right. In August the air is full of the fragrance of the twinflower.

1 hr 8 min On the right, a short path leads to an erratic (a large rock deposited by a glacier) on which a spruce tree grows, apparently without much soil.

1 hr 15 min Follow the hiker signpost once the path emerges onto a pebble and sand beach. Halfway around you must jump over a small stream that cuts through the beach on its way to the pond.

1 hr 30 min At the second hiker signpost, turn off the beach and follow the path through the trees and over a small hill. It becomes muddy in parts and there are some roots underfoot.

1 hr 50 min Cross the large bridge over the brook.

2 hr Just before Snug Harbour the trail passes through a primitive campsite. There is a pit toilet on the left and a sign to Boil Water Before Drinking. The name Snug Harbour was given to the little cove by the fishermen who sheltered there during storms. Have a picnic on the gravel and coarse sand beach, but leave no garbage for the bears that live in the area.

Trail 4: North Rim Ascent

Take trail 3 to Snug Harbour, then walk left along the beach to the second clump of rocks.

2 hr 10 min Turn into the path marked by an orange survey ribbon and head uphill along the primitive path. It is very muddy and wet with plenty of roots and rocks underfoot and with some fallen trees partially blocking the way.

2 hr 23 min The path is lost in a large, wet area with many fallen trees. Veer left over the first clump of fallen trees, then right over more fallen trees and head towards an uprooted tree where you should hit an obvious trail. The difficult walking continues with lots of roots and windfalls across the path. The trail becomes steeper and you must crawl under a big fallen tree blocking the path. It is very strenuous, but as the ascent increases look back over the treetops and enjoy the view of the lowlands and the sea.

2 hr 35 min The steep boulder climb ends, but the path continues uphill over rocks and roots before commencing another steep climb. Very big birches grow in the boreal forest alongside the spruces and firs.

2 hr 45 min The steepness eases for a short section, then returns to challenge again. The trees begin to get lower and over their tops the view of the lowlands, ponds and sea can stretch more than 50 kilometres.

2 hr 52 The path leaves the forest and continues through metre-high coniferous shrubbery, sheep laurel and blueberries. At last there is respite from the intense steepness, but the roots and muddy patches continue to make the going tough. On the right Western Brook Hill (on the south flank of the gorge) stands tall.

2 hr 55 min As you come over the crest of the hill, St. Pauls Inlet creeps out on the coastal lowlands below and then disappears behind the hill again. The path incline is gentle but the cumbersome roots and branches of the dense shrubbery still persist. Once above the treeline, the path continues across a carpet of blueberries, Labrador tea and mountain alder.

3 hr 5 min A two-pronged waterfall cascades down the hill opposite. There are no trees, so it can be very windy until the path returns into the shelter of another spruce forest. It continues to be muddy, rocky and uneven underfoot.

3 hr 25 min When the trail disappears in a large boggy patch, stay to the right until you reach the boulder and root path. The vegetation becomes dense and low as the path ascends steeply. Look back for the views.

3 hr 35 min An orange survey ribbon marks the point where the steep section emerges from the treeline, and up on the far right a cairn marks the trail.

3 hr 40 min Continue climbing very steeply uphill over the rocky, muddy path towards the cairn.

3 hr 45 min Pass the first small cairn on the right and head towards the second one on the large erratic. From here on there is no trail and directions are difficult. With your back to the cairn, St. Pauls Inlet directly behind you and Western Brook Pond to your right, head up the middle of the hill for 100 m/yd towards a mat of disturbed soil beyond the band of hip-high tuckamore (direction south-southwest). Next, follow the rough moose path through the tuckamore until it fizzles out (if you cannot find the paths through the tuckamore bands, do not attempt to plough through them, but skirt around, even if it means going a fair bit out of your way).

4 hr Once through the first band of tuckamore, keep bearing left uphill until the way is blocked by a second, larger band (if you see two small wallow holes, you are too far to the left). At the second band, walk right along its edge to where it begins to narrow and take the path through. Once through, continue in a straight line uphill over the mat of low alpine vegetation. The sea is on the right, the top of Western Brook Hill peers over the rising plateau and the second cairn is behind you. Continuing on this line you should hit the next band of tuckamore exactly at the point where another path cuts through. Once through, bear left uphill and head for the tip of the south rim as it appears over the horizon.

4 hr 30 min Arriving at the rim, the plateau falls away dramatically to reveal the gorge and the pond 650 metres below. The coastal lowlands and blue sea look smooth and flat so far below, and on the dark waters of the pond the tour boat silently glides — a tiny spot before a widening wake. At the height of summer when the days are longer, you can continue uphill along the rim for another hour for even better views of the fjord. Turn back and retrace your steps to the parking lot.

Background Notes:

The scale of Western Brook is overwhelming. The mountains through which the gorge cuts rise 851 metres. The cliff elevation is 717 metres above sea level with the height above the pond surface at 686 metres. Cutting approximately 16 kilometres into the Long Range Mountains, Western Brook Pond is a spectacular formation.

The Long Range Mountains are part of the same mountain range that encompasses the Appalachian Mountains and were heaved out of the surrounding land mass by the immense forces of continental collision. During the last Ice Age the weight of glaciers pressed parts of the island below sea level, and when the climate warmed and the ice receded it exposed glacially cut canyons. As the glaciers melted,

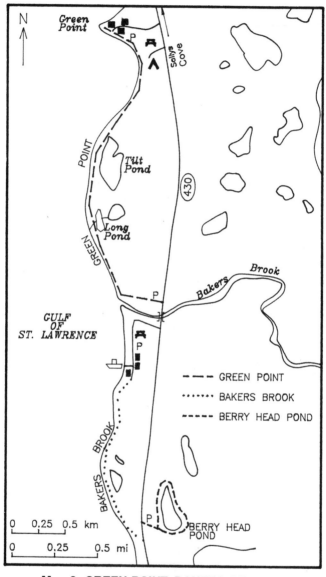

Map 6: GREEN POINT, BAKERS BROOK & BERRY HEAD POND

GREEN POINT

BAKERS BROOK

BERRY HEAD POND

the sea level rose more than 100 metres and flooded the newly carved valleys. Some, like Trout River Pond, Bonne Bay and Western Brook Pond, were connected to the sea, while others such as Ten Mile Pond and Bakers Brook Pond probably were not. Relieved of the ponderous weight of the ice, the land rebounded and the coastal lowland emerged, cutting off the fjords from the sea.

Erosion within the fjord continues today. The natural destruction of running water, frost and wind can cause cliff faces to fracture with no warning and plunge into the water. Occasionally, maybe once every hundred years, these can be so great that a whole rock face will break away and crash into the water. The most recent rock falls can be identified by the lack of all vegetation including lichens and mosses. As erosion continues its destructive work, the pinnacle on the south rim called the Old Man will eventually find its large nose worn away.

For more information on the geology of Gros Morne, see the excellent booklet called *Rocks Adrift,* which is available at the Visitor Centre.

GREEN POINT
(map 6)

Time: 1 hr 10 min
Distance: 5.25 km
(3.2 mi) one way
Difficulty: easy;
good for children

Condition: maintained;
boardwalks in wet parts;
cobbles

Summary of Trail:
This trail is another section of the old mail road

which was the lifeline of the small communities from Deer Lake to Flowers Cove during the winter months. It runs from Bakers Brook to the Green Point campground along the cobble beach and the grass terrace behind, and cuts a path through the dense tuckamore. A further section has been reconstructed and opened as the Shallow Bay trail. A kilometre past the campground, and accessible from the beach and a gravel road, a small group of sheds cluster around a harbour. Beyond lie interesting rock formations — sections of the continental slope of the ancient Iapetus Ocean. With two cars, this trail can be walked one way.

How to Get There:
To start at Bakers Brook:
- Take Route 430 north from Rocky Harbour.
- Pass the parking lot for Berry Head Pond on the right.
- After 2.2 km (1.3 mi) turn left immediately after the bridge at Bakers Brook and park in the small clearing with a No Camping sign.

To start at Green Point:
- As above until Bakers Brook.
- Continue for the next 2.8 km (1.7 mi) and pass the turning on the left to Green Point campground.
- After a further 300m/yd turn left into the gravel road to the fishing premises. There is no signpost except when the park has its guided Green Point Walk.

Trail Directions:
Take the cart track through the alders towards the sea. There may be some large muddy patches.

5 min Just before the brook flows into the sea, ignore the right fork (not very clear) and stay on the cart track as it curves onto the cobble beach. The sea swirls around clusters of rocks and boulders, and piles of driftwood mark the high-water line. To the south, the Lookout Hills are a misty outline, and inland, the flat coastal plain extends towards the mountains.

8 min Take the boardwalks over the wet ground and then follow the path marked by cobbles. Gulls pose on the rocks around the small ponds on the right and black crows craw loudly. Driftwood covers the cobble beach.

10 min Cross the stream that flows from the bog on the right. Follow the path marked by cobbles, around which tiny pale blue flowers of the sea lungwort curl and beach peas grow in green clumps.

15 min Pass parallel to Long Pond.

25 min Long Pond, including the silted-in last third, ends at a hill where densely packed conifers grow in a huge, thick mat of tuckamore. Bleached tree stumps and twisted trunks hurtled by an angry sea lie on the grassy terrace and along the beach of cobbles and boulders. Cobbles continue to mark the route of the old road.

30 min Tilt Pond (also known as Gully Pond) lies in a hollow on the far right. Cross the brook that flows from the pond to the sea. Continue along the grass terrace and veer inland along the marked trail through the tuckamore. Boardwalks cross over wet areas, after which the gravel path exits the trees and heads towards Green Point campground.

40 min Pass around the barrier of the campground, and turn left at the gravel by site 18. Walk through the campground and turn left to site 1 and the loop of open sites overlooking the sea.

45 min At the fence, take the long bank of steps from the top of the terrace down to the beach.

50 min At the bottom, turn right and walk along the cobble beach (it is quite rough walking). Fifty metres/yards later pass the second set of steep steps up to the campground.

55 min Pass the long mound of driftwood that covers the upper part of the beach.

1 hr On the left, a rock breakwater protects the small harbour. Long wooden slipways of lodge poles lashed together and weighted down with rocks extend from the fishing sheds into the water. Boats lie upturned on the cobbles and gutting tables stand where they were last used.

1 hr 5 min Pass up from the beach onto the gravel road by the fishermen's sheds. Turn left and walk to the end of the road and onto the rocks below the overhanging cliffs. Thin diagonal lines like stacks of paper run down the cliffs and along the flat shelf out to sea. These tilted layers of shale and limestone breccia stretch for hundreds of metres offshore. The shale ridges are paper thin and crumble to the touch, while the limestone breccia project above the shelf like walkways of concrete. Long, narrow pools lie between the ridges. Microscopic mussels and barnacles cling to the rocks and yellow and brown kelp fill the water.

Background Notes:

Millions of years ago the geology of the earth was shaped by the movement of massive continental plates. As the plates moved, oceans were created and destroyed. With the movement of the eastern plate (that of Eurasia and Africa) and the western plate (later to become North America), the Iapetus Ocean narrowed and was eventually destroyed. As the eastern landmass slid over the western one, an arc of volcanoes was formed. Rocks from the ancient ocean floor were pushed into stacks, and slices of oceanic crust and mantle were pushed up onto the land.

As described in *Rocks Adrift*, the underwater

shelf at the edge of the eastern continent hardened and the steep outer face collapsed in underwater avalanches. The larger pieces of limestone fell to the bottom of the sea, eventually cementing together with lighter dust particles to form a solid mixture called breccia. Mud particles filtered down more slowly and formed thinner layers of shale. Deep sea organisms were trapped within the layers, and today a fine sequence of fossils spanning two geological periods can be seen at Green Point.

For those interested in the geology of Green Point, the park organizes a guided walk as part of its interpretive programme and sells *Rocks Adrift* at the Visitor Centre.

BAKERS BROOK
(map 6)

Time: 40 min
Distance: 3 km
(1.8 mi) one way
Difficulty: easy;
good for children

Condition: not
maintained; cart track
and cobble beach

Summary of Trial:
As with the Green Point and Shallow Bay trails, this walk follows the route of the original footpath that linked the small settlements along this coastline. Starting before a cluster of summer fishing premises at Bakers Brook, the path passes sheds and cabins that were part of the community of the same name. As the path follows the coastline southwards, it hugs the cobble beach where massive chunks of bleached driftwood lie at the high-water line. All along the

coastline the beaches are littered with battered lobster pots and fishermen's paraphernalia. With two cars, this trail can be walked one way.

How to Get There:
- Take Route 430 north from Rocky Harbour.
- Pass the parking for Berry Head Pond on the right.
- After a further 2.2 km (1.3 mi) turn left for Bakers Brook picnic area.
- Continue 500 m/yd along the gravel road, round the sharp left bend and park at the second picnic shelter.

Trail Directions:
From the picnic shelters, take the gravel road through the summer fishing premises of Bakers Brook. During the summer, cod dries on the flakes and wooden platforms, lobster traps are piled around the fishing stores, cabins and trailers, and upturned boats lie on the cobble beach. Pass the Landwash Boat Tours sign on the shed on the right.

5 min The sheds end and the gravel road continues as a cart track. Fishermen's nets lie drying on the small meadow where wildflowers and strawberries grow. The track passes a small dump and continues beside the piles of bleached driftwood on the cobble beach. Tuckamore hugs the contours of the slope behind the beach. Blue harebells and beach peas bend against the winds, and mats of juniper grow amongst the driftwood.

20 min Pass the pond on the left and follow the track. Although it is level, it is uncomfortable walking wherever it crosses cobbles.

22 min In the distance, the entrance to Bonne Bay is marked by the white lighthouse at Lobster Cove Head, and a tiny pond on the left marks the spot where Philip Decker's father once built a fence to keep the cattle from Bakers Brook separate from those of Rocky Harbour. On the left rises a low hill of tuckamore; to the right the piles of driftwood, broken lobster pots and huge tree trunks lie on the beach. In the distance a tiny white cabin peers out of the tuckamore. A piece of the *Balsam Lake*, a barge that broke her tow cable and came aground at Berry Head in 1943, lies on the beach.

30 min Once at the white cabin, turn back (you can continue further along the beach, but two rocky headlands prevent you getting all the way to Lobster Cove Head). If you don't want to return along the beach, scramble up the rocks left of the cabin and take the gravel track out on Route 430 opposite the parking lot for Berry Head Pond. Return along the road.

Background Notes:

In her book *Gros Morne: A Living Landscape*, Pat McLeod recalls a charming story about the small community of Bakers Brook. Bakers Brook was made up largely of the Decker family, who had been amongst the first settlers to this region. They had a reputation of never being at a loss for words or backing off from a challenge, so when Tom found out the government was offering to supply communities with purebred rams, he wrote away for one for Bakers Brook. The reply came back saying that Bakers Brook was too small to qualify. Furious at the reply, the outspoken fisherman wrote back to the government official saying he did not want a ram for his people but for his sheep. The ram arrived shortly afterwards.

The lobster fishery was the mainstay of the families at Bakers Brook and all the others living along this coastline. The rocky underwater ledges were particularly lucrative for fishing, but the communities were lacking in many basic amenities (the area was still without electricity in 1963). All the tiny settlements were very isolated, especially in the winter, with the only land link being the path behind the beach. Over years of use the tucks and cliffs were smoothed out to form a well-trodden route that served as a cart track, footpath and dog-team track. This lifeline was often the only means by which news of the outside world was carried, and it was not until the 1950s and 1960s, when the new highway was built, that it was no longer needed. The path can still be walked to the north and south of Bakers Brook, and at Shallow Bay and Green Point where it has been upgraded into a trail.

On a sunny day the viciousness of the sea is not obvious, but further up the coast at Martin's Point lie the remains of one of its victims, the *SS Ethie*. A dramatic rescue of its crew and passengers on 10 December 1919, included a baby's being rescued in a mailbag.

BERRY HEAD POND
(map 6)

Time: 35 min
Distance: 2 km (1.2 mi) loop
Difficulty: easy; good for children

Condition: maintained; boardwalks and gravel path

Summary of Trail:
Berry Head Pond is the only trail in Gros Morne with wheelchair access to part of it. With this in mind, be advised that the boardwalk comes close to

the water, projecting over it in places. In the pond a lone beaver can sometimes be seen swimming, or a duck feeding among the lily pads. When it is not close to the water, the trail passes through forest and bog habitats on its circumnavigation of the small pond. At the far end of the pond a series of bogs house shrubby cinqefoil, meadow rue, bakeapples and flag iris, and possibly the odd moose.

How to Get There:
- Take Route 430 north from Rocky Harbour.
- After 6.5 km (3.9 mi) turn right into the parking lot for Berry Head Pond.

Trail Directions:
From the parking lot, follow the wide boardwalk through the dense spruce trees. Ignore the gravel path on the right.

2 min At the pond, a viewing platform with a bench overlooks the water. Turn left on the boardwalk and follow it alongside the pond. Pass a bench and small viewing area. Under the trees grow the fragrant twinflowers, and lilies grow in the pond.

5 min Pass a second platform and seat overlooking the pond. Take the two steps down to a short section of gravel path, which is followed by a long wooden bridge with steps, a short continuation of the boardwalk and the resumption of the gravel path. The pond flickers through the spruces and firs on the right. Twinflowers, crackerberries and bluebead lilies grow along the sides of the path.

10 min Follow the sharp left bend away from the pond and into the trees for a short distance, and then return to the pond where pitcher plants, flag iris and leafy white orchis all grow. Young spruce stand 10-15 metres high in dense clumps, and in open areas a new growth of balsam firs, birches

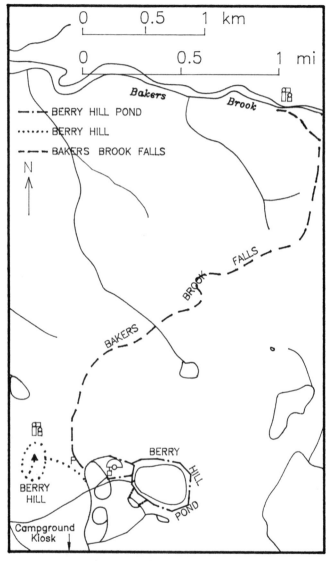

**Map 7: BERRY HILL POND, BERRY HILL
& BAKERS BROOK FALLS**

and maples is sprouting. Several small paths on the right lead to the water's edge.

15 min A long boardwalk begins and eventually exits the spruce forest and crosses a fen of grasses, scraggly trees and bog-loving plants including leafy white orchis, bog cottons and bakeapples.

20 min The path returns to the water's edge across the pond from the bridge. Electricity cables and poles pass nearby. The boardwalk ends and the gravel path resumes.

22 min Follow the short boardwalk.

24 min Take another boardwalk over an area of open bog about 100 m/yd left of the pond. In the distance the Long Range Mountains provide a framework to the picture.

28 min Pass the viewing platform on the right; shortly afterwards the boardwalk returns to the forest, where it ends at the gravel path.

35 min The gravel path ends at the boardwalk and the loop is completed. Turn left to return to the parking lot.

BERRY HILL POND
(map 7)

Time: 30 min

Distance: 1.8 km (1.1 mi) loop

Difficulty: easy; good for children

Condition: maintained; packed gravel and earth

Summary of Trail:
This short trail within the Berry Hill campground has been designed as a pleasant before-breakfast or

after-dinner stroll for campers. The path is well-maintained, level, accessible from several points within the campground, and loops around a small woodland pond. I find early morning the best time to walk it, before the campground awakens and while silence and tranquillity still reign. If you want to see the beavers by their lodge, the best time to come is dusk or dawn.

How to Get There:
- Take Route 430 north from Rocky Harbour towards Cow Head.
- After 3 km (1.8 mi) turn right into Berry Hill campground.
- Continue for 2 km (1.2 mi) to the campground kiosk where, if you are not a camper, you may need to obtain a free day pass.
- Enter the campground and follow the road for 3 km (1.8 mi) to the trailer dumping station opposite the children's playground. There is no parking lot for the trail, so park where you can.
- If you are a camper, the trail is accessible from opposite the parking lot and to the right of site 13, between site 20 and the kitchen shelter/toilets, between sites 29 and 28, between site 70 and the firewood store, between sites 132 and 131 (left of the playground) and from the group camping site.

Trail Directions:
Starting at the path between sites 132 and 131, take the trail through the trees to the pond.

3 min At the pond, turn right and cross the bridge over the beaver dam at the outlet of the pond. As the bridge ends, a path on the right joins from site 70 and there is a signpost on the left.

4 min Turn left. A path joins ahead from sites 28-29

(loop B) and there is a signpost on the right. The pond can be glimpsed through the dead fir trees draped with old-man's beard (a harmless lichen that grows on dead branches in places where the air is very pure). Mosses and twinflowers grow on the ground.

8 min Two paths join from the left, one to sites 18 and 19, the other to site 17. These walk-in sites are right by the water's edge and hidden in the dense fir and spruce forest.

9 min The path from sites 20-38 (loop B) and the toilets joins from the right, followed by the path to sites 15 and 16 on the left (also walk-in).

10 min The path from sites 1-13 (loop A) and walk-in site 14 joins from the right. Continue straight and return close to the water's edge. Water lilies and rushes grow in the pond and skeletal trunks stand in the water.

14 min Cross the two small bridges over a brook and a boggy area.

18 min There is a large beaver lodge on the left, and felled trees in the forest indicate the presence of beavers there. Dusk and dawn are the best times to see the beavers. There are several points where you can get very close to the lodge, but please do not walk on it.

23 min Continue over the short boardwalk bridge. In the distance, Gros Morne Mountain and Rocky Harbour Hills frame the pond.

24 min Continue along the boardwalk.

25 min Pass the path on the right to the group camping sites and a small jetty on the left. Swimming is not safe because of submerged rocks.

27 min The loop is completed. Turn right to return to the campground.

30 min Back at the playground.

BERRY HILL
(map 7)

Time: 25 min
Distance: 1.3 km (.8 mi)
Difficulty: strenuous but
short; good for children

Condition: maintained;
packed gravel; banks
of steps; steep

Summary of Trail:

After the last Ice Age, when the coastal plain was
under the sea, Berry Hill was an island. Locally
known as "The Hummock," it projects 60 metres
above the surrounding lowlands. The trail climbs
steeply to the top, but the use of steps and benches
along the way has made it easier. Even three- and
four-year-olds can make it to the top. Once at the
summit there are viewing platforms with long views
towards the mountains and sea, so choose a clear
day. The trail is within Berry Hill campground.

How to Get There:

- Take Route 430 from Rocky Harbour towards Cow
Head.
- After 3 km (1.8 mi) turn right into the Berry Hill
campground.
- Continue 2 km (1.2 mi) to the campground kiosk
where, if you are not a camper, you will need to
get a free day pass.
- Follow the paved road for 800 m/yd into the camp-
ground.
- At the first sharp right bend, turn left and park in
the area in the parking for Bakers Brook Falls and
Berry Hill.
- Take the trail on the left (south) side of the parking
lot (the one on the right is to Bakers Brook Falls).

Trail Directions:

Take the hard-packed gravel path signposted Berry Hill. Walk through the forest of maples, birches and firs.

4 min The path ascends slowly to a very long bank of steps (there is a bench halfway and at the top), followed by another shorter bank. After the steps, the path continues ascending steeply through the spruces, draped in old-man's beard, and the young firs.

12 min Fork in the path; this is the loop at the top, so you can go either way. Look for bluebead lilies (a solitary stalk with yellow flowers which are replaced by dark blue, poisonous berries in the fall) and crackerberries (carpets of shiny green leaves with white flowers in the summer replaced by clusters of red berries in the fall), and the clump of trees seemingly growing from the top of a rock. In July and August the fragrance of twinflowers at the edge of paths fills the air. Three viewing points look out across the lowlands. One has a bench. Northward, the forested lowlands and ponds stretch as far as the eye can see. Westward lies the Gulf of St. Lawrence. Eastward, the campground access road meanders through the forest, and in the distance stand the peaks of Gros Morne Mountain and Big Level.

16 min Rejoin the path you came up and go downhill.

25 min Back at the parking lot.

BAKERS BROOK FALLS
(map 7)

Time: 1 hr 15 min
Distance: 4.8 km
(2.9 mi) one way
Difficulty: easy;
good for children

Condition: maintained;
boardwalks and
packed-earth path

Summary of Trail:

This popular trail within Berry Hill Campground passes through a largely coniferous forest of white and black spruce, balsam fir, tamaracks and birches. In July and August assorted flowers blossom under the canopy of the trees and in the bogs. Old-man's beard hangs from dead branches and adds an ethereal quality to the forest. At the end of the trail a bench overlooks the falls and provides a good resting place.

How to Get There:

- Take Route 430 north from Rocky Harbour.
- After 3 km (1.8 mi) turn right into the Berry Hill campground.
- Continue for 2 km (1.2 mi) along the paved road to the campground kiosk (if you are not a camper you will need to obtain a free day pass).
- Enter the campground and continue for 800 m/yd to the first right-hand bend. Turn left into the small parking lot and park.
- Take the trail on the right (north) side of the parking lot (the trail on the left leads up Berry Hill).

Trail Directions:

Start at the sign for Bakers Brook 4.8 km by the park information board and take the boardwalk into the forest. In the surrounding bogs grow leafy white orchis, blue flag iris, pitcher plants, showy lady's-slippers, Labrador tea, spruces, tamaracks and firs.

10 min Immediately at the end of the boggy area and boardwalk there is a large abandoned beaver lodge in an overgrown pond on the right. It is difficult to see, but the tell-tale signs of chiselled branches and trunks give it away. Continue along the packed-earth and boardwalk sections with forget-me-nots growing alongside the path and crackerberries and ferns growing under the trees. Squirrels chatter warnings from the safety of higher branches.

35 min The boardwalk resumes as the trail leaves the sheltered forest and crosses an open bog. The Long Range Mountains form a backdrop, but to the left the Gulf of St. Lawrence is barely visible. Stunted, knee-high tamaracks and firs struggle to survive but bakeapples (also known as cloudberries) grow in abundance. In mid-August their solitary white flowers grow into peach-coloured berries that are popular for pies, sauces and jams. Please do not pick any in the park.

50 min The open area and boardwalk end and the trail returns to the forest. Birds sing and in July and August the fragrance of the twinflower (moss-like mats with tiny, very pale pink flowers growing over rocks and stumps) fills the air. Under the trees another distinctive flower blooms. The bluebead lily (also known as clintonia and corn lily) produces a solitary stalk from the pair of large, pale green leaves in June and early July. By late summer the delicate yellow flowers wither and are replaced by dark blue, poisonous berries or beads.

55 min Pass the small pond on the left where ducks swim amongst the lily pads and woodpeckers beat rhythmically against the trees.

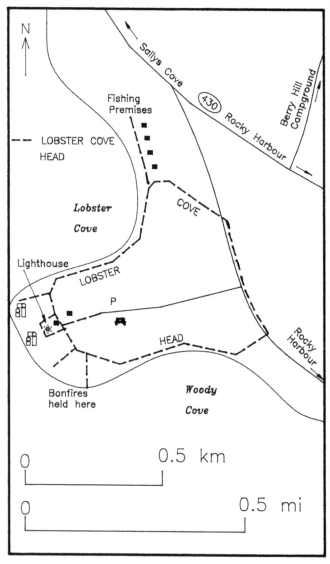

Map 8: LOBSTER COVE HEAD

1 hr Round the left bend with the large black and white arrow and hiker symbol, and take the steps down. The falls become faintly audible.

1 hr 5 min The first view of Bakers Brook appears through the trees as the path meanders parallel to the river's banks.

1 hr 10 min Take a look at the smaller falls from the first viewing platform, then follow the sign Bakers Brook Falls 500 m. Continue along the hilly path, down a couple of long banks of steps and past a pit toilet.

1 hr 15 min At the second viewing platform overlooking the main falls you can rest on the bench and have your picnic.

LOBSTER COVE HEAD
(map 8)

TRAIL:

Time: 50 min

Distance: 2.75 km (1.7 mi) loop

Difficulty: easy; good for children

Condition: maintained gravel path; rock and cobble beach

DETOUR 1:

Time: 5 min

Distance: 1 km (.6 mi) loop

DETOUR 2:

Time: 5 min

Distance: 1 km (.6 mi) one way

DETOUR 3:

Time: 5 min

Distance: 1 km (.6 mi) one way

DETOUR 4:

Time: 5 min

Distance: 1 km (.6 mi) loop

Summary of Trail:

Outside the Lobster Cove Head lighthouse, which marks the entrance to Bonne Bay, there are several short trails. They can be walked individually or linked together into a longer hike. The area directly around the lighthouse is rocky and exposed, though the trails are well maintained, and there are several short detours to viewing points or down steep steps to rocky beaches. At low tide you can walk north from this sheltered cove, around the headland and along the beach to the small cluster of sheds and cabins of the abandoned community of Lobster Cove. Access along the cobbles is easy but can be tiring.

Before leaving stop at the lighthouse, which houses the Living on the Edge exhibit about how this coastline was inhabited and harvested from as far back as 4,000 years ago (see page 35 for hours).

How to Get There:

- Take Route 430 north from Rocky Harbour.
- After 3 km (1.8 mi) pass the turning on the right to the Berry Hill campground.
- 1 km (.6 mi) later turn left onto the gravel road signposted Lobster Cove Head.
- Continue 700 m/yd (ignore the gravel road on the right) and turn right onto the paved road signposted Lobster Cove Head.
- Continue 500 m/yd to the parking lot by the lighthouse. The lighthouse can also be reached directly from Rocky Harbour.

Trail Directions:

From the aerial map outside the lighthouse, turn left down the gravel path and steps. At the fork, turn left (right is detour 1, a five-minute loop to a fenced lookout below the back of the lighthouse).

1 min Turn left at the second fork (right is detour 2

to the small cove where the park staff organize campfires as part of the interpretive programme. With extreme caution, and not at high tide, it is possible to walk north from the cove and around the headland).

2 min Take the left fork through the tuckamore and the grassy clearings (right fork is detour 3, also to the rocky beach).

5 min Walk down the bank of 30 steps to the beach. Turn left on the beach and walk in the direction of the dilapidated shed. Scramble over the large assortment of patterned cobbles, boulders and rocks. A steep bank of grass and tuckamore rises behind the beach and piles of seaweed lie scattered near the waterline. The dark shadows of the Lookout Hills loom through the mist on the far side of Bonne Bay, and on the slopes behind Rocky Harbour stand the colourful traditional houses of Newfoundland outports. In the distance, the profiles of Gros Morne Mountain and the Rocky Harbour Hills glisten in the brilliant blue sky.

15 min Turn left up the gravel track before the small fishing shed. Meadows of wildflowers have reclaimed the site of Woody Cove, but the depressions where houses used to stand can just be made out.

17 min Turn left onto the gravel road from Rocky Harbour.

18 min Ignore the paved road on the left signposted to Lobster Cove Head, and take the next left turning onto the gravel road towards the fishing sheds and cabins.

23 min At Lobster Cove, turn left by the fishing sheds and walk out onto the beach. Fishermen still use the old buildings in the summer months. Their boats are moored behind the breakwater or lie upturned on the cobbles, and piles of lobster traps stand next to the sheds. Their children play on the cobbles, poking at fish skeletons and urchins. Further along on the grassy embankment behind the beach, the remains of the old sawmill lie in an overgrown pile of twisted metal.

45 min A bank of timber steps leads up the embankment and a gravel path leads back to the lighthouse. Turn left at the fork (right is detour 4 to a viewing point).

50 min Back at the lighthouse.

Background Notes:

In 1889, an article about the concerns people in Bonne Bay had about the lack of navigational aids in the area was published by the First Legislative Assembly. Although this prompted plans for a lighthouse at Lobster Cove Head, it took a further eight years before they came to fruition and the lighthouse became functional. Cast in a foundry in St. John's, the light tower was installed at Lobster Cove Head in 1897. For the next 73 years it was maintained by three lighthouse keepers. The first of these, Captain Robert Lewis, was appointed caretaker on November 26, 1897, at a salary of $504 per year. The second, William Young, followed in the 1900s, and he was succeeded by his son George from 1941 until 1970, when the light was automated.

Lobster Cove, north of the Head, was first settled in 1856 by the Deckers, long before plans for a lighthouse had surfaced. Until the late 1970s the family continued running a small sawmill in the cove. Woody Cove to the south also housed a small community, with the last inhabitants also leaving in the late 1970s. Rocky Harbour, southeast of Lobster Cove Head, is the largest community in the area.

With the establishment of a trading post and a market for fish, the settlement began to grow more rapidly. The extensive inshore rocky ledges also proved lucrative, and in the 1860s the lobster fishery was introduced by Nova Scotia merchants aware of the demand for lobster in the markets of Boston.

In the 1950s the cod fishery began to decline. Held together by the lobster fishery, the community survived, but Rocky Harbour began to look away from the sea for a living. With the coming of the park in the 1970s, the community found an alternative direction. A new road was built to Deer Lake and another, (the Viking Trail,) was proposed up the Northern Peninsula. This area was barely accessible by land until the new road was built in the 1980s — infact, the journey of the first car to reach Rocky Harbour in 1926 included a train link from Channel-Port aux Basques and the crossing of the Humber River on a log raft and of Bonne Bay astride two motor boats. Rocky Harbour found itself in a central position within the park. The park headquarters were located in the community which took over from Woody Point as the administrative and service centre for Bonne Bay. Many families from the relocated communities moved to Rocky Harbour, and its population swelled. New houses were built and services were brought in to cope with the influx of people. With the new road to Deer Lake, residents no longer needed to rely on the ferry connection to the south shore of Bonne Bay, and in 1985 it was terminated. Since then the ferry has had a chequered history of openings and closures, and its long-term future is still unknown.

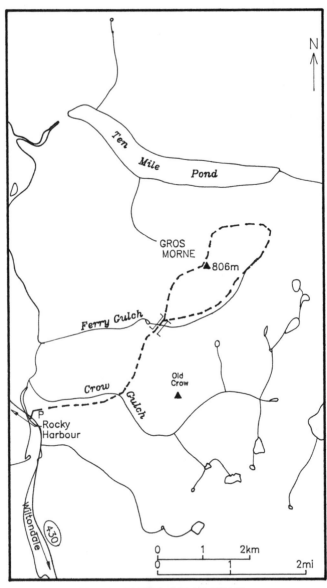

**Map 9: JAMES CALLAGHAN
(Gros Morne Mountain)**

JAMES CALLAGHAN
Gros Morne Mountain (map 9)

Time: 5 hr 15 min
Distance: 18 km
(10.8 mi) loop
Difficulty: very strenuous;
not suitable for children

Condition: maintained;
steep gully; open rock
plateau; long rocky
descent (wet and slippery)

Summary of Trail:
The first section of this gruelling trail leads to the base of Gros Morne Mountain, and although it is a slow uphill walk, it is not strenuous. Next follows the most difficult section up the steep scree gully to the plateau above. Once at the top of the gully, a gentle uphill walk across the rock fields brings you to the summit. The trail across the top is marked by cairns and passes along the edge of a deep U-shaped valley containing Ten Mile Pond. The trail then loops around the back of the mountain and into Ferry Gulch. This section is rocky and wet, and some parts are slippery, requiring constant care and vigilance. It continues through scraggly forests and across slopes of quartzite on the flank of the mountain until it rejoins the trail to the car park by the gully. Strong hikers only should undertake this trail. Choose a clear day for hiking, and carry a compass and map as well as survival equipment.

How to Get There:
- Take Route 430 south from Rocky Harbour for 6.7 km (4 mi) (or north from Wiltondale for 30 km [18 mi]).
- Coming south, cross the bridge over Deer Arm Brook, turn left onto the gravel road signposted James Callaghan trail, and park.

Trail Directions:

From the parking area take the gravel path sign-posted Gros Morne. Pass the pit toilets on the left and continue through the coniferous forest of second-growth trees.

3 min Cross the bridge over Crow Gulch Brook and pass the plaque dedicating the trail to James Callaghan, former prime minister of England. Take the path and numerous steps uphill through the spruce, fir, birch and alder forest.

7 min Take the bank of steps up and another one down and continue uphill along the path and steps.

14 min A short path on the right leads to a small viewing area and bench overlooking Crow Gulch Brook. Continue uphill over the boardwalks and steps.

20 min Pass through the low tuckamore on the crest of a small hillock and have your first glimpse of Gros Morne Mountain. Pass down six steps and return into the trees. Cross through a cutting with overhead cables and continue uphill along the path and steps.

28 min On a small hillock of sheep laurel and low tuckamore stand two benches where you can rest and admire the views of Gros Morne ahead, Old Crow on the right, and Deer Arm and the Tablelands behind.

29 min A short path on the left leads to a pit toilet. The trail re-enters the forest up a few steps.

32 min Pass the large erratic (a large rock deposited by a retreating glacier) on the left. The path becomes rocky underfoot and keeps ascending over steps and boardwalks. Twinflower fragrance fills the air in July and August.

48 min On the right lies a moss-covered erratic with trees growing on the top. A long view stretches across the coastal plain, the arms of Bonne Bay and on to the Tablelands in the distance. The path continues over boardwalks and steps.

53 min A bank of timber steps in three uphill sections is followed by more uphill walking and steps. The distinctive rounded shape of Gros Morne seems close. The long views continue.

56 min Pass the small pond on the left, then an overgrown erratic on the right, followed by three small ponds on the far left. The trail slopes gently uphill and is strewn with big quartzite boulders. Looking at Gros Morne there are two main gullies; the one on the right is the trail to the top. Between Gros Morne and Old Crow lies Ferry Gulch. A rest area with benches and interpretive signs is planned for here.

1 hr 3 min Two bridges span two streams linking the second and third ponds. Once across the bridges, the path continues over the scree spill from the gully.

1 hr 7 min Signpost to Gros Morne, straight, and Ferry Gulch, right. Continue straight and start the steep climb up the gully. It will take about an hour and is easier if you stick to the bigger rocks at the side. It is possible to walk up Ferry Gulch but you must return the same way; it is dangerous to attempt to come down the gully.

1 hr 45 min Pass the big boulder in the middle of the gully. Follow the black and white arrow left.

2 hr The gully ends at a flat stone path. Turn left to continue up the hill towards the summit (turn right and walk back to look at the view of the Lookout Hills and Tablelands). When the flat stone path ends, continue gently uphill over the felsenmeer (a German word meaning sea of rocks), following the cairns capped with small orange boxes. If visibility is poor, it can be difficult to spot some of them.

2 hr 15 min Signpost, You Have Reached the Summit. The uphill work is over. While following the cairns across the felsenmmer to the cliffs above Ten Mile Pond, look out for rock ptarmigan and arctic hare.

2 hr 30 min Ten Mile Pond lies 600 metres below in the glaciated valley. Follow the cairns along the edge towards the back of Ten Mile Gulch.

2 hr 40 min The cairns start leading away from the gorge and across the plateau. Patches of dwarf willows and birches creep in over the rocks. Across the other side of the gorge a waterfall plummets to the valley bottom.

2 hr 50 min You can take a rest on the bench directly across from the hanging valley before descending over rocks, boulders and a very long bank of steps.

2 hr 55 min Bear to the right of the last cairn as the path turns away from Ten Mile Gulch and bends into the back of Ferry Gulch. The slippery, rocky path meanders through the tuckamore.

3 hr 5 min Pass the big boulder on the right and take the left fork steeply downhill towards the pond.

3 hr 8 min Continue alongside the pond (mosquitoes can be a pain here).

3 hr 10 min At the black and white arrow, take the right fork (left to the primitive campground). Pass the pit toilet and continue uphill past another little pond with a small beaver dam. The trail continues downhill through narrow Ferry Gulch. It scrambles over rocks and roots as it passes through the trees and crosses large slides of scree. Streams trickle along the rocky path, making it muddy and slippery. In the gulch below, a brook rushes between small ponds, and across the other side a narrow waterfall cascades down the flank of Old Crow.

3 hr 53 min Cross the small boardwalk at the bottom of the slope, then continue uphill across an open area before going back down into the trees.

4 hr The loop is complete and you are back at the signpost for Gros Morne and Ferry Gulch by the gully. Turn left to return to the parking lot.

4 hr 45 min Pass the two benches.

5 hr 15 min Back at parking lot.

SOUTHEAST BROOK FALLS
(map 10)

Time: 5 min
Distance: 500 m/yd one way
Difficulty: easy; good for children

Condition: maintained; packed earth and gravel path

Summary of Trail:

A friend of mine called this a "beautiful, beautiful trail," and I agree, even though it is but a five-minute walk. The dense fir forest, with mosses and fragrant twinflowers sprawling over rocks and stumps and leafy white orchis that remind me of hyacinths, has a picture-book quality. The falls at the end are especially impressive in the spring and after heavy rainfall when the volume of water increases.

How to Get There:

- Take Route 430 from Wiltondale north towards Rocky Harbour.
- After 8.5 km (5.1 mi), along a steep downhill section of road, turn right into the parking lot signposted for Southeast Brook Falls.

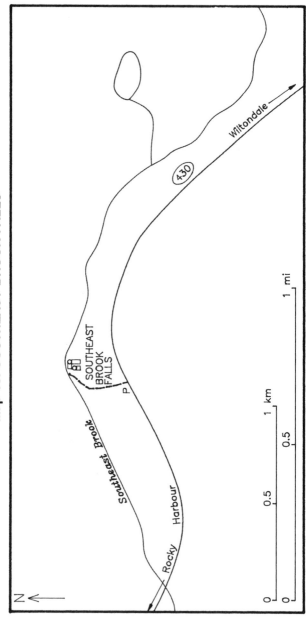

Map 10: SOUTHEAST BROOK FALLS

N

430

Wiltondale

Southeast Brook

SOUTHEAST
BROOK
FALLS

P

Rocky Harbour

1 km
0.5
0.5
0
1 mi
1
0.5
0

Trail Description:

Take the trail from the corner of the parking lot.

2 min Cross the small boardwalk bridge, take the steps down, cross two more small boardwalk bridges, take more steps down and cross the last boardwalk bridge. The waterfall is audible.

5 min Walk along the boardwalk to the fenced viewing area overlooking the tall, narrow falls, about three-quarters of the way up. Visibility is not very good, as you are looking down at the falls at an angle. Turn right up the bank of steps to a second viewing area over the top of the falls. The water is high in tannic and humic acids leached from the soil and vegetation that it flows through. The acids are harmless, but they give the water the colour of weak tea.

LOMOND RIVER
(map 11)

Time: 1 hr 10 min
Distance: 4.75 km
(2.9 mi) one way
Difficulty: moderate;
good for older children

Condition: maintained;
woodland path; hilly

(Add **Time:** 15 min **Distance:** 1 km [.6 mi] if walking to or from the Lomond campground)

Summary of Trail:

The Lomond River and Stuckless Pond trails both pass through an area that was logged intensively from the 1920s until the 1950s. The trails initially follow the same path from the parking lot off Route

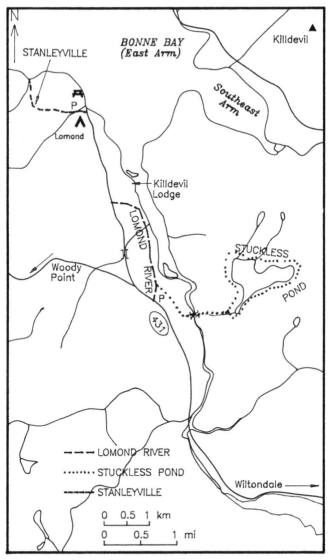

Map 11: LOMOND RIVER, STUCKLESS POND & STANLEYVILLE

431. After the latter trail has turned off, the river trail continues through mixed forests and along the banks of Lomond River to the Lomond campground road. At the end of the trail you can continue into the campground and enjoy the beautiful view across the East Arm of Bonne Bay towards Killdevil Mountain. The grassy meadows are ideal for a picnic, and if you want to extend your hike, pass through the campground and pick up the trail to Stanleyville.

How to Get There:
From Route 431:
- Take Route 431 from the Wiltondale junction on Route 430.
- After 12.5 km (7.5 mi) turn right into the parking lot signposted Lomond River Trail (both the Lomond River and Stuckless Pond trails start here).

From the Lomond campground:
- From the campground kiosk, return 1 km (.6 mi) along the gravel access road. You will pass the turning on the left signposted to the Anglican Church Camp and Killdevil Lodge, formerly the home of the manager of a lumbering company that operated here between 1917 and the 1950's. When the clearing ends and the forest resumes, turn left onto the woodland path marked with a small board and map.

Trail Directions:
From the parking lot, take the trail signposted Lomond River. Follow the boardwalk across the small fen of wildflowers, tamaracks and spruces.
5 min At the junction and map, take the left fork for Lomond River (right fork is for Stuckless Pond).
8 min At the junction, take the left fork (right fork is to the river) and continue over the fen with

showy lady's-slippers and leafy white orchis. Pass into the forest where large trees tower over logged trunks and piles of logs. The trail meanders around the hillside, and after a sharp right bend it drops steeply and descends down some steps to the river.

43 min A small track leads to the river and a wide, angled boardwalk crosses a small brook. Boom piers run lengthways through the barachois (a shallow river estuary or lagoon sheltered from the sea by a sandbar or low strip of land). These piles of rocks in the river were used to anchor floating barriers of wood so as to prevent spillage of logs from the river to the barachois. The trail continues through the forest along the western bank of the barachois. Boardwalks cross numerous small brooks and steps clamber up and down the hilly banks. Sometimes the path remains close to the water's edge; other times it runs further back in the forest where spider's webs collect the early morning dew.

53 min Leaving the barachois and river, take the boardwalk over the brook and follow the path into the forest. Then cross through a small grassy clearing where a sawmill once stood. Continue along the logging track through the tall pines and spruces.

56 min Cross the boardwalk over the brook and walk up the steps.

1 hr Follow the path as it bends to the right (the overgrown logging track continues straight). Tall spruces, pines and maples tower over stumps as the path undulates over short, steep hilly banks.

1 hr 7 min Pass the tiny pond on the left around which beavers have felled trees. Take the left fork (the right fork leads to Killdevil Lodge and the church camp).

1 hr 10 min The trail emerges from the forest onto

the road to the Lomond campground and ends by the board and map. Turn right for the campground where you can picnic, walk the grassy meadows and look for mussels on the beach, all against the beautiful backdrop of the East Arm and Killdevil Mountain.

STUCKLESS POND
(map 11)

Time: 2 hr 40 min
Distance: 10 km
(6 mi) loop
Difficulty: moderate;
good for older children

Condition: maintained;
grass or packed earth and
gravel; some uphill

Summary of Trail:

The Stuckless Pond trail branches off the Lomond River trail shortly after the trailhead and follows an old logging road to the pond. The trail encircles the funnel-shaped trout pond, where signs of past logging operations persist to this day. A grassy clearing marks the site of the winter camp, and cutlines used for dragging logs to the frozen pond scar the hillside. Today young saplings are reclaiming the clearings and wildlife is returning to the pond. Beavers fell trees for their lodge, moose drink at the pond and bears move from one patch of berries to another. The trail is peaceful and still.

How to Get There:

- Take Route 431 from the Wiltondale junction on Route 430.
- After 12.5 km (7.5 mi) turn right into the parking

lot signposted Lomond River Trail (both the Lomond River and Stuckless Pond trails start here).

Trail Directions:

From the parking lot, take the trail signposted Lomond River. Follow the boardwalk across the small fen of wildflowers, tamaracks and spruces.

5 min At the junction and map, take the right fork (left is the Lomond River trail) and follow the boardwalk and gravel path through the dense mixed forest.

15 min The woodland path ends at an old logging road, so turn left at the signpost and continue downhill.

20 min Pass the Fisheries and Oceans sign on the left.

22 min Cross the suspension bridge over Lomond River and walk up the overgrown logging road. Yellow paintbrushes, pearly everlasting, goldenrods, blue vetch, leafy white orchis and an abundance of the showy lady's-slipper grow on either side of the road.

27 min Pass the 1.5 km signpost and continue steeply uphill through the birch and fir forest, where you may see signs of moose and bear.

35 min At the 2 km signpost you can take a rest on the wooden bench.

38 min Continue straight at the fork (right is the return part of the pond loop). Stuckless Pond lies on the right with the outlet of the pond draining over a ruined dam, part of the waterway for the log drive. Stands of white birch grow on either side of the path.

45 min Past the 2.5 km signpost the pond flickers through the trees on the right and aspens rustle in the wind.

1 hr Near the 3.5 km signpost smaller overgrown logging tracks cross over the road.

1 hr 8 min After the 4 km signpost, continue downhill to the site of the logging camp. Before the grassy clearing you can see stumps chiselled by beavers. Past the clearing, the logging road finishes and a narrow path crosses a small brook, turns left onto another logging track and continues gently uphill.

1 hr 18 min Pass the 4.5 km signpost and follow the rocky trail through the small spruce trees at the top end of the pond. Carpets of grey lichen creep along the sides of the logging track. At the crossroads, continue straight in the direction of the hiking sign.

1 hr 25 min Pass the 5 km signpost and walk down the hill and steps towards a second pond. Cross the bridge over the remains of an old dam, also part of the water system for the spring log drives.

1 hr 32 min Pass the 5.5 km signpost and carry on through the forest on the steep eastern side of the pond. Glimpses of Stuckless Pond can be caught through the dense forest on the right. The path descends sharply to the water.

1 hr 39 min Pass the 6 km signpost. There may be some wet patches. The path ascends through the trees and then descends again to the water. The small, white, waxy Indian pipe plant grows beneath the trees. You may see trunks stripped of their bark where moose have been rubbing the velvet off their antlers.

1 hr 46 min By the 6.5 km signpost there are more signs of beavers at work.

1 hr 54 min By the 7 km signpost, near the spout end of the pond, you can see the beaver lodge on the far bank. At the end of the pond lie the remains of the dam used in the log drives.

2 hr Pass the 7.5 km signpost and cross over the bridge.

2 hr 4 min At the junction with the logging road, the loop is complete. Turn left, pass the bench and walk downhill towards Lomond River.

2 hr 11 min Pass the 1.5 km signpost.

2 hr 14 min Cross the suspension bridge over Lomond River.

2 hr 22 min At the arrow, turn right off the logging road (easy to miss) and follow the woodland path through the forest.

2 hr 34 min Follow the boardwalk to the junction with the Lomond River trail. Take the left fork to return to the parking lot.

2 hr 36 min Back at the parking lot.

STANLEYVILLE
(map 11)

Time: 40 min

Distance: 2 km (1.2 mi) one way

Difficulty: moderate; good for older children

Condition: maintained; some wet patches; some uphill

Summary of Trail:

This is a lovely short hike over the ridge from the Lomond campground to the site of the sawmill at Stanleyville in the next cove. The trail passes through mixed forests and ends at the small cove that housed the community. Behind the small pebbled beach, the grassy meadows, a clump of balsam poplar, some poisonous monkshood, apple and plum trees, and scraps of metal are all remnants of the community. Campers and hikers can feast their eyes on the beautiful view of Killdevil Mountain rising steeply from the East Arm of Bonne Bay, its summit often obscured by creeping mists.

How to Get There:
- Take Route 431 from the Wiltondale junction on Route 430.
- After 13.5 km (8.1 mi) turn right for the Lomond campground.
- Continue for 3.5 km (2.1 mi) to the campground (you may have to obtain a visitor's pass if you are not a camper) and proceed to the picnic area behind the pebble beach.

Trail Directions:
The trail begins at the small signpost behind the kitchen shelter of the picnic area. Proceed up the grassy path into the forest.

4 min Cross the small wooden bridge over the brook.

5 min Take the right fork. Continue along the gravel path ascending between the trees. Crackerberries carpet the forest floor — in the summer their shiny green leaves are covered with white flowers, and in the fall these are replaced by bright red berries.

8 min A small track merges from the left as the path continues ascending gently through the forest of white spruce, fir, tamarack, white birch and some red maple.

14 min Climb up the long bank of rough wooden stairs. At the top, the trail levels out and passes through a glade of dead trees.

18 min Take the bank of steps downhill.

23 min Walk along the boardwalk. Throughout the forest there are large rotting stumps of white pine.

30 min The path levels off after a few steps up and is followed by a small boardwalk bridge.

37 min The blue water of the East Arm appears through the trees ahead. The path descends gently through the meadow towards the cove.

40 min The trail ends on the pebble beach. Headlands restrict the cove at either end (at low tide you can scramble around them), and the McKie River flows from the hills into a small pond behind the beach. Wild raspberries and the look-alike queen of the prairie grow on the meadow. On the other side of the East Arm, cars scurry like busy insects along the road to Rocky Harbour. A pit toilet and picnic table are provided for the convenience of campers at the primitive campground.

Background Notes:

At the turn of the century Stanleyville was a small logging and farming community with fewer than 50 residents, half of whom were children. In 1915 the McKie brothers sold all their land holdings and the sawmill on which the families depended to the St. Lawrence Timber, Pulp and Shipping Company. There was no room to expand the logging operation in the small cove, so the new owners constructed a new mill at nearby Lomond (then called Murphys Cove) and the company moved the base of their operation in 1917. At Lomond, a large steam mill, wharves, buildings, houses and a school were built to encourage settlement. This was successful enticement, and shortly after the mill in Stanleyville ceased operating the families moved and the settlement was abandoned.

LOOKOUT HILLS
(map 12)

Time: 1 hr 40 min
Distance: 5.75 km
(3.5 mi) one way
Difficulty: moderate;
good for older children

Condition: maintained;
uphill

Summary of Trail:

This trail to the Lookout Hills is designed to replace the unmaintained, unofficial Big Lookout trail from behind Woody Point. Although it is all uphill, the excellent condition of the trail has made the ascent quite attainable, and the glorious view of Bonne Bay and the Long Range Mountains beyond is worth every last ounce of effort that it takes. And the best is yet to come, for the return journey faces the view that was unseen during the ascent.

How to Get There:

- Take Route 431 towards Woody Point.
- At Woody Point do not continue straight into the village but turn left to follow Route 431 to Trout River.
- After 700 m/yd turn right immediately past the Forestry Management Office (white house with a green wooden fence and an antenna in the yard) and park in the gravel lot. There were no signs for the trail in the fall of 1993.

Trail Directions:

From the parking lot, take the gravel path through the bushes and up the hill. In the fall the turning birches and maples splash pockets of gold and

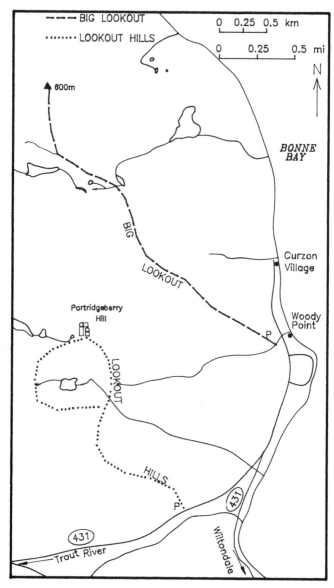

Map 12: BIG LOOKOUT & LOOKOUT HILLS

red against the backdrop of black spruce, giving the mountainside a fiery glow.

5 min At the small boardwalk bridge, look back through the trees for a view of the South Arm lying between the tree-clad hills.

7 min Cross the small boardwalk bridge over the stream and take the two steps up.

7 min From the boardwalk, look back for the spectacular view across Bonne Bay to Gros Morne. The trail continues uphill and the sweat builds up.

20 min Take the log steps around the bend to the right, then take the steps around the bend to the left, and continue snaking up the mountain. Unfortunately, there are no benches for a rest. As the forest becomes denser, the spectacular views are shut out, but after another bend to the right the first view of the Tablelands offers a taste of things to come. Continue up the steps and around the second bend.

25 min Walk along the lengthy boardwalk and look left across Trout River Gulch to Winter House Brook Canyon, sculpted out of the orange peridotite rocks of the Tablelands by glacial action. At this distance there is no sign of the plants that have adapted to the extreme conditions of the Tablelands and the slopes look barren. White, fluffy clouds swirl around the flat summit like freshly picked cotton. The trail continues climbing uphill around bends and up steps. A few red berries remain on the crackerberry carpets, which have turned purple in keeping with the autumnal theme. Yellowing birches dominate the thinning forest, allowing views of Gros Morne in one direction and the South Arm in the other. More steps assist the uphill climb.

35 min A long boardwalk over peat bogs of grasses and thin, scraggly sheep laurel begins its slow uphill meander over the open landscape. On either side trees brace against the winds and form sparse clumps of misshapen tuckamore. Purple pitcher plants stand out against the yellowing grasses and a brook trickles by. It is easy walking on the gentle incline of the boardwalk, but winds build up across the open plateau. The layers of clothing that were peeled off during the climb slowly come back on.

42 min The long, gently ascending boardwalk ends and the trail continues up the hill through shrubbery. Around the next bend a long, steep bank of stairs clambers up the next hillock, suggesting the summit is nigh.

43 min At the junction (this is the loop part of the trail), continue straight towards the stairs. Before you reach them, pass a yellow sign that denotes the park boundary. There may be a wet patch or two here. The splendid view of Bonne Bay and the South Arm continues to delight.

45 min Climb up the long bank of steps and continue over the hill. To the rear, the boardwalk snakes upwards against the backdrop of Winter House Brook Canyon. Across Bonne Bay, Norris Point juts out into the blue waters, and behind it Gros Morne's familiar shape appears and disappears in a halo of mist.

50 min At the lookout platform you can take a rest on the tiered bench if it is not too windy, enjoy the spectacular landscape and look for moose in the clearings far below. Then continue along the loop further around the top of the hill, locally called Partridgeberry Hill. Lichens and mosses creep over the rocks, and sheep laurel and contorted spruces struggle against the weather. As the path descends on the far side of the hill, the crest offers some protection from the wind. However, the contorted skeletons of trees are evidence that on other days it blows against this side, too. Small blue ponds dot the tundra-like landscape, and in the distance the cotton clouds furl and unfurl over the Tablelands. In the rockiest, most barren places the trail is marked by stones.

55 min Another very long boardwalk meanders gently down the largely treeless hillside facing straight into Winter House Brook Canyon. The trickling of a small brook breaks the silence.

1 hr 5 min When the boardwalk ends, the path enters the trees and heads downhill to complete the loop.

1 hr 10 min At the junction, the loop is complete. Turn right and return downhill along the outward path. The views are even better on the return.

1 hr 40 min Back at the car park.

Background Notes:

At the turn of the century, Woody Point had become an important logging and fishing community, with a road to Glenburnie and a ferry to Norris Point. However with the Depression following on the heels of a fire that destroyed most of the waterfront homes and business premises, Woody Point declined. In 1963 there still was no electricity, and in the 1970s, with the advent of the park, Woody Point was bypassed for Rocky Harbour as the administrative centre for the area.

BIG LOOKOUT
(map 12)

Time: 2 hr 50 min

Distance: 6.5 km (3.9 mi) one way

Difficulty: very strenuous; not suitable for children

Condition: not maintained; very rough; very wet sections; steep difficult to follow in parts

Summary of Trail:

This trail starts in Woody Point outside the park boundary and since it is no longer used by park firemen, it has become very rough, overgrown and difficult to follow. There are several long, steep ascents and the higher elevations can be bludgeoned by strong winds. However, the 600 m/yd ascent culminates in spectacular views. Nevertheless for environmental and safety reasons the park is discouraging its use and a new, shorter trail up the Lookout Hills has been recently finished and may be more suitable for most hikers. The weather is changeable, so always carry survival equipment as well as a compass and topographical map. Inexperienced hikers should not undertake this trail.

How to Get There:

- Drive to Woody Point along Route 431.
- At the junction continue straight for 1 km (.6 mi) (left is the continuation of Route 431 to Trout River).
- Turn left onto the small paved road immediately before St. Andrews United Church (before the No Exit sign at the fork to Curzon Village).
- Drive 150 m/yd up the hill towards the green cylindrical water tower (behind a house) with Woody Point painted on the side in large white letters.

- Park before the warehouse on the left (if you are coming from the ferry, turn right as you come off the boat, drive through the town, pass the No Exit fork to Curzon Village on the right, and then turn right after St. Andrews Church and drive up the hill to the water tower).

Trail Directions:
From the warehouse where you left your car, walk up the gravel road on the right of the house and head for the tower. Pass to its right and take the overgrown path on the right into the shrubbery (not clear). After 5 m/yd, push through the bushes on the left (before the stream) and descend the steep bank to Crollys Brook. Cross the brook on the boulders and ascend the other side.

10 min Scramble up the steep path through the trees and take the left fork (not clear). The trail is wet and very overgrown. Continue through the spruces, firs, red maples, sheep laurel and ferns.

35 min Cross the wooded crest of the first hill, from where the mouth of Bonne Bay can be seen through the trees.

40 min The trees start becoming shrubby. The climb is steep and tiring. At the rocky outcrop rest awhile and enjoy the beautiful view. Killdevil is directly ahead and Gros Morne is the more rounded peak to the left. Norris Point nestles on the far side of the bay between the two peaks. On its right lies the little peninsula called Gads Point.

50 min The trail levels off and enters into a grassy clearing and disappears. Look for the overgrown path up the wooded slope in the left corner of the meadow (not clear).

1 hr 5 min Cross over an open area full of sheep laurel.

1 hr 10 min Continue over the wet grassy area with small ponds and puddles.

1 hr 15 min Cross the park boundary (marked by yellow posts). Rocky outcrops, small ponds and string fens are scattered throughout the grassy bogs. A small stream flows on the right, and the trail turns left uphill. It is very wet underfoot, and caribou have made the path even muddier.

1 hr 30 min The path meanders around the ponds and grassy bogs of the plateau. Look out for a small fork (not clear). Take the right path and continue towards Big Lookout. (If you miss this fork you will end up on the left path, which eventually disappears. Don't worry, keep going towards Big Lookout ahead and you will pick up the path 15 minutes later.)

2 hr 5 min The trail bends to the left, away from Big Lookout. Keep with the path.

2 hr 10 min At a tight clump of spruce on the right look for a sharp right, turn into the trees (not clear) and turn into the tuckamore.

2 hr 12 min Scramble up the steep gravel slope and look for a rough path on the left (not clear). Ascend the slope to the ridge. Strong winds can hamper progress.

2 hr 30 min Pass through the patch of spruce and fir.

2 hr 50 min The trail ends at the two repeater stations. There is nowhere to shelter from the wind, but the view is terrific.

TABLELANDS
(map 13)

TRAIL 1: Shoal Brook Road

Time: 1 hr 20 min
Distance: 5.4 km
(3.2 mi) one way
Difficulty: moderate;
strenuous return; good
for older children

Condition: not
maintained; ford;
steep hill down

TRAIL 2: Winter House Brook Canyon

Time: 3 hr 25 min
Distance: 9.25 km
(5.6 mi) loop
Difficulty: very
strenuous; not suitable
for children

Condition: no trail;
rough; very steep climb
and descent

Summary of Trail:

The Tablelands have some of the most fascinating scenery in the park and look more like Nevada than Newfoundland. Both trails starting from the Tablelands exhibit in Trout River Gulch follow the old road as far as Winter House Brook. At this point in order to continue on the first trail you will probably have to ford the stream after which the trail is all downhill towards the beautiful views across Bonne Bay. With two cars this trail can be walked one way.

The second trail turns right before Winter House Brook and heads to the rear of the canyon. There is no trail over the peridotite rocks and boulders, and the steep sides of the canyon rise dramatically. At its rear a steep climb leads to the Tablelands plateau and takes you past the snow patches that can lie in the hollows throughout the entire summer. As you

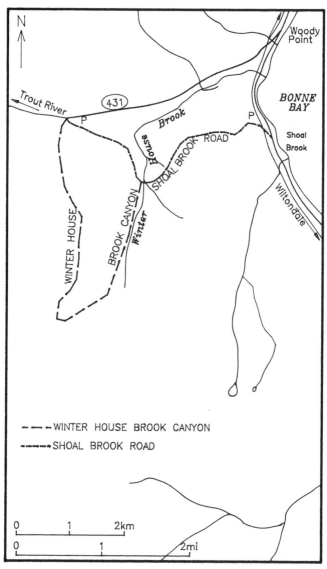

Map 13: WINTER HOUSE BROOK CANYON & SHOAL BROOK ROAD

climb higher you can see the canyon opening into Trout River Gulch. This hike is very strenuous and should not be undertaken lightly. It is recommended that you carry a compass, map and survival equipment in case of a sudden change in weather.

How to Get There:
- Take Route 431 to Woody Point and turn left for Trout River.
- After 4.7 km (2.8 mi) turn left for the Tablelands exhibit and park.

Trail Directions:
Trail 1: Shoal Brook Road
From the parking lot, take the gravel path from the exhibit boards to the bench, then continue gently uphill along the old road. Pass under the electricity cables. Trout River Gulch has a reputation for fearsome January blizzards. In the words of a park interpreter, "the worst I've ever seen, a complete whiteout, and one of the worst places for accidents in Newfoundland." Even in the summer it can be very windy. At first glance the golden rocks look bare of vegetation, but take a closer look.

7 min Cross the bridge and continue on the road.

25 min Either ford or cross Winter House Brook.

35 min Continue on the road. Look back to see the canyon. After the earth's mantle was thrust up from far below the sea, years of erosion flattened the rock. Glacial activity took over, reshaping the landscape into the vast, wide valley of Trout River Gulch and the cirque (a bowl-shaped formation formed by the glacier) of Winter House Brook Canyon.

43 min On the right, the golden peridotite mountain rises. A large erratic (a rock transported by glacial activity) lies among the smaller rocks. On the left, vegetation has taken hold on pockets of richer soil. Alders and wildflowers grow on the side of the road and cable posts run alongside it. Across the gulch the forested Lookout Hills look rich and fertile.

49 min Pass the small pond on the right and arrive at the crest of the hill. The starkness of the Tablelands begins to disappear, and ahead lies the gentler scenery of Bonne Bay. From this point the road descends to the community of Shoal Brook with uninterrupted views. Norris Point lies across the blue water, and behind it Gros Morne's easily distinguishable summit is shrouded in soft mist.

1 hr 20 min The road ends at Route 431 beside the Glenburnie Terminal Station and a sign for Shoal Brook.

Trail 2: Winter House Brook Canyon

From the parking lot, take the old road to Winter House Brook.

25 min At the brook, turn right into the canyon (no trail).

30 min Pass the small waterfall and look for the travertine spring, a smaller version of the springs in Yellowstone Park. Throughout the canyon, black streaks mark the golden peridotite rocks where springs flowed down the cliffs and across the valley floor. Solitary harebells and alpine campions cling to clumps of broken soil.

1 hr 7 min One kilometre (.6 mi) into the canyon the back wall rises steeply. Two or three streams funnel into the brook from patches of snow high up the cliffs. Head up by the one on the right. At the base of the snow, water gushes from an ice cavern and cascades down the hill. It is hard to say which feature is most impressive: the view, the elevation, the peace, the stark beauty of the landscape or the magnificent colours.

2 hr Bearing right all the time, you will arrive at the plateau of golden peridotite rocks. Turn directly north and continue with the canyon on your right. Even up here, arctic flowers and shrubs cling to a precarious existence and birds chirp their songs.

2 hr 10 min The eastern end of the gulch begins to open up in front of you. Bonne Bay and Norris Point lie beyond. Moments later, Woody Point appears. Continue northwards. Bear left of Gros Morne until you locate Big Lookout (the highest green summit with a knob on the top). Head towards Big Lookout and eventually you will start going downhill and will see Route 431 and the old road. At this point, turn west along the edge.

2 hr 50 min When the steep edge gives way to a scree slope, carefully snake down to the parking lot.

3 hr 25 min Back at the parking lot.

Background Notes:

As explained in the park's publication *Rocks Adrift* (available at the Visitor Centre), hundreds of millions of years ago plate tectonics resulted in the formation of a huge sea called the Iapetus Ocean. When the movement of the plates reversed and the ocean narrowed, the eastern plate (Eurasia and Africa) slid over the undersea edge of the plate that has become North America. The converging plates thrust up the Tablelands from 5-10 kilometres beneath the ocean floor. The Iapetus Ocean was destroyed and the reunited landmasses created the new supercontinent of Pangaea. Peridotite rocks from the oceanic lithosphere were trapped in a line down the centre of the new continent. It was largely due to the unique conditions found on the Tablelands and the evidence they offered to the theory of plate tectonics that led to the park's becoming Canada's tenth site on UNESCO's prestigious World Heritage List.

Peridotite rock is low in calcium, potassium and nitrogen which are essential for healthy plant life, and high in concentrations of iron, chromium, nickel and magnesium, which create a toxic environment. Arctic conditions sweep over the rocks, affecting any plants that survive the high toxicity. Frost churning produces a patterned ground of rock polygons and inhibits good root growth. Few plants are thus able to survive on the Tablelands, creating a landscape more visually akin to the deserts of Nevada than the Atlantic island of Newfoundland.

Those plants that do survive have adapted to the unusual conditions and found an alternative source of nutrients. The green mounds sprinkled with pink flowers (moss campion) have extensive root systems to hold them down. Pitcher plants, survivors of low-nutrient areas such as bogs, have a whole ecosystem within their tiny pitchers. Stunted tamarack, ground juniper, dwarf arctic birch and arctic willow survive by growing horizontally on the ground. Lying so squat, they find some protection from the low temperatures (which may reach -30C in the winter), tearing winds and snow. The grey rooty stems that emerge from the clumps of shrubbery are not roots but the trunks of the trees. A juniper trunk one centimetre in diameter was found to be 300 years old.

GREEN GARDENS
(map 14)

TRAIL 1: Short Hike (the first part of Trail 2)

Time: 1 hr 5 min

Distance: 4.5 km
(2.7 mi) one way

Difficulty: strenuous;
good for older children

Condition: maintained;
steep descent to coast

TRAIL 2: Long Hike

Time: 5 hr 10 min

Distance: 14 km
(8.4 mi) loop

Difficulty: very strenuous;
not suitable for children

Condition: as trail 1, then
continues maintained;
lots of steep descending
and ascending; two fords

(You can also hike the trail by walking from the Wallace
Brook parking lot to the second ford and then joining
the loop: **Time:** 5 hr 30 min **Distance:** 15.5 km [9.3 mi]
loop)

DETOUR: Along the Beach (at the end of trail 2)

Time: 5 min

Distance: 500 m/yd one way

Summary of Trail:

The long hike at Green Gardens is a complete loop
which can be started either from Long Pond (signposted Green Gardens) or Wallace Brook. Either
way, you will have to ford Wallace Brook in two
places. To avoid fords, walk from the Long Pond
parking lot down to the coast (trail 1) and then take
trail 2 along the grassy meadows at the base of the
steep cliffs. Continue until the terraces end at Green
Gardens, and when the trail climbs steeply inland,

Map 14: GREEN GARDENS

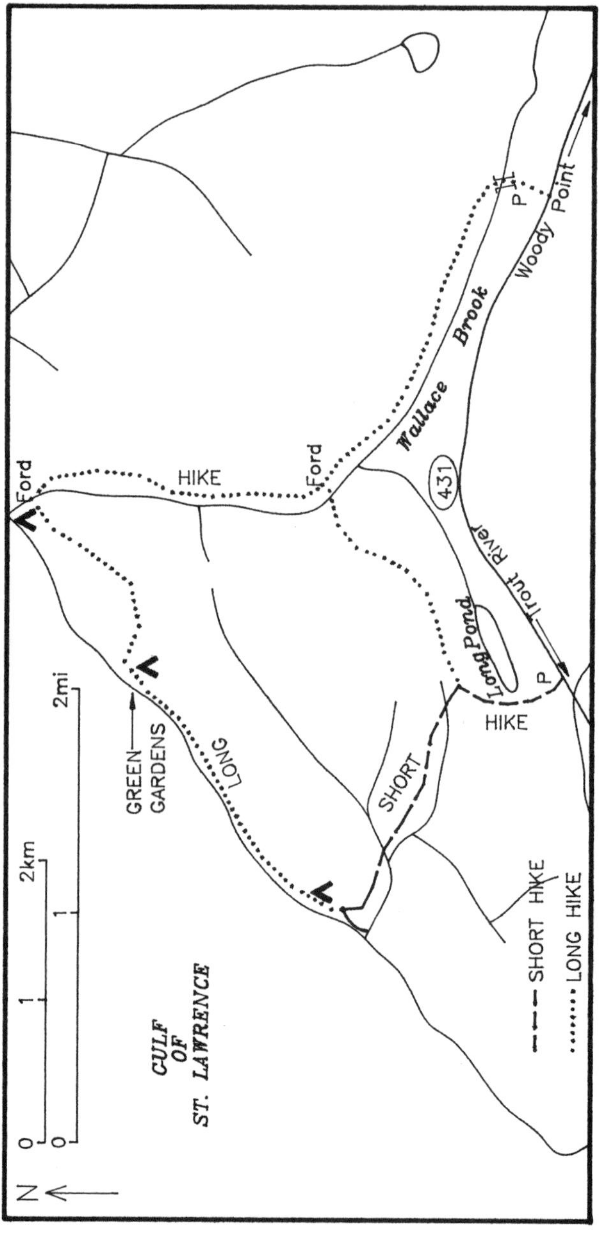

GULF OF ST. LAWRENCE

GREEN GARDENS

Wallace Brook

Woody Point

Trout River

Long Pond

431

HIKE

HIKE

SHORT

LONG

Ford

Ford

P

P

- — - SHORT HIKE
- ⋯⋯ LONG HIKE

N

0 1 2km
0 1 2mi

turn back and retrace your steps. This is a little longer but easier than the complete loop. Another alternative is to walk trail 1 (the short hike), enjoy the short detour onto the beach and come back the same way. Although this makes the hike much shorter, the uphill return is still quite strenuous.

After it turns away from trail 1, the first part of trail 2 follows the coastal terraces overlooking the Gulf of St. Lawrence. At Green Gardens, the meadow terraces terminate at a steep headland. The trail then climbs aggressively to a ridge and scrambles down to the mouth of Wallace Brook. After fording the brook, the trail turns upstream, hugging the riverbanks far above the water. At the point where it descends to cross the brook for the second time, the path forks in two. If you don't want to ford the brook again, continue to the Wallace Brook parking lot and return to Long Pond along the road (Route 431). Aternatively, you can cross to the other side of the brook where a long climb meanders up the hill and rejoins trail 1 at the crest. From there it is but a short walk downhill to the parking lot at Long Pond.

How to Get There:
For the Wallace Brook trailhead:
- Take Route 431 to Woody Point and turn left for Trout River.
- After 9.2 km (5.5 mi) turn right into the parking lot signposted Green Gardens and Wallace Brook.

For the Long Pond trailhead:
- Proceed to the Wallace Brook trailhead, but continue past it for a further 2.9 km (1.7 mi) and turn right into the parking lot signposted Green Gardens. Although it is not signposted as such, this is the Long Pond trailhead.

Trail Directions:
Trail 1: Short Hike

Take the path from the parking lot to the hill behind Long Pond. The landscape looks stark and barren at first glance, but plants that have adapted to the adverse conditions do grow here. Tamaracks, barely 20 centimetres high, grow horizontally in contorted shapes.

17 min At the top of the hill, enjoy the view of glacially carved Trout River Gulch.

21 min At the junction and signpost, take the left fork (right fork is the steep return portion from the second fording of Wallace Brook), cross the hilltop and descend steeply through the woods. In the steeper sections and across the brooks, the steps and boardwalks are useful. In August, look for the tiny pale pink twinflower. You always know when it is nearby because of its strong fragrance. Look also for the Indian pipe plant, a strange plant that looks like it is made of wax. Pink flowers cover the sheep laurel shrub.

43 min Cross the bridge over the brook.

53 min Pass the bench on the left and take the stone steps downhill into the forest.

59 min The path arrives at the coast. Turn right and continue through the trees at the top of the cliffs.

1 hr 5 min The trail emerges onto a grassy meadow and continues through the long grasses. Look back to see the coastline which resembles Hawaii.

1 hr 10 min At the junction, the signpost shows Beach, straight, and 3.3 km Green Gardens, right. You can now either turn back, walk the detour to the beach, or continue along trail 2.

Detour: along the beach

Take the path signposted Beach. At the end of the meadow, descend the bank of steps down the cliffs. Once on the beach, turn right and walk towards the headland where part of the volcanic history of this area is preserved. See the layers of pillow lava that cooled rapidly in a tropical ocean, and the intruded layers of sill. Around the headland, and only accessible at low tide, a large sea cave is cut out of the cliffs. Walking south along the pebble beach, pass the reddish cliffs of trachyte lava and volcanic sea stacks and explore the tidal ponds for crabs and molluscs.

5 min Past the stacks, in a small valley set back into the cliffs, a small waterfall tumbles across the rocks and flows into the sea.

Trail 2: Long Hike

Take trail 1 as far as the signpost showing Beach, straight, and 3.3 km Green Gardens, right. Turn right and continue north along the terrace, taking time to look for whales and dolphins.

1 hr 16 min A small boardwalk crosses a brook near a large, grey stack just offshore. Continue along the terraces of grass, massive raspberry patches, wildflowers and clumps of trees.

1 hr 30 min The terrace ends and a narrow path traverses the cliffs several metres above the beach.

1 hr 37 min Two banks of steps lead to a short boardwalk at beach level, then another bank of steps climbs up to a railed boardwalk attached to the cliffs.

1 hr 40 min The path descends to the beach and immediately turns back up the cliffs. If streams have washed the path away, take the beach. Bleached driftwood lies scattered around and waves roll against the stacks, rocks and black sand.

1 hr 45 min The path descends again to the beach and scrambles over the assortment of coarse, cemented volcanic breccia and bulbous pillow lava strewn there.

1 hr 47 min Take the long bank of steps up the cliffs. The sign at the bottom of the steps points back along beach; the one at the top is marked with a hiker. The terrace at the top of the steps is covered in blue flag iris.

1 hr 57 min Pass a small square wooden pen around a tiny natural basin of water. A sign reads Boil Water Before Drinking. These are the Green Gardens. It is also the second primitive campsite, a favourite grazing area for sheep and a good spot for a break and lunch before the next strenuous section. (If you do not wish to ford Wallace Brook, this is the point at which you should turn round and retrace your steps to the Long Pond parking lot.)

1 hr 59 min Take the steps into the woods at the end of the terrace and begin snaking uphill. Long banks of steps and short boardwalks help with the tiring climb.

2 hr 20 min At a large area of dried spindly trunks, the path levels and then begins the steep descent to Wallace Brook (may be muddy after rain). On a clear day across Bonne Bay, Lobster Cove Head lighthouse sparkles like a white pebble against Berry Hill and the coastal lowlands.

2 hr 35 min Take the banks of steps (totalling approximately 180!) down to Wallace Brook.

2 hr 43 min The path on the left leads to the third primitive campsite at the mouth of the brook (signpost about boiling water), and a huge clump of pink wild roses graces its banks.

2 hr 45 min At the brook, take off your shoes and socks, roll up your trousers and cross on the rocks. Be careful. It may be slippery and the current is fast; it is safer to have something on your feet.

3 hr On the other side, the path runs along the bank

and climbs up the hill over banks of steps (again about 180!).

3 hr 12 min The path levels and continues along the forested hills above the brook and valley.

3 hr 18 min Take the bridge over the brook in a small ravine. Continue through the forest along the hilly path, boardwalks, steps and small board-walk bridges.

3 hr 32 min Walk down the long bank of steps and then another shorter one.

3 hr 34 min Ignore the small track to the brook on the right. Continue with the main trail along the forested banks and pass a small island. The path then bends away from the brook and climbs up several banks of steps.

3 hr 52 min At the junction and signpost, turn right for the Long Pond trailhead and prepare to ford the brook again*. Head for the small orange survey ribbon on the opposite bank (straight leads to the Wallace Brook trailhead; see ** below if you want this option).

4 hr 7 min On the other side, continue into the forest.

4 hr 9 min Cross the bridge over a brook and begin the uphill climb (at the time of writing this section was still being upgraded with new steps and boardwalks, so they are not included).

4 hr 28 min When the path finally levels, it comes out of the forest and crosses an open area of tamaracks, low conifers, sheep laurel and marsh grasses.

4 hr 43 min Peridotite rock begins to appear as the trail gets closer to the Tablelands. The vegetation lies close to the ground and the path is marked by a row of rocks.

4 hr 48 min At the junction with the outward-going trail the loop is completed. Turn left and continue over the hill and down to the Gulch.

5 hr 10 min Back at the parking lot.

From ** to Wallace Brook trailhead

3 hr 52 min At the junction continue straight (right to ford the brook and return to Long Pond trailhead, see * above). The trail continues up the hill through the largely deciduous forest. Numerous boardwalks and some steps help with the ascent. The first kilometre is the steepest and most tiring.

4 hr 10 min The steepest section ends and the path continues along a curved boardwalk through a small clearing of shrubby cinquefoil. This small shrub has yellow flowers throughout the summer. The Tablelands appear through the trees as the trail continues downhill.

4 hr 18 min Cross the large bridge over a small ravine and brook.

4 hr 33 min The trail leaves the forest and follows a long, curved boardwalk to Wallace Brook.

4 hr 38 min Take the suspension bridge over Wallace Brook. On the far side there is a small picnic area.

4 hr 39 min Cross the small bridge over a tributary to the brook and take either fork (they join shortly). Continue the last 300 m/yd over the peridotite rocks.

4 hr 42 min There is a pit toilet at the Wallace Brook parking lot. To return to the Long Pond parking lot, turn right along the road and walk for about 3 km (1.8 mi).

(If you are starting at the Wallace Brook parking lot, you will be walking this section in reverse. At the ford and junction you can join the trail 2 loop [see * above] and walk it clockwise or anti-clockwise.)

TROUT RIVER POND
(map 15)

Time: 1 hr 45 min
Distance: 7 km
(4.2 mi) one way
Difficulty: moderate;
good for older children

Condition: maintained;
packed gravel and rocks;
hilly

Summary of Trail:

Trout River Pond lies in another beautiful fjord. The 16-kilometre-long pond is divided by the Narrows into Upper (or Big) Pond, and Lower (or Small) Pond. The trail starts from the day-use area by the boat tour landing and continues along the pond's northern slopes. The first part runs along a hilly gravel path through mainly coniferous forests. About halfway along the trail the rocks of the Tablelands, which have been creeping in from the left, finally swamp the path. The trail ends rather abruptly in the middle of the peridotite valley, with the end of Upper Pond still a fair distance away. Another interesting way to see the pond is to take the 2 hr 30 min-boat tour from the day-use-area (see page 36 for details).

How to Get There:

- Take Route 431 to Trout River.
- At the end of the 431 turn left for Trout River campground.
- After 1.25 km (.8 mi) take the left fork for the picnic area and boat tour and park.

Trail Directions:

Facing the pond from the parking lot, take the gravel path on the left by the toilets, then take the left fork by the small hiker signpost. Continue across

Map 15: TROUT RIVER POND

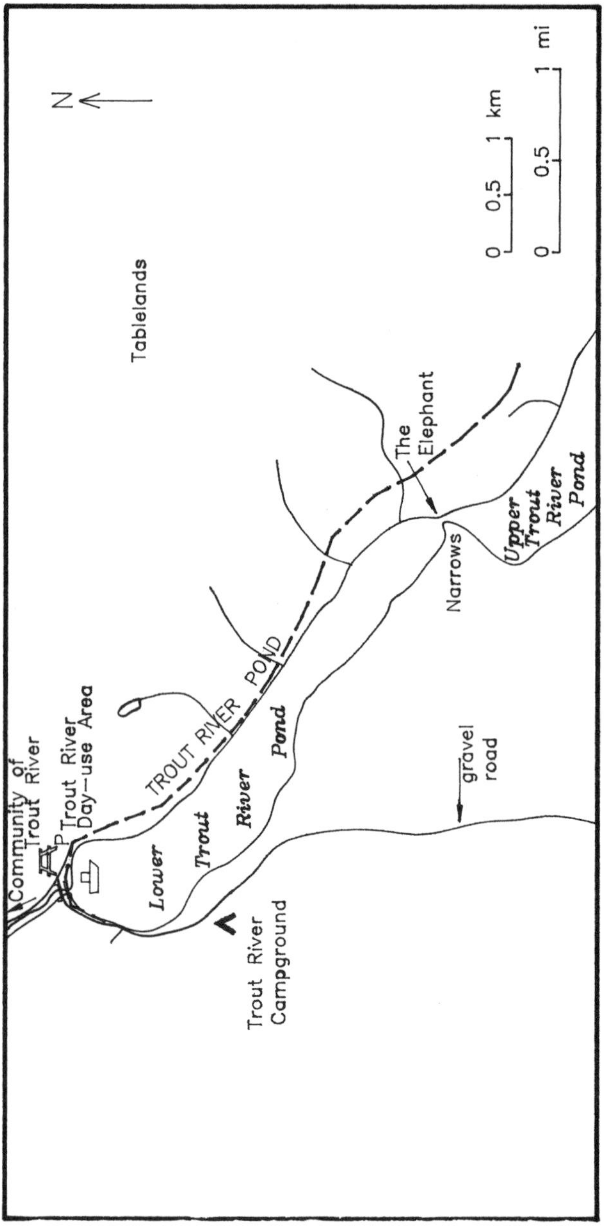

N
Tablelands
Community of Trout River
P
Trout River Day-use Area
TROUT RIVER POND
The Elephant
Narrows
Lower Trout River Pond
Upper Trout River Pond
gravel road
Trout River Campground
0 0.5 1 km
0 0.5 1 mi

the open picnic area, across the bridge, past another hiker signpost and onto the boardwalk. Trout River Pond stretches lengthways towards the Narrows, and you are at the short edge.

2 min The boardwalk ends as the trail enters the woods. Follow the path through the hilly woodlands on the slope above the pond. Boardwalks and steps make it a quick and easy walk.

6 min At the 0.5 km signpost, keep on through the forest. In some places there is no undergrowth, in others crackerberries and sasparilla grow under the trees. Numerous run-offs trickle into the pond.

13 min At the 1.0 km signpost, pass the small pebble beach beside the path. Wildflowers grow in open spots. You might find the shrubby cinquefoil with delicate yellow flowers, goldenrods, thistles, asters, ferns and bluebead lilies.

20 min Ahead of the 1.5 km signpost, grey vertical cliffs tower over the Narrows. Amongst the forest of small twisted spruce grow dogberries, birches and alders, and clumps of pink wild roses blossom.

27 min Pass the 2.0 km signpost.

33 min After the 2.5 km signpost, take the boardwalk across the brook flowing over the cobble beach.

40 min At the 3.0 km signpost the first view of the Tablelands creeps in from the left. A large Eastern white pine grows by the path and a brook flows over it. Past the brook the vegetation changes. Junipers, tamaracks, pines and spruces grow in contorted shapes. On the left the slopes of grey oceanic crust are being replaced by golden peridotite.

47 min Cross the stream on the rocks.

49 min Pass the 3.5 km signpost.

50 min Pass the pit toilet on the left. As the trail runs through the forest, Upper Pond appears beyond the Narrows and in the foreground a large cobbled spit projects from the southern bank of the pond.

55 min The path cuts across the spit. Tamaracks, spruces, birches, junipers, sheep laurel and blueberries grow in shrubs.

56 min Pass the 4.0 km signpost.

1 hr Cross the brook on the rocks. Eastern white pines grow in spreading, stunted forms. Shrubby cinquefoil finish flowering by the end of August, and in the fall small maples add a splash of red. Streams gush down from the Tablelands and moose leave prints in the soft mud.

1 hr 5 min Pass the small basin formed by a travertine spring.

1 hr 9 min After the 4.5 km signpost, the path ascends over the peridotite rocks. On either side tamaracks, dwarf birches, junipers and alders grow horizontally along the rocks. Streams trickle over bare rocks, making them slippery. A large solitary rock of grey gabbro lies in the middle of the valley of peridotite.

1 hr 12 min If you are at the 5.0 km signpost at the right time, you may see the tour boat manoeuvring through the shallow Narrows.

1 hr 22 min After the 5.5 km signpost, the ascent up the peridotite slope is steeper and the path is marked with small rocks. From the flat top of the hillock, you can see the far end of Upper Pond framed by the slopes of mountains.

1 hr 30 min Past the 6.0 km signpost, continue steeply downhill, take the boardwalk over the stream and marsh, and then walk up the other side.

1 hr 37 min Pass the 6.5 km signpost.

1 hr 43 min Pass the 7.0 km signpost.

1 hr 45 min The end of the trail is in the middle of

nowhere. You want to carry on towards the pond, but there is no trail — it just ends at a square of rocks laid out on the peridotite. So sit down on the rocks, listen to the silence and enjoy the stunning scenery.

Background Notes:
Trout River stands on a terrace of gravel deposited by melting ice. As the ice melted and the land rebounded, sea stacks and marine terraces were left far above sea level, giving a grey, quarry-like feel to the scenery around the community. The fishing premises and early homes sit on the shallow ledge between the sea and the first 30-metre-high terrace. There is little room to expand along this narrow ledge, so more homes and gardens stand on the wide valley that cuts through the marine terraces and once linked the pond to the sea. The fish plant and harbour are huddled around the north of the Trout River, so called because of the abundance of sea trout at the time the community was first settled.

By the turn of the century Trout River had become the largest lobster producer in Bonne Bay, with farming also maintaining importance. However, with less community pasture available since the establishment of the park in the 1970s, farming has decreased. Fishing is still important, though it is affected by the state of the fishery in Newfoundland.

PUZZLE POND TRAIL:
Puzzle Pond. BM

TERRA NOVA NATIONAL PARK

Unlike her younger sister Gros Morne National Park, who has made herself a worldwide reputation, Terra Nova National Park is relatively unknown outside Newfoundland. Even within Newfoundland, all too many people pass by seeing only what is visible from the Trans-Canada Highway — rolling hills cloaked in forests stretch as far as the eye can see, and at first glance the park appears little more than one huge mass of grey-green conifers. Seeing Terra Nova from the car does not do it justice. Terra Nova needs time. Time to walk through the forests and around the ponds where logs from distant drives still lie jammed, and beavers chisel where men once sawed and chopped. Time to sit on barren hilltops and feel the wind on your face and look out over the islands and bays where native peoples lived in coastal camps. Time to take a boat trip to remote coves where rusty wheels and engines attest to the sawmills and communities that once flourished there. Time to watch bald eagles and ospreys, perhaps see a minke or pothead whale or an iceberg.

Terra Nova National Park is situated on the northeast coast of Newfoundland. Its 400 sq km spread over sheltered islands and inlets lying across the mouth of Bonavista Bay, and are protected from the windy Atlantic Ocean by the Bonavista Peninsula. Bisected by the Trans-Canada Highway, the park is a three-hour, 210 km (126 mi) drive from the city limits of St. John's, 650 km (390 mi) along the Trans-Canada Highway from the year-round ferry crossing at Channel-Port aux Basques, and 180 km (108 mi) from the ferry crossing at Argentia (operates only in summer). It is also accessible by boat, and there are several small wharves within the park boundary. Established in 1957 and officially opened in 1961, Terra Nova is Newfoundland's first national park.

The Terra Nova landscape is a heritage from the last Ice Age. The massive ice cap that covered southwestern Newfoundland 8,000-12,000 years ago gouged out valleys, deepened rivers and scooped out hollows. When it melted, a land of fjords, coves, tidal flats, rocky cliffs and sandy beaches was revealed. Streams of melting ice filled the hollows, forming ponds as numerous as holes in a colander. Many silted up to become fens and bogs. Boreal forests slowly took hold on the shallow soil, though in some places conditions were too adverse and the bald, windswept hilltops remained. From this melting pot of ingredients emerged the landscape of what is today Terra Nova National Park.

The boreal forests support only trees that can survive the low winter temperatures, short summers and poor soil conditions of Newfoundland. The scraggly black spruce dominates the forests, crowding its more shapely sister the white spruce. The familiar Christmas-tree silhouette of the balsam fir provides foliage, fullness and colour. In the fall, the tamarack (also known as the larch, a deciduous conifer), and birches and aspens provide attractive splashes of gold and yellow on the predominantly coniferous forests, with solitary maples adding a flame of red.

Within the forests, whole glades of spruce are draped in an ethereal curtain of pale, wispy lichen known as old-man's beard. Harmless to the trees, it grows on dead branches where the air is extremely clean. Underfoot, carpets of lime-green moss tumble over rocks and stumps. Mats of crackerberries grow wherever a little sunlight filters to the forest floor. Clumps of ferns appear in the summer and a variety of fungi proliferate. The tops of the trees rustle in the wind, while beneath them the trails remain still. Moose tread lightly through the tangle of trees, never catching their massive antlers on branches that snag sweaters and hair. Lynx silently stalk snowshoe hare, and black bears forage in berry patches.

In the mornings the mist hovers low over the ponds, fens and bogs that are a trademark of boreal lands. Fifteen percent of the park's land area is covered by sphagnum-based bogs and sedgy fens dotted with islands of twisted tamarack and spruce. Newfoundland's provincial flower, the insect-eating pitcher plant, thrives under these wet conditions. Many ponds nestle in sheltered corners, others create waterways between hills of trees once valued for their lumber. Streams, tainted brown by tannic and humic acids, flow from the ponds and bogs and form new ponds behind sturdy beaver dams. Water is a dominant theme throughout the park.

From the bald, windswept hilltops of Blue Hill and Ochre Hill, and from vantage points on Malady Head and Mount Stamford, the theme of water takes on a new perspective. Thirty percent of the park's area is covered in seawater, and its shoreline of 200 km comprises numerous islands and three deep fjords that penetrate into the dark hills and forests. These three prongs are the Southwest Arm of Alexander Bay, Newman Sound and Clode Sound. They are accessible from land, but the wilder, unpopulated outer reaches of the park, where Maritime Archaic Indians, Paleo Eskimos and Beothuck Indians made their camps, cannot be reached without a boat. An excellent, highly educational boat tour from Newman Sound (see page 148 for details) takes visitors to these inaccessible places whose rocky beaches support sea urchins, starfish, mussels, periwinkles and rock crabs. Further offshore, whales and dolphins are attracted by the presence of squid and capelin. Sometimes they swim into the inner sound and perform antics in the quiet waters. Icebergs periodically drift into deep waters, although they appear more often as specks on the horizon.

The boreal forests meet the blue seawater behind the ribbonlike sandy beaches and rocky shores of the fjords. Sea urchins, jellyfish and clams abound in the intertidal zone. Over the waters, bald eagles and osprey glide in the wind looking for food, and migrating birds seeking shelter from the Atlantic storms take temporary refuge along the fertile estuaries.

Formerly the domain of Maritime Archaic Indians, Paleo Eskimos and Beothuck Indians (the original "red indians," so called because of the red ochre used to paint their bodies, clothes and utensils), today several coastal sites in the park have yielded prehistoric artefacts dating back to 3000 BC. Europeans did not arrive in these parts until the 16th century, when pirates found the coastline to their liking because of the numerous coves and inlets in which they could find refuge. Sailors came from France and Portugal to prey on the colonies of great auk which were found in such proliferation on the granite islands off the northeast coast of Newfoundland. Fishermen came and settled around Bonavista Bay because of the bountiful fish stocks. In the 16th and 17th centuries the British began to build settlements, and in time logging, lumbering and shipbuilding became important activities, reaching their heyday in the 1920s and 1930s and then declining to virtually nothing by the time the park was established in the late 1950s. With the arrival of the park, new opportunities developed, and today the communities around Terra Nova benefit from the jobs and tourism-related openings that the park has brought.

Within the boundaries of Terra Nova, camping is available at the Newman Sound campground (Malady Head campground is now closed) and a few primitive campgrounds in the more remote areas. The latter are accessible by hiking or by boat. Otherwise, the surrounding communities provide board and lodging in the form of cabins, hospitality homes and motels.

Once in the park, it is useful to stop at one of the two Visitor Centres to purchase a vehicle permit, pick up a copy of *Terra Nova Sounds* (a pamphlet about facilities in the park), and obtain the latest information on the interpretive programme and scheduled events organized by the park. Twin River Visitor Centre is on the Trans-Canada Highway at the southern entrance to the park and includes a small nature bookshop run by the Terra Nova Heritage Foundation for Terra Nova National Park. The second Visitor Centre also has a few books and is just off the Trans-Canada Highway on the road leading to Newman Sound. This area is the hub of the park, with the campground, small convenience store, laundromat, administration, activity centre, picnic area, several trails and boat tour all within a two-kilometre radius.

Throughout the park there are several picnic areas in attractive locations overlooking ponds, brooks and inlets. There are a number of trails, though some are in need of upgrading and the trail signs can be confusing. However, traffic is very light, and if you are looking for solitude, hiking in Terra Nova fills the criteria. In the words of D.E.

Schuler, superintendent in 1970, "visitors come primarily to picnic, swim, camp and enjoy the more social aspects which make superficial use of the park. These people see only what can be viewed from the 26 miles of the Trans-Canada Highway, or from the various vantage points, camping and picnic areas or park HQ. There are relatively few people who are using the many nature trails."

Sandy Pond has the park's only supervised swimming area. The white sandy beach is especially popular with families, and unlike the trails it can get crowded. In addition to the beach, there are canoe, kayak and paddle boat rentals at Sandy Pond, which is also the start of the main canoe route in the park. A short portage links Sandy Pond to Dunphys Pond, from where another portage takes the route out of the park and into Pitts Pond. A third portage connects the latter with the Terra Nova River, and from there the route negotiates white water to Glovertown and Alexander Bay. This is a dangerous and difficult route and should only be undertaken by experienced canoeists and kayakers.

Ocean canoeists can paddle the secluded waters of the Southwest Arm from the Southwest Arm picnic area to the mouth of Alexander Bay. Newman and Clode sounds also offer excellent canoeing and access to tiny coves where small family-run sawmills once thrived. Take note that the wind can be a hazard here. Another way to see the more remote parts of the park is by taking the Ocean Watch Boat Tour from Headquarters Wharf (see page148). Not only does it enable visitors to see otherwise inaccessible parts of the park, but it is also very informative. You may find yourself jigging for cod, trawling for plankton, hauling lobster traps or observing the antics of young bald eagles.

There are several ponds within the park which

are identified as fishing holes. Most of these are within easy walking distance of the Trans-Canada Highway along very wet paths. Anglers wishing to fish in the park must purchase a National Parks fishing licence and be aware of bag limits. If salmon are to be fished, a National Parks salmon fishing licence is also required. Licences are not required for salt-water fishing.

Bikes can be rented from the small convenience store at the Newman Sound campground, although cycling is restricted to the roads around Newman Sound, the Trans-Canada Highway and the Boundary (Blue Hill West) and Dunphys Pond trails.

On the banks of the Northwest River at the southern entrance of the park there is an 18-hole golf course which prides itself as being "one of Canada's most scenic." Lessons can be arranged and equipment rentals and sales are available, and after your game you can have a shower and dine in the clubhouse.

During the winter Terra Nova becomes a wonderland of snow. The Newman Sound campground remains partially open, and it is also possible to camp in the wild after first registering with the park staff. There are both groomed and ungroomed trails for cross-country skiing enthusiasts, or you can travel your own route. Snowshoeing along the trails is a wonderful way to observe the winter habitat of moose, lynx and snowshoe hare. In mid-January, ice fishing commences on the Southwest Arm, Dunphys Pond and Big Pond. The latter two require a National Parks fishing licence.

Visitors to Terra Nova are sure to see moose during their stay, for they are quite common in the park. In fact, they have become quite a problem on the Trans-Canada Highway and wander into the neighbouring communities during the winter months. The park is conducting a study, due to end in 1994, to map moose movements and to count their numbers. Visitors are asked to participate in the study by reporting any moose sightings and noting if they are wearing transmitting collars. Do not approach the animals if you cannot see from a distance. A similar study is under way tracking bear movements. Sightings of black bears (there are no grizzlies in Newfoundland) have increased over the last few years, and the study hopes to determine why this is so. Bear sightings should also be reported. Never approach a bear. Stand still and back off slowly. If necessary, leave something on the ground to try and distract it. Do not run as it will outrun you, and since it is an efficient climber, climbing a tree will not help. Enjoy the wildlife but do not approach or feed it.

Terra Nova is a special place. It is quiet, gentle and peaceful. None of the hiking trails are very challenging, although each person must know his or her own capabilities. Its weather is amongst the best on the island. When St. John's is buffeted by winds and horizontal rain, Terra Nova is enjoying sunshine. When snow turns to slush on the Avalon Peninsula, destroying any cross-country skiing plans, Terra Nova's trails remain crisp and white. Terra Nova must be used to its fullest before it can be appreciated. It is not enough to drive along the Trans-Canada Highway and stop at a picnic area or campground. When you have walked the trails, got your feet wet in the bogs and felt the morning mist on your face, then you can say you have been to Terra Nova.

How to Get There:
- When travelling eastwards on the Trans-Canada Highway, the north entrance of Terra Nova is approximately 70 km (42 mi) past Gander. From the

north entrance it is a further 11 km (6.6 mi) to the Newman Sound intersection.

- When travelling westwards on the Trans-Canada Highway, the south entrance of Terra Nova is approximately 30 km (18 mi) west of Clarenville. From the south entrance it is a further 30 km (18 mi) to the Newman Sound intersection.
- From the Newman Sound intersection it is 2.2 km (1.3 mi) to the campground. (It is 41 km [25 mi] along the Trans-Canada Highway from the north entrance to the south entrance.)

Useful Information:

Terra Nova National Park:
Glovertown, Newfoundland, AOG 2LO
Tel: (709) 533-2801.

When to Go: The park is open year round in that hiking and skiing are available. However, only a section of the Newman Sound campground is open in winter, but it is not known whether the washrooms will continue to provide hot water. If you stay in some of the surrounding accommodations, the park is beautiful in winter. Once the thaw comes in April, the trails become exceedingly wet, and some of the ones beside streams and rivers become flooded. By mid-May most trails are walkable with the exception of the Outport, which needs more time to dry out. Fall is a very good time to hike in Terra Nova, with warm autumnal colours adding an extra softness to the landscape. Summer is usually quite sunny and the weather can be very pleasant.

Visitor Centres: Newman Sound has a Visitor Centre (off the Trans-Canada Highway) and there is another on the Trans-Canada Highway at Twin Rivers by the south entrance. The season is from mid-June to Labour

Day, when the centres are open daily 10:00-20:00. Pick up a copy of *Terra Nova Sounds*, the park's information pamphlet, and an update of the interpretive programme. A map of the park can be purchased and there are bookshops run by Terra Nova Heritage Foundation.

Activity Centre: This centre opened in 1992 and is in one of the buildings by the old park cabins. It houses slide shows and exhibits, and some interpretive events are scheduled there. There is a small souvenir/book counter run by the Terra Nova Heritage Foundation.

Vehicle Permit: A permit is required from mid-June (start of school holidays) to Labour Day (first weekend in September). 1993 prices were $5.00 daily, $10.00 for four days, $20.00 for an annual Terra Nova permit, and $30.00 for a permit that covers all Canadian National Parks. Canadian seniors get their passes free.

Park Campgrounds: There are two campgrounds within the park, but Malady Head is currently closed so no details are given. Reservations for Newman Sound can be made in advance. There are no electrical, water or sewage hook-ups, although there are hot showers, flush toilets, a laundromat, a convenience store, bike rentals, kitchen shelters, phones, an outdoor theatre and a picnic area. Newman Sound is open year round. 1993 prices (inc. GST) were one night $10.00, four nights $30.00 and one week $50.00 (subject to change). A number of sites adjacent to an enclosed kitchen shelter are designated for winter camping and are available at no charge from mid-October (the Tuesday after Canadian Thanksgiving) to mid-May. In addition to Newman Sound, four primitive campsites are located in the more remote areas of the park (free of charge), but back-country campers must register with park staff before setting out. Pit toilets, fireplaces, firewood, and picnic tables are provided. The backcountry sites are as follows:

MINCHINS COVE: accessible from the Outport trail or by boat.

SOUTH BROAD COVE: accessible from the Outport trail or by boat.

OVERS ISLANDS: off-shore island camping accessible by boat, although there is no wharf.

DUNPHYS POND: island camping on a pond, accessible by canoe or kayak.

Private Campgrounds: There is a private campground in Eastport which operates during the summer season (more information at the Visitor Centres).

Accommodation: The park cabins have been closed for a few years and they are not due to be reopened, but private accommodation in the form of cabins and hospitality homes can be found outside the park in Charlottetown, Eastport, Glovertown, Traytown and Port Blandford. There are listings in the Newfoundland and Labrador Travel Guide available from the Department of Tourism, 1-800-563-6353 or (709) 729-2830, and there are many pamphlets in the Visitor Centres.

Interpretive Programme: The park runs an excellent interpretive programme, so it is worth picking up the latest schedule at the Visitor Centres or from the campground kiosks. Events consist of evening programmes at the Newman Sound outdoor theatre, guided walks and tours, and a children's programme. Special events such as canoe demonstrations, coastguard demonstrations, talks on endangered species and a folk festival are also scheduled. All events are free. In the event of bad weather some activities may have to be postponed, so it is always wise to check at the campground kiosk. Bring along a blanket and some insect repellent.

Boat Tours: Ocean Watch Tours are based at HQ Wharf at Newman Sound. Season: June 20 to Labour Day. Schedule: In 1993 there were four different daily tours which varied from 1 hr 30 min to 3 hours. 1993 prices were about $19-$26 adult, children under 12 half price. Tours are part of the park's interpretive programme, are educational and take place in the sheltered waters of Newman Sound. Reservations and information, (709) 533-2884 or 533-2801.

Wharves and Boat Launches: Saltons Brook on Newman Sound has a wharf and boat launch as well as washrooms and sheltered kitchens. Check with the park for current mooring rates. Minchins Cove, South Broad Cove (both on Newman Sound) and Park Harbour (Clode Sound) have a wharf (no charge for mooring). Green Head on the Southwest Arm (by the causeway on Route 310 to Eastport), has a boat launch and there is also one in Charlottetown (Clode Sound).

Canoeing and Kayaking: Ocean canoeing can be done on the waters of Southwest Arm, Newman Sound and Clode Sound. The latter two are subject to winds. The main freshwater route through the park starts at Sandy Pond, from where a 75-metre portage links it to Beachy Pond and Dunphys Pond. On the latter, a small primitive campsite on an island provides total seclusion. A second portage links Dunphys Pond to Pitts Pond where the route leaves the park. It can, however, be continued to the village of Terra Nova, from where there is white-water canoeing along the Terra Nova River to Glovertown and Alexander Bay. This route is only for experienced kayakers and canoeists, who should check with the Visitor Centres for up-to-date information and maps.

Canoe and Kayak Rentals: These are available at Sandy Pond from Victoria Day to Labour Day (weather permitting). Rentals can be hourly, daily or weekly, and 1993 prices varied from approximately $5.30 per hour to $92.20 per week (inc. taxes). A maximum of two persons is allowed in a canoe and one per kayak. Life jackets are included.

Swimming: Swimming is only supervised at Sandy Pond from the last weekend in June to Labour Day. There is no charge to use the beach, but lounge chairs cost around $5.20 per day and paddle boats can be rented for about $4.90 per hour (inc. taxes). There is a small sandy beach with shallow water at the Malady Head picnic area opposite the Malady Head campground entrance (closed) on Route 310, but it is not supervised.

Fishing: There are several fishing ponds in the park. Arnolds Pond, Kellys Pond, Chatman Ponds and Trout Pond are all signposted from the Trans-Canada Highway and can be reached by short trails, as can Davey Anns Pond. These are usually very wet and not recommended for walking other than as access to the ponds. Ochre Hill Ponds also have good fishing and are along the Ochre Hill trail. National Parks fishing licences are required for freshwater fishing and bag limits are set for most species. No licences are required far saltwater fishing. January 15th marks the start of ice fishing on Big Pond and Dunphys Pond. For up-to-date information contact the Visitor Centres.

Golfing: Twin Rivers Golf Course is situated at the southern entrance to the park. It is an 18-hole, par 71 championship course. Lessons are available, and there are rentals, power carts, a pro-shop, club-house and casual dining. Reservations and enquiries, (709) 543-2626.

Bike Rentals: Newman Sound campground convenience store. Biking is restricted to the Boundary (Blue Hill West) and Dunphys Pond trails, the Trans-Canada Highway and the roads around Newman Sound.

Groceries: Although there is a small convenience store in the Newman Sound campground for emergency supplies, it is best to come prepared with your own. The nearby communities have convenience stores, but for supermarkets and other stores you need to go to Clarenville or Gander.

Laundromat: Newman Sound campground.

Banks: In Glovertown there is a Bank of Nova Scotia with a cash stop. Eastport has a Credit Union, and Clarenville and Gander have banks.

Propane: Ultramar gas station (by Splash-n-Putt Cabins) at the north entrance of the park.

Sewage Dumping Stations: The dumping station at the Newman Sound campground is open from mid-May to mid-October. The Malady Head campground dump is currently closed.

Medical Clinics and Hospitals: There are medical clinics in Glovertown and Eastport, and Clarenville and Gander both have hospitals.

RCMP: Glovertown: (709) 533-2828.

Newfoundland and Labrador Department of Tourism: 1-800-563-6353

Terra Nova Heritage Foundation: (709) 533-2884 or contact the park.

Map 16: TERRA NOVA NATIONAL PARK

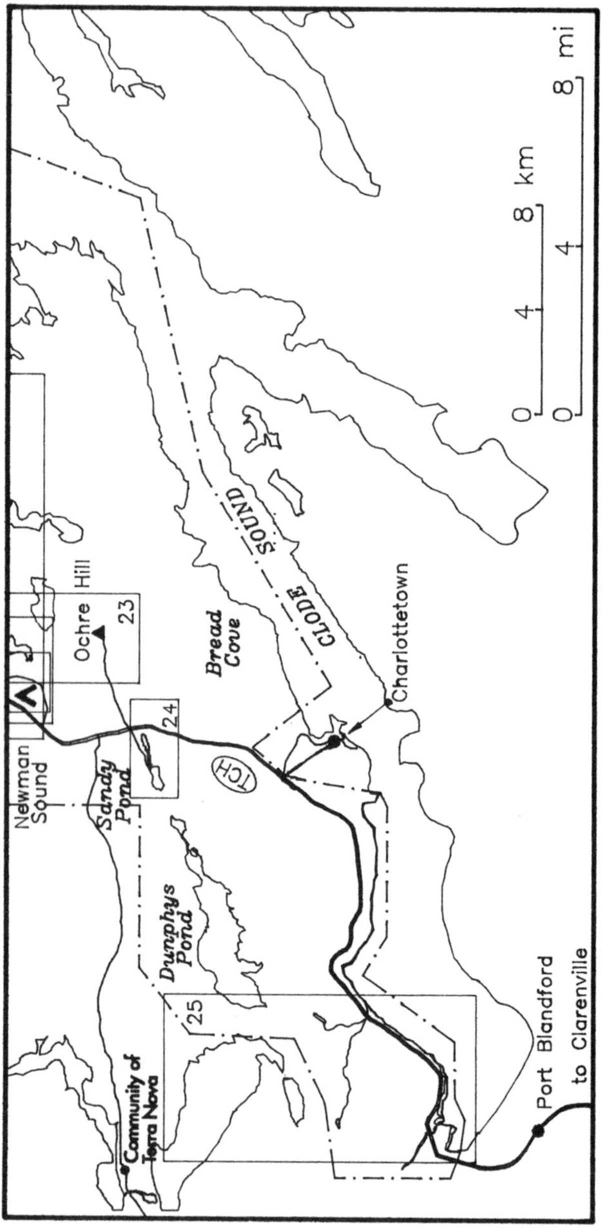

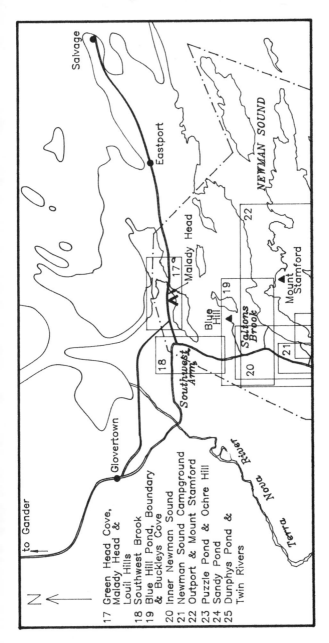

N ←

to Gander

Salvage

Eastport

Glovertown

17 Green Head Cove,
   Malady Head &
   Louil Hills
18 Southwest Brook
19 Blue Hill Pond, Boundary
   & Buckleys Cove
20 Inner Newman Sound
21 Newman Sound Campground
22 Outport & Mount Stamford
23 Puzzle Pond & Ochre Hill
24 Sandy Pond
25 Dunphys Pond &
   Twin Rivers

NEWMAN SOUND

Malady Head

17

17

18

19

20

21

22

Blue Hill

Saltons Brook

Mount Stamford

Southwest Arm

Terra Nova River

TERRA NOVA NATIONAL PARK   153

TERRA NOVA - Trails at a Glance

Trail Name	Time* hr:min	Distance* (approx)	Difficulty
Green Head Cove (map 17)	0:40	2.25 km (1.4 mi)	moderate
Malady Head (map 17)	0:45	2.25 km (1.4 mi)	moderate
Louil Hills (map 17)	1:10	5 km (3 mi) loop	easy (except for short spur)
Southwest Brook (map 18)	0:35	2 km (1.2 mi)	easy
Blue Hill Pond (map 19)	0:50	3 km (1.8 mi)	easy
Boundary (Blue Hill West) (map 19)	1:05	5 km (3 mi)	easy
Buckleys Cove (map 19)	1:00	4.8 km (2.9 mi)	moderate
Inner Newman Sound (Coastal Trail)			
Trail 1 (map 20)	1:10	5.5 km (3.3 mi)	easy
Trail 2 (map 20)	0:30	2.5 km (1.5 mi)	moderate
Newman Sound Campground (map 21)	1:30	6 km (3.6 mi) loop	easy
Outport (excludes Mount Stamford) (map 22)	5:20 (+2:30 boat trip)	18.5 km (11.1 mi) loop	strenuous
Detour to Mount Stamford	0:30	1.5 km (.9 mi)	strenuous
Mount Stamford (map 22)	3:00	10.5 km (6.3 mi)	moderate (strenuous spur)

Trail Name	Time* hr:min	Distance* (approx)	Difficulty
Puzzle Pond (map 23)	1:55	7.8 km (4.7 mi)	easy (moderate return)
Ochre Hill (map 23)	2:00	8.25 km (5 mi) loop	moderate
Sandy Pond (map 24)	0:45	3 km (5 mi) loop	easy
Dunphys Pond (map 25)	1:15	4.75 km (2.9 mi)	easy
Twin Rivers (map 25)	0:10	800 m/yd	easy
Fishing Holes (directions not included)			
Arnolds Pond	0:10	1 km (.6 mi)	easy
Kellys Pond	0:25	1.8 km (1.1 mi)	easy
Davey Anns Pond	0:15	600 m/yd	moderate
Chatman Ponds	0:50	2.5 km (1.5 mi) loop	easy
Trout Pond	0.05	300 m/yd	easy

*unless stated otherwise times and distances are one way

Map 17: GREEN HEAD COVE, MALADY HEAD & LOUIL HILLS

ALEXANDER BAY

Eastport

P

GREEN HEAD COVE

Wings Brook

Day-use Area

P

MALADY HEAD

183m
Malady Head

SOUTHWEST ARM

Northeast Arm

310

TCH

LOUIL HILLS

--- --- GREEN HEAD COVE
··········· MALADY HEAD
——— LOUIL HILLS

N

0   0.5   1km
|————————|————————|
0   0.5   0.5   1mi

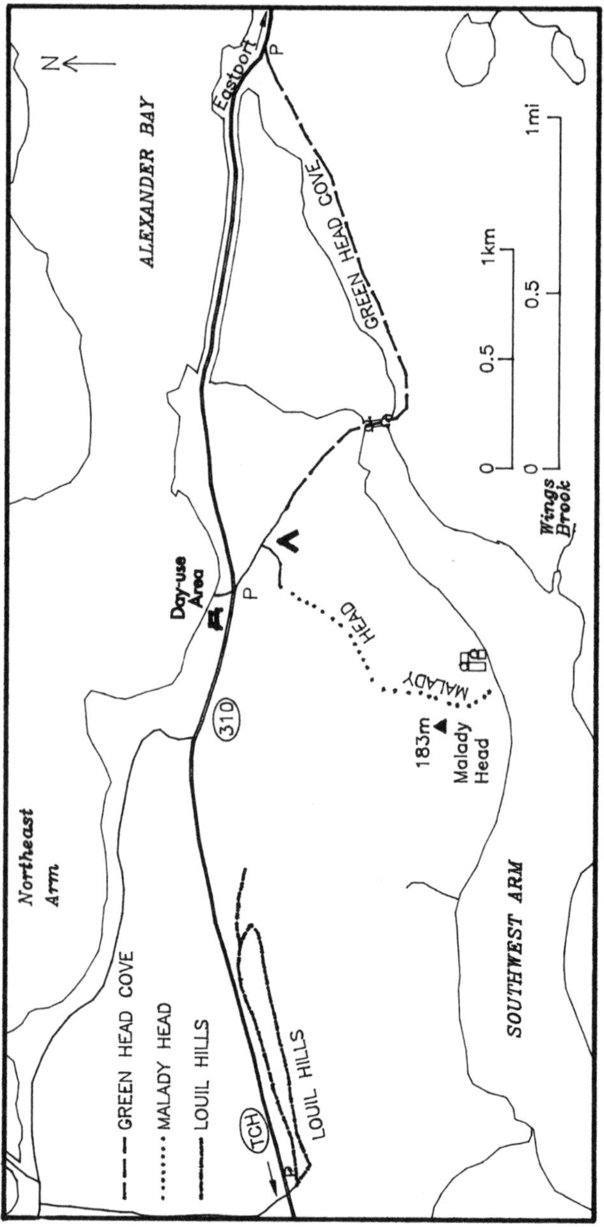

GREEN HEAD COVE
(map 17)

Time: 40 min
Distance: 2.25 km
(1.4 mi) one way
to causeway
Difficulty: moderate;
good for older children

Condition: maintained;
steep in parts; mostly dry

(**Time:** 1 hr **Distance:** 3.25 km [2 mi] to campground)

Summary of Trail:
The Green Head Cove trail follows an abandoned section of the old Eastport road. Skirting the slopes above Broad Cove and Southwest Arm, it runs through a woodland of deciduous and coniferous trees and descends to the old causeway and a pedestrian bridge to the north shore. The setting of the causeway is picturesque, and the highlight of the trail. Across the causeway a trail continues north to the Malady Head campground (campground is closed), from where another trail climbs Malady Head. With two cars, the trail can be walked one way.

How to Get There:
- From the north entrance of the park continue south along the Trans-Canada Highway for 500 m/yd.
- Turn left onto Route 310 to Eastport, Traytown and Glovertown. Continue for approximately 7 km (4 mi) passing Malady Head picnic area on the left, Malady Head campground on the right and cross the causeway.
- Turn right into a small turning opposite a rock outcrop in the sea (the turning is easy to miss). A

notice board marks the trail and a chain restricts access to vehicles.

Should you want to start from the Malady Head campground (closed), head to site 148, where the trail is incorrectly signposted Old Eastport Road and Malady Head, and not Green Head Cove as expected. Add a further 20 minutes from site 148 to the causeway.

Trail Directions:

Pass around the chain and ascend along the over-grown old road. The trail runs gently uphill with some short level and downhill sections. Banks of alders grow on either side and balsam firs and birches limit the view of Alexander Bay.

28 min From the crest of the hill the trail descends towards the causeway through the mixed forest of spruce, fir and birch. On the right, views of the Southwest Arm flicker through the trees.

40 min Left of the causeway, Malady Head looms out of the water. Named My Lady's Head by local fisherman, it later became MA-lady's Head and then Malady (pronounced ma-LADDIE) Head. There is said to be a trail along the south bank (left of the causeway) to Wings Brook opposite Malady Head, but I have never found it. On the far right, the present-day Eastport road follows the new, long causeway that crosses Alexander Bay. To continue to the Malady Head campground (closed), or to connect with the trail to Malady Head, continue across the suspension bridge within the causeway and carry on up the hill.

1 hr The trail comes out in the campground by site 148. To connect with the Malady Head trail, walk towards the exit of the campground, and before the section downhill to the kiosk, turn left (signposted for the theatre) and immediately left again up the gravel road. Follow the signs for site 62 (from site 148 this is about a 15-minute walk).

Background Notes:

Terra Nova has 200 km of spectacular shoreline. Part is rugged, but parts, like the finger-like prongs of Alexander Bay, Newman Sound and Clode Sound, have quiet secluded waters. The intertidal zone is the area that becomes exposed between high and low tides and which harbours species that have adapted to the challenges of their environment. Spending half of their time submerged in water and the other half exposed to air, these species have to cope with changes in oxygen, temperature and the salt content of the water. Mobile species like crabs will move out of the area at low tide or head for tidal pools, while others like barnacles, mussels, limpets and periwinkles close their shells tightly in an effort to control the changes in temperature and salt level. The creatures of the intertidal zone in the Southwest Arm do not have to contend with the destructive force of the pounding waves which poses such problems to organisms living in more rugged spots. However, they still have to develop a means of withstanding such wave action as there is. This varies from cementing themselves in place (barnacles), to swaying with the movement of the water on suckerlike roots (seaweed), to burrowing into the sand and mud (clams).

MALADY HEAD
(map 17)

Time: 45 min
Distance: 2.25 km
(1.4 mi) one way
Difficulty: moderate;
good for older children

Condition: maintained;
mostly dry; steep in parts

(add **Time:** 20 min **Distance:** 1 km [.6 mi] one way if walking through the campground)

Summary of Trail:
Our trail begins inside the Malady Head campground (although the campground is closed, the trail is still accessible on foot). It winds through boreal forests of spruce, birch and fir that shade carpets of crackerberries and moss. Old-man's beard (also called maldow) drapes over dead spruce trees like ragged curtains. Ascending steadily, the trail culminates in a lookout near the top of Malady Head. Chose a clear day to enjoy the view across the hills, ponds and fjords of the park.

How to Get There:
- From the north entrance of the park continue south along the Trans-Canada Highway for 500 m/yd.
- Turn left onto Route 310 to Eastport, Traytown and Glovertown (ignore turnings).
- After approximately 4 km (2.4 mi) turn right into the Malady Head campground, park by the kiosk (campground closed), enter the campground, and follow signs to site 62 (the walk takes approximately 20 minutes).

Trail Directions:
The trail begins by the notice board to the left of site

62. Walk around the barrier, up the gravel road and turn left onto the path signposted Malady Head 2 km. Cross the overgrown rock outcrop and take the bank of wooden steps down into the forest. Old-man's beard hangs limply over the spruces and firs, and green moss covers the fallen trees and rocks. In the early summer, white flowers sprinkle the mats of crackerberries like petals, whereas in late summer they are replaced by shiny red berries. Although the berries are edible, they are tasteless and, as with anything that grows in a National Park, should not be picked. The red squirrels chatter excitedly (they were introduced to the island in the 1960s, and their raiding of bird nests is thought to be responsible for the declining bird populations on the island), and prints and droppings indicate the presence of moose. Bluebead lilies with their poisonous blue berries rise on long single stems from a bed of shiny, green leaves (the beads are yellow flowers in early summer).

5 min Take the boardwalk over the small brook and continue uphill through the woods. In early summer there may be some wet patches.

12 min Another boardwalk and steps up, followed by a signpost to Malady Head.

16 min Boardwalk and steps up, followed by more boardwalks.

20 min Boardwalk and steps down. The path ascends gently. It becomes rougher underfoot but uses boardwalks where necessary.

28 min A handrail assists as the path ascends steeply. Pass the bog on the right and the obstructed path on the left.

35 min Continue up the three banks of stairs (with handrail). Listen for the woodpeckers and maybe take a rest on the moss-covered rock on the left past the second bank of steps. It looks like an arm-

chair. Continue uphill with the aid of the hand
rail and pass the moss-covered cliffs on the right.
42 min The path begins to descend, and through the
trees there is the promise of superb views. The path
ends on a wooden lookout far above the Southwest
Arm. Be careful if you have small children with you
as the railings around the lookout are very open.
Sit on the rocks, rest a while and enjoy the view.

Background Notes:
Standing on the platform on Malady Head and looking out over the park, thoughts of the first peoples
who walked these shores and fished the sheltered
coves and inlets spring to mind. Even though to date
there has not been much archaeological activity
within the park, the preliminary studies that have
taken place indicate that aboriginal markings in the
area date back nearly 5,000 years.

In 1979 and 1980, archaeological studies, by James
A. Tuck and Anna Sawicki respectively, resulted in
some tentative conclusions about the aboriginal
people who occupied the park area. Most of the
coastal sites were badly eroded, but the archaeological teams were able to find several artefacts
including projectile points, flakes, chipped stones,
burned bone, charcoal, celts and scrapers dating
back to 3000 BC. These suggest the presence of
Maritime Archaic Indians, Dorset Eskimos and more
recent peoples, probably Beothucks and Micmacs.
For more information, see Tuck's *Archaeological
Survey of Terra Nova National Park*. It is known that
the Beothucks occupied this area when the first
Europeans arrived in the 16th century, and that the
next 250 years saw the demise of these native
people. It has been suggested that some of the place
names around Alexander Bay may reflect the conflict

between the Beothucks and the Europeans. Sha-
nawdithit, who died in 1829, was the last of the
Beothucks.

LOUIL HILLS
(map 17)

Time: 1 hr 10 min
Distance: 5 km
(3 mi) loop
Difficulty: easy (except
for short spur to summit);
good for older children

Condition: maintained;
parts very wet in early
summer; short steep spur

Summary of Trail:
In early summer the lower, alder-filled part of the
trail can have several large, wet spots, but as the
trail enters into the spruce, fir and birch forest the
path is solid and dry. Old-man's beard drapes over
dead, dry branches of spruce in grey, ghostly
stands.The spur to the top of one of the hills is a short,
steep climb and leads to a rocky outcrop at the summit with long views overlooking Alexander Bay, the
outports of Traytown and Glovertown, and Southwest
Arm. The continuation of the spur to the second hill
is too overgrown to follow.

How to Get There:
- From the north entrance of the park continue south
   along the Trans-Canada Highway for 500 m/yd.
- Turn left onto Route 310 to Eastport, Traytown and
   Glovertown.
- After approximately 1.2 km (.7 mi), turn right into

the parking lot signposted Louil Hills (opposite the road on the left to Traytown).

Trail Directions:

From the parking lot, take the wide gravel path past the barrier and posts and turn left at the signpost for Louil Hills. Follow the grassy path through the alders (in early summer this area can be muddy). Turn left at the signpost with a hiker to Louil Hills (this sign had fallen over in 1993), and continue through the tall alders. The path soon becomes gravel and packed earth, passing beneath spruce trees with an undergrowth of sheep laurel. In early summer the attractive, pink-purple flowers of the sheep laurel are in bloom.

5 min Pass the signpost with a hiker and glimpse the view of Alexander Bay, Traytown and Glovertown through the trees on the left. Enjoy the birds singing amongst the full, green fir trees.

7 min Pass the signpost with a hiker. The old-man's beard grows on the dead branches of tall black spruces. Along the flat trail, moose spoor lies in small piles. I am told that if it is firm and shaped like small eggs, it is spoor from winter feeding, while if it is softer and more bulky, and you wouldn't dream of picking it up, it is spoor from summer feeding. Grey reindeer and caribou mosses grow in drier places beneath the sheep laurel, and green mosses grow in the damp under the trees.

13 min The trail bends left after an uphill incline and then runs gently downhill through the forest and sheep laurel. Alexander Bay shimmers through the trees. There may be some wet patches.

20 min The trees become denser and the path follows a stream bed gently uphill. It can be muddy.

23 min At the signposts for Louil Hills and the viewpoint, turn left into the trees. This spur to the summit of one of the hills is rough and steep, though short. It leads to uninterrupted views of Alexander Bay, Traytown, Glovertown and the northern end of the park.

27 min Once out of the woods and on the exposed rock outcrop, head past the rock with graffiti and across the summit. Small paths crisscross over the rocks and through the light undergrowth of sheep laurel and mosses. None of them lead anywhere. After inhaling the views and bracing the blustery winds, return to the shelter of the forest at the junction with the main trail.

37 min Turn left onto the main trail and follow the path through the spruce trees. Old-man's beard hangs all over the dead branches and trunks of standing and fallen trees, and green mosses spread over the forest floor between the sheep laurel. The trail begins flat before sloping gently downhill. Some windfall may lie across the path.

50 min At the signpost to Louil Hills 1.75 km, emerge from the forest and continue through the area previously destroyed by fire and subsequently taken over by alders.

1 hr 2 min Emerge from the alders opposite a small pond or large puddle by a signpost to Louil Hills. The trail is not very clear at this point. Ignore the path on the right and continue straight along the right bank of the pond, circumnavigating the very wet section as best you can.

1 hr 10 min Although you don't realize it, you are back on the outward-going path. When it comes to the gravel road, turn right at the junction and reach the barrier by the parking lot.

Background Notes:

In the hundred years from the 1850s to the 1950s, the area around Alexander Bay changed substantially. Then between the 1950s and today it changed again, and after a period of settlement and expansion the coves and inlets are once more silent. Traytown and Glovertown have survived, but little of the lumbering operations and fishery that they supported are in evidence. Even the firetower that stood at the summit of Louil Hills has gone, but the view of Alexander Bay (once called Bloody Bay) is almost as tranquil as it was before the arrival of Europeans.

In *Terra Nova National Park, Human History Study*, Kevin Major writes that as the communities along northern Bonavista Bay became more populated with settlers arriving from the West Country of England, existing families moved further south along the indented coastline in search of new fishing grounds. Older communities such as Barrow Harbour, Broom Close and Salvage (northeast of the park) had increased extensively, and the arable land and good fishing grounds further south became very inviting to many. As the settlers moved, Eastport, Sandy Cove and Happy Adventure (northeast of the park) were established and eventually outgrew the communities that had fed them. Salvage still exists today, but Barrow Harbour and Broom Close have long since been abandoned.

The pioneers of the Bloody Bay area were Richard Stroud and his family, who arrived from England in the 1830s to establish a salmon fishery. In the 1890s the salmon and cod fisheries were surpassed by lumbering operations, and by the early 1920s there were 19 sawmills in the area. After a tremendously destructive fire in 1946, the mills ceased to operate.

SOUTHWEST BROOK
(map 18)

Time: 35 min
Distance: 2 km
(1.2 mi) one way
Difficulty: easy;
good for children

Condition: maintained;
mostly dry

Summary of Trail:

This pretty hike along the banks of the Southwest
Brook can be started at either the Southwest Arm or
the Southwest Brook picnic areas. The trail passes
through largely coniferous forests of spruce and fir,
crosses a large suspension bridge and passes through
reedy marshes as it approaches the estuary of the
Southwest Arm. Along the Shady Hollow section of
the trail, there are two beaver dams and a lodge. At
the Southwest Arm end of the trail, Malady Head
looms out of the blue waters. At low tide the mud
flats are uncovered, and shorebirds dig for insects
and small molluscs. With two cars, this trail can be
hiked one way.

How to Get There:

- Take the Trans-Canada Highway north from the
  Newman Sound turning.
- After 6 km (3.6 mi) turn right into the Southwest
  Brook picnic area, and park.

Trail Directions:

Walk through the grassy picnic area and take the
  path by the water tap (boil before drinking). Follow the gravel path through the spruce forest
  alongside the brook.

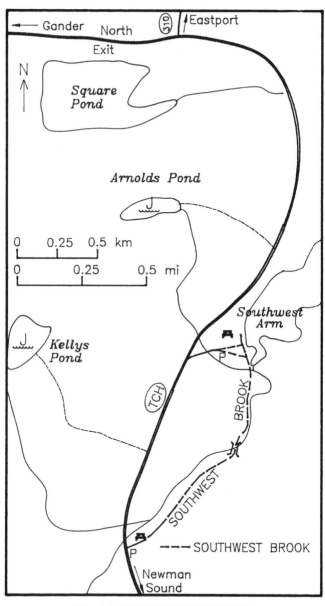

Map 18: SOUTHWEST BROOK

3 min Cross the boardwalk bridge (the rails were broken off at time of writing) over a tributary and take the steps up into the forest on the far side. Once in the trees, a rough barrier partially cordons off the steep bank to the brook below. Some crackerberries grow in the woodland shade. In August and September their white bracts are replaced by bright red berries. From its large smooth leaves the long thin stem of the bluebead lily supports a solitary yellow flower and then a large blue berry. Birches grow around the streams, and you may find some boletus mushrooms.

6 min A few steps down are followed by three short boardwalks (some wet patches may remain between the boardwalks in early summer).

13 min Go along the lengthy boardwalk (as the ice melts in April the boardwalks along this section of the trail are frequently uprooted and moved by flood waters from the brook), and continue through the spruce forest, across the boardwalks and past the railings. Carpets of green moss grow under the trees and some old-man's beard drapes over the dead lower branches and trunks. The trail ascends gently along the banks above the brook and runs parallel to it. In early summer some wet patches may linger on stubbornly, but they are not usually a great problem. The intermittent drone of traffic on the Trans-Canada Highway is more frustrating.

18 min Cross the large suspension bridge across the brook. On the far side, the alders are frequently flooded in the springtime, and the boardwalk can get swept away. Climb up the steps and continue across the small boardwalk bridge with one rail over the stream. The old-man's beard grows black and dense on the dry, lower trunks while the crowns of the trees remain green and full. The moss carpet spreads indiscriminately over fallen trees and rocks as boardwalks assist over minor wet patches. An island is formed by the two arms of the brook, and further downstream a blind tributary ends abruptly. The path continues along the water's edge. Ignore the path from the Southwest Arm parking lot which joins from the left.

23 min Cross the boardwalk over the meandering stream. The still, blackened trunks resemble victims of horrific battles. The boardwalk runs alongside the river where churning waters are alive and burbling.

28 min At the Closed sign across the path, detour to the left of the giant beaver dam along which the path used to go. Cross the small stream and return to the boardwalk next to the brook. On the left a graveyard of dark grey trunks projects out of the marsh like ancient headstones. Two short boardwalks lead to a bend where the path turns away from the brook and follows a long curved boardwalk over the marsh. The beer-brown waters of the brook continue rushing towards the estuary.

30 min At the junction in the boardwalk, turn left along a short spur towards the graveyard of trunks and a large beaver lodge looming out of the destruction. Do not walk on the nearby dam, but return to the main trail, from where the dam can be clearly viewed. Continue along the boardwalk path as it meanders over the marshes of the Southwest Arm estuary. Ignore the turning on the left unless you want to get to the car park at Southwest Arm before reaching the end of the trail. This part of the trail is called Shady Hollow.

34 min Pass another turning on the left to the Southwest Arm parking lot and continue straight to the wharf.

35 min At the wharf you can enjoy the tranquillity

of the Migratory Bird Sanctuary, where birds flying south for the winter sometimes take a rest before continuing on their long journey. Across the blue water, Malady Head rises in the distance. At low tide the mud flats are revealed, and shorebirds sit on the rocks and wade in the shallow pools. Look for the bittern, a brown heron-like bird that inhabits the reedy marshes of the estuary. Across from the wharf on the far bank, an unmaintained trail used to follow the water's edge to Wings Brook bridge (across from Malady Head) and to the old Eastport road causeway. However, apart from the immediate problem of how to cross the water to reach the trail, it is too overgrown to follow. By the wharf, one path leads to the kitchen shelter, pit toilets and car park and the other along the bank to a few picnic tables.

Background Notes:

A hardworking beaver chiselling away at a tree near a peaceful pond holds a tender spot in many a Canadian's heart. So much so that beavers are considered an unofficial mascot of Canada and have been designated as the symbol denoting all the National Parks. Prized for their thick fur coats, beavers very nearly became extinct in Canada during the fur-trapping era of the 1800s, but today they are strictly protected and their numbers are recovering.

Signs of beavers are found in several places in the park, although the best places to see them vary from year to year. Shady Hollow has a large dam and lodge and at one time was a good spot for beaver watching. Another old haunt is Burnt Point, by the Malady Head picnic area, but again the beavers have not been seen there for a couple of years. Cobblers Brook, by the shores of Clode Sound, has a dam, but for the past two years the best place to see

Map 19: BLUE HILL POND, BOUNDARY (BLUE HILL WEST) & BUCKLEYS COVE

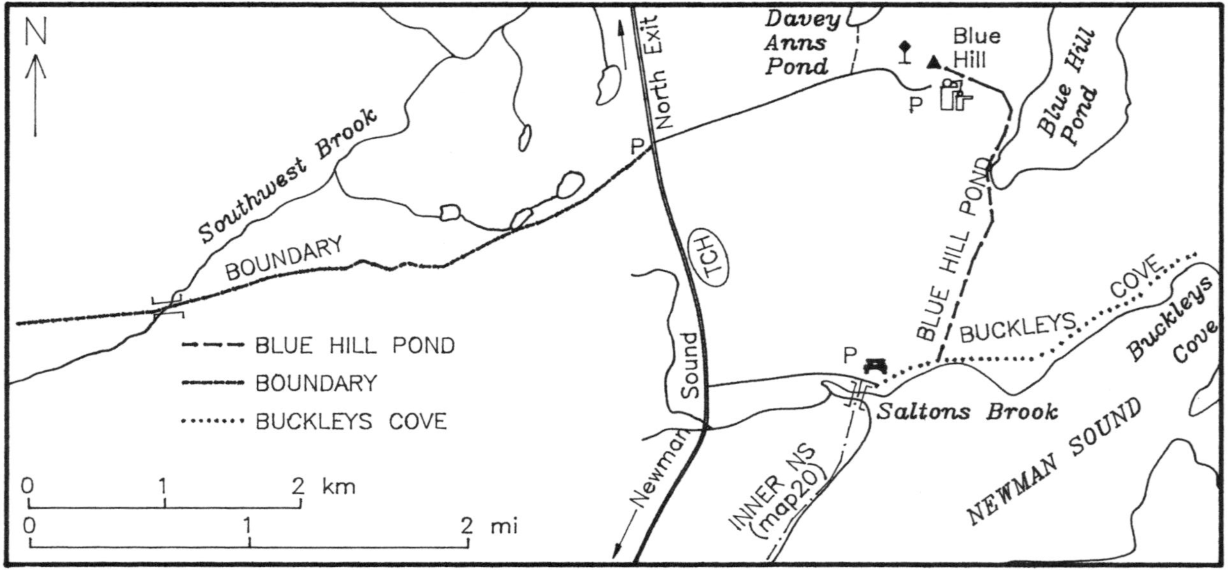

BLUE HILL POND
BOUNDARY
BUCKLEYS COVE

beavers has been the roadside pond opposite the Twin Rivers Visitor Centre. During the summer, dusk and dawn are the most fruitful times to see the beavers, though they can sometimes be seen during the day. In the winter it is difficult to see them at all as they stay hidden in their dens, only leaving to make trips to their food stores.

BLUE HILL POND
(map 19)

Time: 50 min
Distance: 3 km
(1.8 mi) one way
Difficulty: easy;
good for older children

Condition: maintained;
very wet in parts; peat
bogs and woodlands

Summary of Trail:
The first part of the trail from the Saltons Brook picnic area and wharf is shared with the trail to Buckleys Cove, and then it splits off to a slow ascent through peat bogs and spruce and fir forests. Although there are many boardwalks, it can be very wet, especially in early spring. In the fall the needles of the tamaracks turn yellow in a vibrant splash of autumnal colour. Nestled between densely forested hills, the pond is a favourite spot for fishermen, and children may enjoy a brisk paddle in the cold water. The section of the trail past the pond and up to Blue Hill is no longer maintained and can be dangerous.

How to Get There:
- Take the Trans-Canada Highway north from the Newman Sound turning.

- After approximately 3.5 km (2.1 mi) turn right to Saltons Brook.
- Drive 1.5 km (.9 mi) to the day-use area and park.

Trail Directions:

Take the path from the parking lot (the signpost distances are incorrect) and follow the main gravel path into the spruce forest. In late May and June the thick undergrowth of sheep laurel displays lilac-pink flowers. Through the trees Mount Stamford can be seen as the tallest hill across the tranquil, blue waters of Newman Sound.

5 min Follow the path as it bends away from the water.

9 min Cross the bridge over the brook, and at the junction follow the signpost to Blue Hill and Blue Hill Pond (straight), not Buckleys Cove (right). Keep walking gently uphill through the spruce forest. Boardwalks assist in places but the trail is very wet, especially in early summer. At first the trees are quite sparse, but the forest becomes denser and old-man's beard hangs limply over dry branches and trunks.

20 min The path emerges from the forest and veers to the right of an old cut-line. The trees thin out into an open area covered in sheep laurel and where bakeapples (small peach-coloured berries that are considered a delicacy by Newfoundlanders, who use them in jellies, jams and pies) can sometimes be found. Hills frame the peat bog on the far left as the trail cuts through the scrub and continues uphill over many boardwalks. Even with the long boardwalks there are still some very wet areas which can be difficult to circum-navigate. Before the boardwalks end, the sheep laurel closes in on the path and the scraggly spruce and tamarack become denser once more. As the path becomes drier, more reindeer and caribou mosses grow over the forest floor and firs are mixed in with the trees. Old-man's beard appears to be strangling the trees.

35 min Catch the first glimpse of Blue Hill Pond backed by Blue Hill.

38 min At Blue Hill Pond a signpost reads Alexander Bay, Louil Hills and Blue Hill, left, and Saltons and Buckleys Cove, right (i.e., the way you have come). A narrow, overgrown fishing track hugs the pond edge, but the main trail turns left and runs around the pond behind a narrow sandy beach and a low bank of moss and sheep laurel. The path is gravel and packed earth, but there may be some wet patches. Short boardwalks cross the small streams that flow into the pond, and crackerberries and green moss grow under the trees and beside the path.

42 min Turn left, away from the pond, and cut across the small peninsula, then continue on the path along the edge. The pond stretches long and narrow below Blue Hill, and a narrow sandy beach skirts the edges of the clear blue waters. At one time this was a popular haunt of fishermen who climbed down the steep trail from the fire lookout on Blue Hill. For safety reasons this section was closed in 1993.

45 min Continue through the wet forest as the path skirts the pond. Unfortunately the boardwalks are not adequate, and in places the trail is still very wet but navigable. Cross the streams and tread carefully around the moose droppings.

50 min At the junction, a signpost says Blue Hill Pond and the trail ends. The trail up the hill to the left is the closed section. It is very steep and rough, and it takes over half an hour to climb the wet and slippery path (at the time of writing there was nothing at the trail's end to indicate that this part was closed). The narrow, unmaintained trail straight ahead is just a fishing path alongside the pond. Before retracing your steps, sit for a moment in the tiny clearing and look out over the peaceful pond. Remember to first douse yourself with insect repellent against the mosquitoes and blackflies.

BOUNDARY
Blue Hill West (map 19)

Time: 1 hr 5 min
Distance: 5 km
(3 mi) one way
Difficulty: easy;
good for children

Condition: maintained;
very wet sections

Summary of Trail:
This trail is impossible to walk without a pair of rubber boots because of a large wet section towards the beginning. The trail passes by some of the largest birches in the park — they stand heads above the spruces and firs. In 1986 large sections of the forest were damaged by fire, and stands of grey, leafless trunks rise sombrely out of the regenerating forest. Towards the end, a bridge takes the trail across Southwest Brook and uphill to the park boundary, where the hike ends in a sandy clearing by a cutline.

How to Get There:
- Take the Trans-Canada Highway north from the Newman Sound turning. After 3.5 km (2.1 mi)

pass the turning to the Saltons Brook picnic area and wharf.
- After a further 1.75 km (1 mi) turn left (opposite the turning to Blue Hill) and park before the barrier and notice board.

Trail Directions:

Go around the barrier and follow the grassy fire road. Pass across the cutline beneath the electricity cables and bear left into the spruce forest. Prints on the soft earth and the dry, egg-shaped droppings from winter foraging and bulkier, wetter droppings from richer summer forage indicate the presence of moose.

10 min Under the path a stream flows through a double culvert. This section is very wet and rubber boots are an uncomfortable necessity. The dry spruces are prone to being knocked over by the wind and sometimes lie across the road. They can be circumnavigated or stepped over. Beneath the spruces, shrubs of sheep laurel blossom from late May to early July with lilac-pink flowers.

30 min Sections of this forest were ravaged by fire in 1986. The blackened trunks of the trees on the left show the damage. The trail descends gently through the fire-damaged section and returns to the forest.

33 min A culvert passes under the road. The leaves of large birches and aspens rustle overhead. Beneath them stand the dry, grey trunks of trees destroyed by the flames. Many have been knocked over by winds that sweep around the recently exposed area. On the ground the forest is regenerating and covering over the ugly scars.

40 min Alders are among the first to reclaim the forest after the fire and grow in large shrubs alongside the wet section of the trail.

45 min Cross the culvert (barely visible). The largest birch trees in the park grow along this section. Smaller spruce and firs fill the spaces between the large trunks, and alders have become established in the wet sections in the middle of the path.

1 h Bridge over Southwest Brook. You can cross the brook and continue the short distance to the boundary, but it is quite a disappointing ending to the trail, so I suggest you stop at the brook and don't bother with the last few metres.

1 h 5 min If you decided to continue, you are now at the park boundary marked by the overgrown boundary/cutline (although it is possible to follow the boundary all the way to Terra Nova Village road, it is very wet and overgrown and is not recommended).

Background Notes:

One of the most popular questions that the park wardens get asked by visitors to the park is about "that yellow and black stuff killing the trees?" What they mean is the old-man's beard, or maldow, which hangs over dead spruce trees like ragged fairy's breath draped over Christmas trees. This twisted tangle of green-yellow and black fibre is a lichen and only grows where the air is exceptionally pure. It does not harm the trees which died as a result of spruce budworm infestation in the 1970s.

This is only one type of lichen found in the park. Others live in areas where plants have trouble surviving. Look at rocks in exposed high places and you see the wily lichens surviving against all odds. They produce their own chemicals to create their own soils and thus can even grow on rocks that are washed twice daily by seawater. Lichens come in three basic types: fruticose (like old-man's beard), foliose (flat and broad like leaves) and crustose (forming hard crusts on rocks). They are often mistakenly thought of as plants, but they are not. They are made up of fungus and algae. The fungus gets its food from the algae, and the algae — tiny plants that use the sun to make food — get the necessary water, shelter and nutrients from the fungus. This symbiotic relationship enables the lichen to grow in places that would otherwise be inhospitable.

BUCKLEYS COVE
(map 19)

Time: 1 hr
Distance: 4.8 km
(2.9 mi) one way
Difficulty: moderate;
good for older children

Condition: maintained; muddy sections; rough and steep in parts

Summary of Trail:
The Buckleys Cove trail starts and ends at the Saltons Brook day-use area. The first part of the trail runs close to Newman Sound and is shared with the Blue Hill Pond trail. After the trails divide, the one to Buckleys Cove follows the beach beside a large barachois and enters the forest of dry spruces draped in old-man's beard. Ascending and descending between stream beds and coves, the rocky trail terminates at picturesque Buckleys Cove. On the other side of the sound Mount Stamford rises out of the forested hills.

How to Get There:
- Take the Trans-Canada Highway north from the Newman Sound turning.

- After approximately 3.5 km (2.1 mi) turn right to Saltons Brook.
- Drive 1.5 km (.9 mi) to the day-use area and park.

Trail Directions:

Take the gravel path from the corner of the parking lot (distances on the signpost are incorrect) and follow it through the spruce forest (ignore the thinner trodden track on the left). Mount Stamford stands out clearly across the blue water, and in July the sheep laurel shrubs display their delicate pink flowers.

5 min Follow the path as it bends away from the water.

9 min Cross the bridge over the brook, and at the junction turn right and follow the signpost to Buckleys Cove (Blue Hill and Blue Hill Pond, straight). Continue along the path — first it is gravel, then boardwalk — as it skirts the edge of the cove towards the barachois.

12 min At the end of the boardwalk, turn left onto the beach towards the ochre boulders. Just before the boulders, turn left by a signpost with a hiker. Walk up into the forest and cross over the stream. The trail becomes rougher underfoot and ascends up the hill. Wispy old-man's beard cocoons dry spruce trunks in a thin, ragged blanket. Fallen trees lie in untidy clumps of shattered timber. Sheep laurel spreads along the forest floor, and although boardwalks go over the wet patches, in late spring and early summer the path can be muddy.

27 min Descend steeply to the junction and the signpost with the hiker. Take the left fork away from the sound. Immediately cross the small brook and continue uphill through the forest.

38 min Descend steeply to a small brook, cross it and ascend the other side. The path can be wet here.

40 min Cross the lichen-covered rock outcrop and descend steeply to the boardwalk across the bog. Fresh glimpses of the sound lure you on.

45 min Descend to the boardwalk over a small brook.

55 min Cross the brook and the boardwalk with steps.

1 hr As you walk down the hill to Buckleys Cove, the trees sweep aside to reveal a small cove. Waves tumble from the sound and meet the tiny stream as it meanders lazily over the sandy beach. As the sun peers out of the clouds, smoothed rocks brighten to a warm ochre. Years ago a trail ran from the cove to the headland and a sawmill probably stood on the grassy meadow behind the beach, but today the sawmill has gone and the trail is too overgrown to find. The wind tousles your hair and forms small whitecaps on the waves. A small boat churns through them, leaving a trail of white foam on the blue water. On the other side of the sound Mount Stamford beckons for another day.

Background Notes:

Although red squirrels are commonly seen in Newfoundland, they are not native to the island. They were introduced in 1963 near Roddickton on the Northern Peninsula, and again in 1964 in the Notre Dame Bay area. They have spread rapidly and their chatter is frequently heard throughout the park. They are entertaining to watch but they can be a nuisance, so be wary of them. They are apt to chew holes in all sorts of things and to get into unwanted places. Last year it was reported that a man drove all the way to St. John's without knowing he had a nest of squirrels underneath the hood. Mercifully the squirrels survived (and so did all the hoses of the engine) and were returned to their natural habitat. Do not encourage squirrels, and remember that it is illegal to feed any form of wildlife in the park. In-

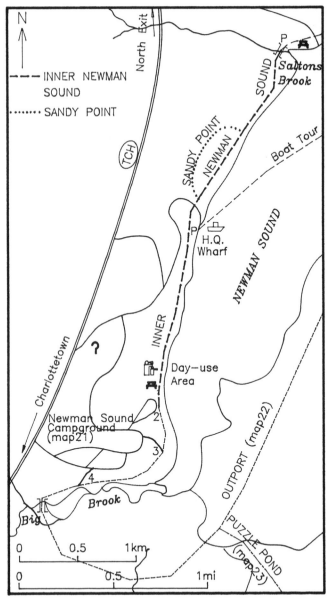

Map 20: INNER NEWMAN SOUND

cidentally, they bite. There is no rabies on the island, but squirrels are rodents and have nasty, scissor-sharp teeth.

INNER NEWMAN SOUND
Coastal Trail (map 20)

TRAIL 1: Newman Sound picnic area to HQ Wharf

Time: 30 min

Distance: 2.5 km (1.5 mi) one way

Difficulty: easy; good for children

Condition: maintained; wooded slope by the sound

TRAIL 1 (cont.): HQ Wharf to Saltons Brook

Time: 40 min

Distance: 3 km (1.8 mi) one way

Difficulty: easy; good for children

Condition: maintained; wooded slope by the sound; section along the beach

TRAIL 2: SANDY POINT NATURE TRAIL (from HQ Wharf)

Time: 30 min

Distance: 2.5 km (1.5 mi) loop

Difficulty: moderate; good for older children

Condition: maintained; wooded slope by the sound; section along the beach

Summary of Trail:

The Inner Newman Sound trail runs along the shores of the sheltered sound. It consists of two parts which can be walked in sequence, on their own or incorporated with the Ocean Watch boat tours from HQ Wharf (for details see page 148). The trail can be accessed from the Newman Sound campground and picnic area, HQ Wharf and Saltons Brook (the trail directions below take you from the Newman Sound picnic area). The length of the trail runs along the forests on the slopes above the water. In places the trail crosses beaches of rounded boulders and coarse sands, boardwalks, and sites at abandoned settlements, sawmills and ship building yards. If you are short of time you may prefer to walk the Sandy Point nature trail from HQ Wharf, which loops back along the Coastal trail. With two cars, this trail can be walked one way.

How to Get There:
To start at Newman Sound picnic area:
- Take the Trans-Canada Highway to the Newman Sound turning (approximately 12 km [7.2 mi] from the north entrance of the park and 31 km [19 mi] from the south entrance).
- Turn, and after 700 m/yd turn right for the campground.
- After approximately 2.5 km (1.5 mi), immediately before the campground kiosk, turn left for the picnic area and take the gravel road down the hill to the parking lot. (If you are camping, the Newman Sound Campground trail links with this one from site 17.)

To start at HQ Wharf:
- As above, but after the Newman Sound turning do not turn right for the campground but continue straight following signs for the boat tour and wharf (ignore all turnings).

To start at Saltons Brook:
- Take the Trans-Canada Highway north from the Newman Sound campground junction.

- After approximately 3.5 km (2.1 mi) turn right to Saltons Brook.
- Drive 1.5 km (.9 mi) to the day-use area and park.

Trail Directions:
Trail 1: Newman Sound picnic area to Salton's Brook (via HQ Wharf)

At the notice board by the parking lot, turn left along the gravel path. With the sound on the right, cross the open grassy picnic area (popular with families picnicking and children playing), pass the lookout platform (with telescope and interpretive boards), the playground, picnic shelter, fenced enclosure, toilets, second picnic shelter and another wooden lookout platform.

3 min At the No Cycling sign, follow the boardwalk into the trees. (Left leads to the parking lot for the outdoor theatre. The schedule of events is available from the Visitor Centre and campground kiosk.) Cross the bridge over the stream and take the left fork to the theatre arena (the right fork was the direct route leading behind the theatre, but since the bridge collapsed it has been closed). Pass behind the stage and pick up the original gravel path. Cross the short boardwalk bridge and pass the steep cliffs on the left (rail on the right) followed by two more railed sections.

8 min Take the bank of steps down to beach level, cross over the base of the sand spit and up the bank of steps on the other side. Follow the path over the slope of coniferous and deciduous trees.

13 min Cross the wide base of the second sand spit where a wheel and engine from an old sawmill lie by the path. Follow the trail across the stream and through the alders that are reclaiming the old road from the sawmill to the shipbuilding enterprise.

18 min Pass the concrete foundations on the left, continue through the tall alders, cross the small boardwalk bridge and walk through grassy clearing full of raspberries. Take the steps up the wooded slope.

23 min The trail continues below some cabins. These used to be park concessions available for holiday rentals, but for the last few years they have been closed and the dining hall has become the Activity Centre.

26 min Past the last cabin, take the bank of steps down the hill, pass the narrow sandy beach behind the trees on the right and see HQ Wharf beyond.

28 min Ignore the two paths on the left (first one is from the cabins; the short second one is to Pissing Mare Falls, where you can rest on the bench, look at the waterfall and contemplate the imaginative name). Cross the wooden bridge over the stream from the falls and take the boardwalk out of the woods around the large lawn at HQ Wharf and walk up the road to the parking lot.

30 min: From HQ Wharf, take the trail behind the notice board in the parking lot *. By the hiker signpost to Sandy Point, take the right fork. (If you wish to follow the shorter Sandy Point loop, see trail 2 below.) Pass the signpost marked Coastal Trail and continue along the gravel path and boardwalks. The trail runs through the forest of aspens, spruce and fir on the edge of the sound. This walk is especially beautiful on sunny days when the dark green forested hills on the far bank frame the intensely blue water of the sound.

35 min Take the bank of steps up the hill and continue through the trees. Follow the boardwalk around the bend just above the beach, pass the signpost to Saltons Brook (you can also walk onto the beach and follow it along the sound) and take the few steps up along the boardwalk. In early summer there may be some minor damp patches as the path runs through the woodland, across longer and shorter boardwalks, over small streams, up and down steps and along the gravel path. Blue irises nod their heads in the breeze and sheep laurel flowers in blanket of pink. In the fall, goldenrods add a splash of yellow.

42 min When the path ends at the beach, turn left and walk along the coarse sand. Pass two signposts (the first says Headquarters, the second Coastal Trail) after which a path comes out of the trees on the left (it is easy to miss - this is the Sandy Point nature trail from HQ Wharf, so those wanting a shorter walk may return this way **). Continue along the beach, and after a further two minutes, turn left into the trees at the signpost to Saltons Brook and walk up the two banks of steps (if you miss the turning off the beach, continue along the sand for a further five minutes and take the steps up to the path).

48 min Take the steps down to the bridge over the ravine and then up the other side.

52 min Pass the bank of steps down to the beach and continue with the sound on your right. Mount Stamford is the highest hill across the water (see Outport and Mount Stamford for the trail that leads to the summit and the spectacular views of the fingerlike Newman Sound fjord and the outer reaches of the park.)

1 hr Follow the bank of steps down and continue through the forest before coming to another bank of steps down. Then walk through a grassy avenue of alders. Pass a white post, then a hiker signpost (both on the right), and catch glimpses of Saltons Brook through the shrubbery.

1 hr 5 min Come out into a clearing overgrown with high shrubs of alder. Pass the kitchen shelter on the left and head towards the large bridge across Saltons Brook.

1 hr 8 min At the far side of the bridge, pass the signpost (South Broad Cove 17 km and Mount Stamford 13.75 km, but the distances are incorrect). Turn right and walk towards the washrooms and wharf.

1 hr 10 min End the trail at the wharf. It always seems windy at Saltons Brook, so windproof clothing is useful. However, it is also a great place to fly a kite, have a picnic and look at the boats.

Trail 2: Sandy Point Nature Trail:

Start from HQ Wharf as for trail 1 (see * above) and take the left fork (you can take the right fork, too, and walk the loop counter-clockwise). There are no views of the sound from this upper part of the trail as it meanders through the forested hills, crossing streams and rising and falling over tucks and hillocks.

18 min The path runs steeply downhill towards the sound and emerges onto the beach. You have now joined the Coastal trail. Turn right and walk along the beach to complete the walk and return to HQ Wharf. (If you wish to continue to Saltons Brook, turn left and follow the directions in trail 1 from ** above.) Shortly after turning right onto the beach, after passing a signpost for Headquarters and another for Coastal Trail, turn right off the beach into the fores. You are now walking in reverse over the section of the coastal trail from HQ Wharf as described above from * to **. This trail runs closer to the sound and there are constant views and glimpses of the blue water through the trees.

30 min Exit the forest by the parking lot at Saltons Brook immediately after the outward-going junction signposted Sandy Point (** on trail 1).

Background Notes:

From the 1910s to the 1940s, lumbering and ship-building provided plenty of work around Newman Sound. According to Kevin Major's *Terra Nova National Park, Human History Study*, three main sawmills and a pitprop operation supplied most of the work during this period, but other, smaller sawmills also had plenty of work for those wanting to work independently. The work was hard but there was no shortage of it. The cutting took place during the winter months, with the men living in small camps scattered throughout the woods. Some brought their families with them, but many only saw their wives and children during periodic visits home. Once the sound froze over, the men and women were virtually isolated, but life in the camps was simple and happy.

NEWMAN SOUND CAMPGROUND
(map 21)

Time: 1 hr 30 min
Distance: 6 km (3.6 mi) loop
Difficulty: easy; good for children

Condition: maintained; woodland path; sand and gravel

Summary of Trail:

In early morning or at dusk it is not uncommon to come across moose along this trail. The full loop

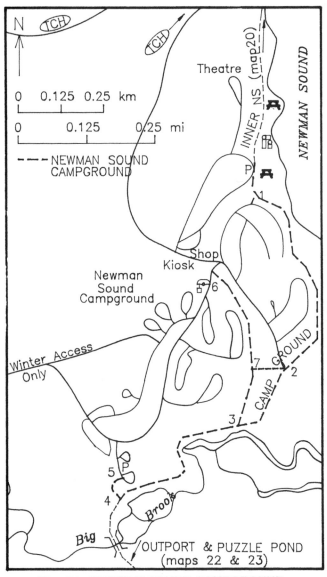

Map 21: NEWMAN SOUND CAMPGROUND

around the campground takes about an hour and a half, but there are several alternatives for shorter strolls. The trail runs along a ridge, above the Newman Sound estuary and salt marshes. After taking the long banks of steps off the ridge the trail skirts the banks of Big Brook. If combined with the Outport and Mount Stamford and the Puzzle Pond trails to the south or the Inner Newman Sound trail to the north, this trail can be extended to fill a whole day or even include a night stop.

How to Get There:
- Take the Trans-Canada Highway to the Newman Sound turning (approximately 12 km [7.2mi] from the north entrance of the park and 31 km [19 mi] from the south entrance).
- Turn, and after 700 m/yd turn right for the campground.
- After approximately 2.5 km (1.5 mi) turn left before the campground kiosk and take the gravel road down the hill to the Newman Sound day-use/picnic area and theatre. (If you are camping the trail is accessible from beside sites 17, 84, 253 and opposite the trailer dumping station. It also connects with the Outport and Mount Stamford, and the Puzzle Pond trails by site 253, and the Inner Newman Sound trail by site 17.)

Trail Directions:
From the notice board by the parking lot (where the Inner Newman Sound trail also begins), take the gravel road up the hill (with your back to the sound this is the road on the left). At the yellow pedestrian sign, turn left and walk up the long bank of steps. At the junction at the top (1 on map 21), turn left onto the trail before the gravel road. Follow the dry sandy path through the spruce

trees and sheep laurel shrubs behind the campsites. Ignore any tracks crossing the main trail. Far below on the left the estuary waters spill over the mud flats.

7 min The campsites disappear behind the trees and shrubs on the right, but the view of the estuary continues on the left. Keep ignoring the smaller paths trodden out by campers and continue along the main sand and gravel path.

15 min At the junction (2 on map 21), take the long bank of steps down the ridge on the left (the path on the right leads to the gravel road near site 84 where it is marked by two signposts: one has a hiker and the other says Mount Stamford 12.8 km). At the bottom of the steps, follow the level gravel path over the silted-up estuary, now overgrown with sheep laurel and lone scraggly spruces.

20 min Take the sharp right bend at Big Brook (a short path leads down to the brook, but anglers must have a National Park fishing licence, available at the Visitor Centres and campground kiosks). Pass the Environment Canada Parks notice allowing trout fishing only and continue along the forested, sandy banks of Big Brook. The meandering brown waters cut into the banks on one side and deposit the sediment in sandy spits on the other. The water is brown because of the high content of tannic acid seeping in from the surrounding peat bogs.

24 min Cross the railless boardwalk bridge and pass another Environment Canada Parks notice.

25 min At the junction (3 on map 21), you can choose from one of the many options this hike offers. The trail log continues straight, past the Environment Canada Parks sign and along the banks of the brook, but you may prefer to shorten the loop by turning right and following the woodland path back to the campground. Taking the first option along the banks of the brook, the path weaves through the spruce and fir forest. Small boardwalks cross streams and wet areas and cautionary rails protect hikers from the soft, steep banks. In some places the path runs close to the brook, and in others it turns away into the darkness of the forest.

32 min Take the steps with the rail up the hill and pass the Environment Canada Parks notice and another rail.

35 min After walking through the stand of dry trunks and passing a last Environment Canada Parks sign, emerge from the trees at a junction with an old grassed-over road (4 on map 21). To continue the campground loop, turn right and walk up the road, round the right-hand bend and arrive at the barrier (the path through the trees marked by a signpost is shared by the Outport and Mount Stamford, and the Puzzle Pond trails).

40 min On the campground side of the barrier, the trail is marked by a signpost with a hiker and arrow. Go around the barrier (site 253 is further on the right) and turn left onto the gravel road (5 on map 21). Turn right at the junction and follow the green and white arrows towards the campground exit.

53 min Immediately past the trailer dumping station, but before the Stop sign, turn right into the woods by the hiker sign (6 on map 21; left at the Stop sign brings you to the campground kiosk). Ignore all the tracks that cross the path and continue downhill through the small wooded gulley. Spruces and firs grow in the sandy soil and their needles form a soft carpet between the roots. In sunny spots the sheep laurel flowers, and it is warm and sheltered.

1 hr 2 min After the steep downhill slope, ignore the

rough track up the hill on the left (this is an unofficial shortcut to site 84 at junction 2). Continue
straight (7 on map 21).

1 hr 5 min Back at the river, turn left (3 on map 21)
and retrace your steps beside the brook.

1 hr 14 min At the top of the stairs, turn right (2 on
map 21) and continue along the hilly path.

1 hr 27 min At the junction (1 on map 21), take the
bank of steps down to the day-use area and open-
air theatre (left is the gravel road and site 17).

1 hr 30 min End at the day-use area or continue
along the Inner Newman Sound trail.

Background Notes:

Driving and hiking around Newfoundland you are
bound to see moose either grazing by the side of the
road, silently walking through the forest or wading
in a pond in search of aquatic delights. These huge
animals are quite plentiful and seem very much at
home on the island, but they are not native to Newfoundland. In 1878 an unsuccessful attempt was
made to introduce a pair from Nova Scotia. Another
attempt was made in 1904, and it is from these two
New Brunswick bulls and two cows that the moose
population on the island has developed. In fact, the
moose have been so successful in the Terra Nova
National Park area that the residents of Charlottetown are concerned by the numbers that forage
around the community during the winter. The increasing numbers are also posing a problem on the
roads: in 1992, 24 animals were killed by cars. In
order to get more information about the park herd, a
three-year study was begun in 1992. Field workers are
locating, tranquillizing and fitting the animals with
transmitter collars and other visual identifications,
so if you see a moose, let the park authorities know
where you saw it and if it was wearing a collar. The

best time to see moose is at dusk and dawn; however this is when most accidents occur. The animals become disoriented by car headlights, so please drive carefully and dim your lights if you see a moose.

OUTPORT and MOUNT STAMFORD
(map 22)

TRAIL 1: South Broad Cove to Newman Sound campground

Time: 5 hr 20 min

Distance: 18.5 km (11 mi) loop

Difficulty: strenuous; good for older children

Condition: maintained but rough; very wet in parts; steep sections

(includes **Time:** 1 hr 5 min **Distance:** 4.2 km [2.5 mi] for the last section from the end of the trail at Newman Sound campground to where you parked at HQ Wharf, but does not include 2 hr 30 min for the boat tour to the trailhead at South Broad Cove)

DETOUR: Mount Stamford
Time: 30 min
Distance: 1.5 km (.9 mi) one way

TRAIL 2: Newman Sound campground to Mount Stamford

Time: 3 hr

Distance: 10.5 km (6.3mi) one way

Difficulty: moderate, but with a strenuous spur at the end; good for older children

Condition: maintained but rough

Map 22: OUTPORT & MOUNT STAMFORD

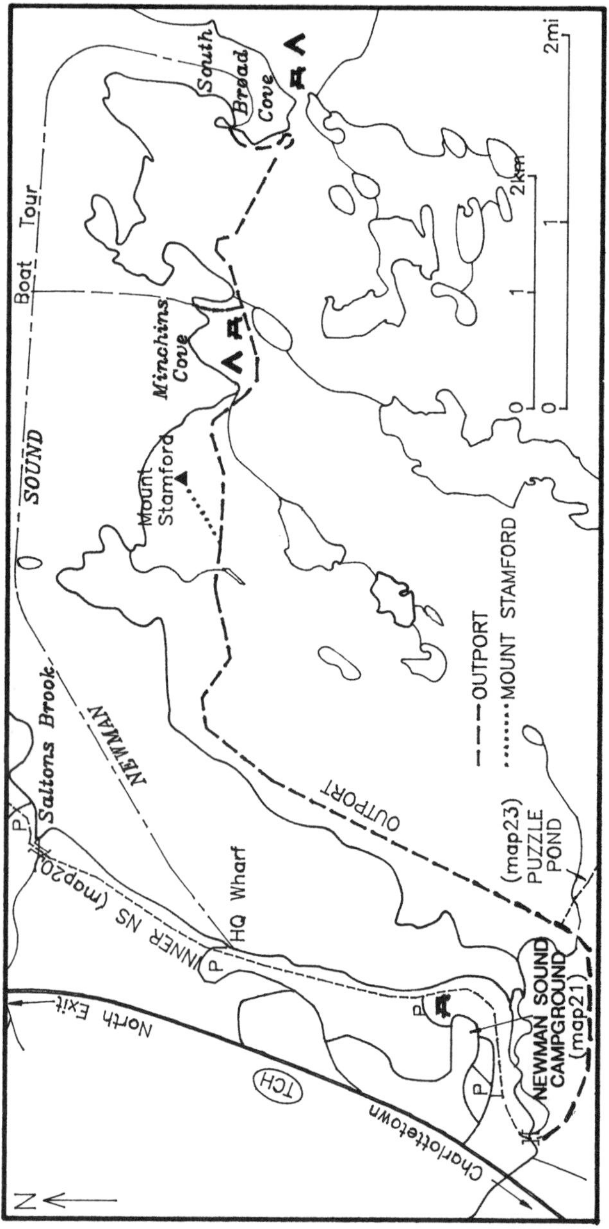

Boat Tour
South Broad Cove
2mi
2km
0 1 2
0 1
Minchins Cove
SOUND
Mount Stamford
OUTPORT
MOUNT STAMFORD
Saltons Brook
NEWMAN
OUTPORT
(map23) PUZZLE POND
HQ Wharf
INNER NS (map20)
P
NEWMAN SOUND CAMPGROUND (map21)
North Exit
TCH
Charlottetown
N

Summary of Trail:

The Outport trail starts at the Newman Sound campground and meanders through forests and coves which once held small logging communities and sawmills, until it reaches the Outer Sound beyond Mount Stamford. The path is rough and wet, making the uphill sections quite strenuous, but the sections along the sound are exceptionally picturesque. Budget time for extra stops and bring sufficient food and drink. The hike can be tiring, so it is not recommended that you walk the trail both ways in one day. Either plan to spend the night at one of the primitive campgrounds, only walk as far as Mount Stamford and return (trail 2), or arrange for Ocean Watch Tours at HQ Wharf to drop you at South Broad Cove or Minchins Cove and walk back from there (trail 1).

The trail to Mount Stamford follows the Outport trail but turns off partway to climb a spur to the summit of the hill. Since it can be walked there and back in one day, it has been included as a separate trail. It follows the easier section of the Outport trail, and although the hike needs most of a day, it is not particularly strenuous. Even the short climb to the summit of Mount Stamford is quite tolerable, and once there, one is rewarded by a spectacular view. But be prepared with some warm clothing; even on warm, sunny days it can be quite cool and windy at the summit.

How to Get There:

Trail 1: To start at HQ Wharf in Newman Sound

- Take the Trans-Canada Highway to the Newman Sound turning (approximately 12 km [7.2 mi] from the north entrance of the park and 31 km [19 mi] from the south entrance).
- Turn for Newman Sound and follow the road to the boat tour and wharf for approximately 2 km (1.2

mi) (ignore all turnings, including the one to the campground).
- Take the 09:00 Ocean Watch Tours boat trip (not all trips go to South Broad Cove, so make arrangements and bookings in advance. See Terra Nova Useful Information, page 148).

Trail 2: To start from the Newman Sound campground
- As above, but instead of continuing to the boat tour turn right for the campground.
- After approximately 2.5 km (1.5 mi) pass into the campground (free visitor permit required for non-campers), drive to site 253 and park opposite the barrier (the trail can also be begun at sites 17 and 84, which are junctions 1 and 2 respectively along the Newman Sound Campground trail; however, they have no parking).

To start at the Newman Sound day use/picnic area
- Follow the above directions to the campground, turn left before the kiosk, and drive to the day-use/picnic area. Follow the Newman Sound Campground trail until it joins the Outport trail before the Big Brook suspension bridge.

Trail Directions:
Trail 1: Outport
After the drop-off at the South Broad Cove wharf (remember: it will take about about two and a half hours for the trip), take the steps up the rocks and turn left among the scraggly spruces (right leads to a small cove and a picnic table), pass the pit toilet and follow the meandering hilly path over the rocks and between the trees. In places it is difficult to follow, but keep parallel to the water's edge and eventually it will bring you to a small

cove. Across the other side of the cove a notice board marks the primitive campground.

10 min At South Broad Cove, turn right (left leads round the cove to the notice board and primitive campground) and take the trodden-down trail inland through the long grass and alders. Sometimes the signpost to South Broad Cove falls down, so don't trust it. The trail bears right through the small valley and ascends very steeply into the forest.

21 min The steep incline ends and the trail continues through an open forest of large trees where a tapestry of green weaves over the forest floor. The small wet patches can be easily avoided as the trail meanders through the forest. Moose tracks are pressed in the soft earth and droppings lie in piles.

23 min A slope of green moss and trees rises on the left.

25 min Cross the tree trunk over the small stream. Pass the pond of rippling blue water on the left and continue uphill through the forest. Lots of dry trees lie on the forest floor. Many trunks are covered in wispy strands of old-man's beard. Pass between a small bog on the left and a rock slope covered in reindeer moss, sheep laurel and trees on the right. The path is uneven, with rocks, roots and constant wet and muddy patches slowing progress.

37 min Descend the short, steep path and cross the semi-stagnant stream spanned by logs. The path remains wet as it continues downhill through the large trees.

42 min Catch a glimpse of Minchins Cove ahead, and once at the water's edge, follow the path left along the river bank. On the cobble beach on the other side of the cove lie the remains of a rusting steam engine from a sawmill. On the grass banks behind, stone cellars mark the sites where frame houses once stood (these can be reached from further along the path). On the far right the park wharf replaces a 300-metre one at which wooden schooners used to moor. These vessels transported pitprops and lumber from the mills and took men to Labrador to fish.

45 min Cross the wooden bridge over the stream flowing into the cove (trout fishing is allowed with a National Parks fishing licence, but salmon must be released). Continue around the back of the cove through the large spruce and fir trees.

50 min Just before the staggered crossroad, two very large maple trees on either side of the path are said to have stood in the garden of a house. However, no foundations or remains have ever been found. At the junction, follow the signpost Newman Sound and Mount Stamford, straight (left is to Minchins Pond, right is to the wharf, the site of the abandoned community and a primitive campground). Access to the cove was mainly by sea but in the winter, when the sound was frozen, the trail from Minchins Cove to Newman Sound was the only lifeline.

55 min Pass through a large, grassy clearing with only a few large trees; one tree on the right is tied with an orange survey ribbon. The wind rushes around the treetops, rustling the aspens and birches, but only a light breeze flutters around the trail. The path ascends slowly through tall, thin spruces bare of all but a modicum of foliage. Thin, grey branches stick out supporting rich deposits of old-man's beard like coat hangers draped in lace. Behind the trees on the right, Mount Stamford faces the winds.

1 hr 10 min Follow the path downhill, glimpsing

Hefferns Cove on the right, but veer left before you reach it. For the next half hour, up to the turning for Mount Stamford, the trail is very wet and mainly uphill. Roots and rocks lie underfoot and a stream trickles along the path, making progress slow and tiring.

1 hr 13 min Pass closer to the water. On the right, overlooking Hefferns Cove, there is a good spot for a break; it is sheltered and sunny and the blue water laps gently against the rocks. Follow the path over the rocks by the water's edge. Rock pools fill small hollows, and bleached driftwood has been thrown up onto the rocks. The steep face of Mount Stamford looms out of the blue water. Turn left into the trees away from the shore, and continue over the short boardwalk and hillock to a small cove. Take the boardwalk over the stream and turn inland. As the path climbs uphill under the trees, a small waterfall burbles on the far right. There may be wet areas.

1 hr 19 min Cross the stream on the bridge with one handrail, and walk along the right bank by the cascading water. Birds sing, indifferent to the hikers struggling up the steep, wet path.

1 hr 45 min At the junction and signpost continue straight to Newman Sound and Ochre Hill. The worst uphill is now over. (The right fork is for Mount Stamford;* see trail 2 below.)

1 hr 50 min Pass to the right of Mount Stamford Pond. Cross the stream trickling out of the pond and follow the trail along the bank where large, leathery leaves of water lilies move gently on the blue water. Turn away from the pond and continue uphill. Pass the large, uprooted tree on the left and around the fallen trees blanketed in green moss. Pass into a forest of green trees where the old-man's beard is thriving on dry lower branches and trunks, and a rough trail threads a narrow path over the green moss.

2 hr 14 min Take the inadequate crossing of logs and sawn lumber over the small stream, trying to avoid the mud on both sides.

2 hr 22 min Crossing over several small boardwalks and wet patches, the path continues through a forest of scraggly black spruce decked in old-man's beard.

2 hr 24 min The trail becomes very straight, dry and level like an overgrown logging road. Small young conifers grow on either side. Mosses and blueberries provide a covering and pink lady's-slippers bloom with their delicate flower.

2 hr 33 min The straight, dry section ends and the path bends to the right through a mature forest of large trees.

2 hr 37 min The first glimmer of blue water means Newman Sound is nearby. Continue downhill through the trees, crossing the streams on the boardwalks.

2 hr 42 min At the sound, the path bears left at a point directly opposite HQ Wharf and runs along the forest slopes (at the bend a short path leads to the beach, where there are many good places to rest on the boulders).

2 hr 47 min On the left, pass the tree with the misshapen trunk. Everyone has an opinion, but I think it looks like the head of a gazelle or donkey. The trail continues through the forest, crossing boardwalks and muddy patches. At low tide the mud flats are revealed and shorebirds trudge around and pose on the uncovered rocks. In August a large clump of wild roses blossoms in a flush of pink.

2 hr 52 min Pass an uprooted tree on the left and cross a small stream. The sound is behind the trees for a while, then the path returns close to the water and follows a long boardwalk overgrown with grass. Blue flag irises grow in the wet soil and three more boardwalks provide a less than adequate surface over the mud.

3 hr Turn inland away from the water and walk uphill through the forest. It may be wet at first. Big aspens and birches grow between the black and white spruce. Bluebead lilies, wild lily of the valley, crackerberries and mosses grow in the shade.

3 hr 10 min The hill levels and the path continues along another overgrown logging road that runs gently downhill through the forest. This straight section lasts for about the next 35 minutes, crossing a few streams and wet patches on the way. Sheep laurel, blueberries and crackerberries grow beneath the large spruces and birches. In wet open areas tamaracks add a splash of autumnal colour. Members of the larch family, they are the only coniferous trees that shed their leaves.

3 hr 45 min Continue straight, ignoring the turning on the left to Ochre Hill. This is the Puzzle Pond trail.

3 hr 46 min At the big bridge over the stream the straight section ends and the trail returns to meandering through the trees.

3 hr 50 min Cross the second bridge and pass through a large open basin of sheep laurel, scattered spruce, tamarack and grey mosses. The path is dry and sandy.

3 hr 54 min At the junction, take the right fork. The sandy path is sheltered and mosses and sheep laurel grow in abundance. In mid-June the pretty pink-purple flowers of the sheep laurel blossom on the shrubs. The old-man's beard is almost black and covers only the tops of the trees, leaving the lower branches green. Usually it is the other way around. Ignore any small tracks to the left and continue downhill along the sandy path until it enters the forest. A fire access road runs behind the trees on the left.

4 hr 6 min Descend through a wet, grassy hollow of alders and pass into the stands of tall trunks bare as bristles. Lots of trees lie in the long grass and clumps of alder are taking over. A short boardwalk leads to a second similar stand, from where the path meanders through the alders and crosses a grassy cutline. The big suspension bridge on Big Brook comes into view.

4 hr 12 min Cross the suspension bridge and continue along the sandy path between the dry trunks and alders until it reaches a crossroads with a grassed-over road.**

4 hr 13 min At the crossroads there is a signpost with a hiker. To get to HQ Wharf, continue straight over the grassy road and take the path into the trees by the Environment Canada sign. (For the quickest return to the campground, turn left up the grass road, bear right around the bend and enter the campground by site 253. Then turn left and follow the gravel road and the green arrows to the exit.) This next section is part of the Newman Sound Campground trail (map 21) by Big Brook, where trout fishing is allowed with a National Parks licence, and where families come to paddle. Follow the sandy path and boardwalks through the trees on the bank of the brook.

4 hr 24 min At the junction (3 on map 21), continue straight (left returns to the campground entrance). Another Environment Canada sign reminds anglers of fishing restrictions. Cross the boardwalk bridge over a small stream and pass another Environment Canada sign. The brook meanders between the sandy banks, undercutting the outer edges and depositing the sand as beaches on the inner sides. The water is the colour of thick beer due to the tannic acid seeping in from the surrounding bogs. Beavers use the fallen trees to build dams in the brook.

4 hr 30 min The path turns sharply to the left by another Environment Canada board. It turns away from the brook and crosses an open area covered in sheep laurel and a few scraggly trees. In the distance on the right the river continues meandering through salt marshes and enters the estuary of Newman Sound.

4 hr 35 min Go up the long bank of steps. At the top, turn right and continue along the ridge (left at the top leads to the campground by site 84 and the Mount Stamford 12.8 km signpost — junction 2 on map 21). As the trail follows the hilly, sandy ridge, the campground is behind the trees on the left. Ignore all the small paths on the left. On the right, below the ridge and across the marsh, the mud banks of the estuary are exposed at low tide.

4 hr 45 min Take the long bank of steps on the right (this junction 1 on map 21; left is the campground road by site 17) down to the gravel road, and go down to the Newman Sound day-use area.

4 hr 50 min At the notice board the Newman Sound Campground trail ends and the Inner Newman Sound coastal trail (map 20) begins. With the sound on the right, take the path past the lookout platform, playground, kitchen hut, fenced enclosure, toilets, a second kitchen shelter and another wooden lookout platform. The area is open and grassy, with picnic tables scattered throughout, and it is popular with families picnicking and children playing.

4 hr 53 min At the No Cycling sign, take the boardwalk straight into the trees (the boardwalk left leads to the parking lot for the outdoor theatre; a schedule of events is available from the Visitor Centre and campground kiosk). Cross the bridge over the stream and take the left fork to the theatre arena (the right fork is the direct route behind the stage but at the time of writing the bridge had collapsed, so it was closed), pass behind the stage and pick up the original path. The gravel path continues along the wooded slopes of the Inner Sound. Cross the short boardwalk bridge and pass the steep cliffs on the left (rail on the right) followed by two more railed sections.

4 hr 58 min Take the bank of steps down to beach level, cross over the base of the sand spit, and up the bank of steps on the other side. Follow the path over the slope of coniferous and deciduous trees leading down to the sound.

5 hr 2 min Cross the wide base of the second sand spit, where a wheel and engine from an old sawmill lie in the bushes by the path. Follow the trail across the stream and through the alders that have taken over the old road from the sawmill and shipbuilding enterprise that once occupied this spot.

5 hr 7 min Pass the concrete foundations on the left and continue between the tall alders. Cross the small boardwalk bridge and enter a grassy clearing full of raspberries. Take the steps up the wooded slope from the clearing.

5 hr 12 min The trail continues below some cabins. These used to be park concessions available for holiday rentals, but for the last few years they have been closed and the old dining hall is now the Activity Centre.

5 hr 15 min Past the last cabin, take the bank of steps down the hill, pass the narrow sandy beach behind the trees on the right and see HQ Wharf beyond.

5 hr 17 min Ignore the two paths on the left (the first

one is from the cabins and the short second one is to Pissing Mare Falls, where you can rest on the bench, look at the waterfall and contemplate its imaginative name). Cross the wooden bridge over the stream from the falls and take the boardwalk out of the woods and around the large lawn of the HQ Wharf.

5 hr 20 min Find your car and give yourself a pat on the back for walking the longest trail in the park.

Trail 2: Mount Stamford:

The Mount Stamford trail is a segment of the Outport trail, walked in reverse. For a fuller description, read from ** to *, pages 201-204.

Pass around the barrier by the hiker signpost (this is junction 5, map 21, Newman Sound Campground trail) and walk down the wide, grassy old road. Round the bend to the left and continue towards the river.

5 min Just before the river, turn right at the hiker signpost (junction 4 on map 21) and follow the narrow path through the stand of dry trees. This is now the Outport trail (map 22), the first section of which is shared with the Puzzle Pond trail.

6 min Cross the suspension bridge over Big Brook.

10 min Cross over the grass cutline that intersects the path and pass through the large clump of alders (the trail may be wet). Climb the bank into the forest and follow the sandy path up the hill to the ridge. Ignore the small tracks to the fire access road behind the trees on the right.

24 min At the junction, ignore the right fork and continue straight along the sandy path across the open basin.

30 min Cross the bridge and meander through the spruce forest.

32 min Cross the big bridge over the stream.

33 min Ignore the path on the right signposted to Ochre Hill (the Puzzle Pond trail) and follow the sign to Mount Stamford and South Broad Cove up the overgrown logging road through the forest. This section, about 35 minutes long, crosses a few streams and wet patches, but mostly it is easy walking.

1 hr 8 min The rough, overgrown road ends and the trail descends gently through the forest. The path may be wet towards the bottom of the hill.

1 hr 18 min With the sound directly ahead, the path bears right and for approximately the next 20 minutes runs along the banks. Sometimes it is far from the shoreline, other times the water laps right up to boardwalk. Across the sound, HQ Wharf and Saltons Brook intrude on the wooded slopes. Despite the boardwalks, sections of the path may be wet. Here you'll see the tree trunk that resembles the head of a gazelle, or maybe it's a donkey.

1 hr 36 min At a point directly opposite HQ Wharf, the trail turns inland and heads up the hill through the forest.

1 hr 45 min The path becomes straight, dry and level, like an overgrown road.

1 hr 54 min The straight road section ends and the trail continues over small boardwalks and wet patches.

2 hr 4 min Take the rough log and sawn-lumber crossing over the small stream and mud patch.

2 hr 20 min Cross the stream draining out of Mount Stamford Pond and follow the trail around the low banks of sheep laurel shrubs.

2 hr 28 min The trail leaves the pond and continues through the forest.

2 hr 33 min At the junction, turn left for Mount Stamford. (Straight is the continuation of the Outport trail. Do not be tempted to follow it unless you are going to camp at the primitive camp-grounds, as you will not have enough time and energy to get there and return to Newman Sound before dusk.) Continue through the forest for the next kilometre. It will take about half an hour, with only the last 20 minutes ascending more steeply.

3 hr min At the summit of Mount Stamford, enjoy the views while trying to hide from the winds.

PUZZLE POND
(map 23)

Time: 1 hr 55 min
Distance: 7.8 km (4.7 mi) one way
Difficulty: easy (moderate return); good for older children

Condition: maintained, but boardwalks in need of repair; very wet sections

Summary of Trail:

Before beginning the hike take ten minutes to walk around Ochre Hill and enjoy the panoramic view from the fire lookout. The first part of the trail follows the very overgrown remains of an old logging road. It then meanders through boreal forests, over marshes and brooks, by Puzzle Pond, past a water-fall or two, through spruce forests, along a sandy ridge, and down to Big Brook and Newman Sound campground. The trail can be extended into a longer hike by connecting with other trails in the area. At the time of writing the Puzzle Pond trail was closed due to its poor condition. Repairs to the trail were said to be imminent. With two cars, the trail can be walked one way only.

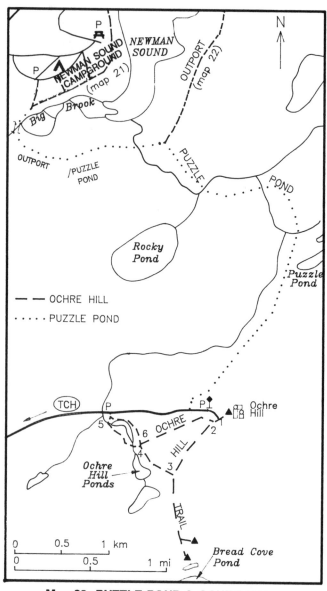

Map 23: PUZZLE POND & OCHRE HILL

How to Get There:
To start at Ochre Hill:
- Take the Trans-Canada Highway south from the Newman Sound turning.
- After 6 km (3.6 mi) turn left at the crossroads by the sign for Ochre Hill (right is the road to Sandy Pond). No trailers allowed.
- Continue up the gravel road. After 2.2 km (1.3 mi) pass the lower parking area for Ochre Hill Ponds and continue for a further 3 km (1.8 mi) to the parking beneath the fire tower.

To start at Newman Sound:
- Take the Trans-Canada Highway to the Newman Sound turning (approximately 12 km [7.2 mi] from the north entrance of the park and 31 km [19 mi] from the south entrance).
- Turn for Newman Sound and after 500 m/yd turn right for the campground.
- After a further 1.5 km (.9 mi) pass into the campground (you will need a free day-pass if you are not a camper) and drive to site 253 (you can also reach the trail from the Newman Sound Campground trail, day-use area and from campground — see map 21).

Trail Directions:
Before hiking the Puzzle Pond trail, first take the short walk around Ochre Hill. Climb either bank of steps from the parking area and walk around the rock outcrop. Enjoy the views and the interpretive boards. Look through the telescope and climb the firetower, and return to the parking lot.

10 min From the parking lot, walk down the road to the Max 50 sign (about 150 m/yd).

13 min At the notice board and trail board (on which the distances are inaccurate), turn right and take the path into the forest. The strange, wispy lichen called old-man's beard hangs from dry branches and around the trunks of the tall spruces. In the filtered sunshine, crackerberries grow in green carpets speckled with white flowers or red berries (depending on the season). Lilac-pink flowers decorate the sheep laurel shrubs and the bluebead lily displays its yellow flower or single poisonous, dark blue berry. The outcrop of Ochre Hill towers above the trees as the path descends. A new growth of coniferous trees pushes up the thick mosses and on the distant horizon lurk the shadows of hills. The surface is uneven underfoot and can be very wet, especially in early summer. It can be windy on blustery days.

22 min The path crosses a small rock outcrop and bears right, down to a small boardwalk and sign-post. Take the left fork towards South Broad Cove (the right fork is a ski trail signposted to Halfway Cabin). The path narrows to a single track and the trees become thicker. Bluebead lilies and mosses thrive in the dim light and sheep laurel encroaches on the rocky path. To avoid the wet and muddy patches, walk along the banks on either side of the path, for there are only a few short boardwalks.

30 min Continue over the longer boardwalk and on through the undergrowth of sheep laurel and the scattered spruces and tamaracks. Grey, reindeer and caribou mosses spill onto the path. Moose have left prints in the muddy path as it undulates over the wooded hillside. Throughout the park there are constant signs of these large animals. They include droppings, tracks and trees on which they have rubbed their antlers, but they are expert at hiding and it is not often you see them on the trails. The best place to see moose is the Newman Sound campground at dusk or along the Trans-Canada Highway.

35 min Cross the small boardwalk and walk across the open area framed by distant hills. A boardwalk descends over three steps and then the path climbs a small hillock covered in sheep laurel. It then leaves the open area and re-enters the dense forest. Green moss covers the rocks, roots and fallen trees in a blanket of colour. There may be wet patches.

42 min Follow the long boardwalk with three steps towards Puzzle Pond. The path becomes muddy and is encroached upon from both sides by sheep laurel. It veers to the left of the water's edge and continues over a rickety old boardwalk that is overgrown by long marsh grasses. Be careful of loose planks and holes.

45 min Follow another old boardwalk, also very overgrown and rickety, over the flat marsh around the pond. As the path bends left, the pond disappears from view and the sheep laurel shrubs resume beneath the scattered spruces and tamaracks.

48 min The pond appears on the right again and the path continues over another rickety boardwalk. Be careful crossing the partially collapsed section in the middle. It can be pleasantly warm around the pond, although there are no obvious places to sit down and enjoy the sun. The next section of path through the sheep laurel and grey mosses is sandy and dry and enters a stand of skeletal spruces. Many trees have fallen over and are smothered with old-man's beard.

51 min Continue downhill and cross the boardwalk bridge over the stream. The water is the colour of strong beer because of the seepage of tannic acid from the surrounding peat bogs. Past the bridge the path is muddy and wet until it reaches the next boardwalk. Heavily overgrown with marsh grasses, the boardwalk leads to a drier section.

55 min Cross the tiny boardwalk bridge and follow the wet path overgrown with marsh grasses. The grasses thrive in the damp soil and swamp the sheep laurel and tamaracks. After the small rickety boardwalk bridge, continue gently uphill.

58 min The path passes through the open forest of tall trees; many have been cut or have been blown over and some may lie across the path. Trickling water punctuates the silence. The trail continues downhill to the stream and meanders alongside for the next 20 minutes. Sometimes the trail follows along its bank, other times it is far from the stream. Wet patches and dry sections alternate, and although there are boardwalks in strategic positions the conditions are generally wet and muddy.

1 hr 10 min A long rickety boardwalk with several broken boards crosses the stream. It runs alongside the water and cuts through a small, grassy marsh. It can be windy in this open area. When the boardwalk ends, the trail continues beneath the spruce trees, cutting a narrow path in the green moss and the undergrowth of sheep laurel. Old-man's beard hangs on the trees and bluebead lilies grow in the shade.

1 hr 16 min Beware of the hole in the small curved boardwalk. Further on, cross the stream on the bridge with one rail and continue on the far bank. Take the small boardwalk over the tributary and continue up the hill into the forest. Windfall may lie across the path.

1 hr 21 min Between the two short boardwalks, stop to see the small waterfall on the left and then continue parallel with the water as it bubbles downstream.

1 hr 25 min Pass around the Closed sign at the junction with the Outport trail (the sign may be removed if the trail has been upgraded) and follow the signpost left to Newman Sound (Mount Stamford and South Broad Cove, right, and Ochre Hill, back from where you came).

1 hr 26 min At the big bridge over the stream, the straight section ends and the trail returns to meandering through the trees.

1 hr 30 min Cross the second bridge and pass through a large open basin of sheep laurel, scattered spruce and tamarack, and grey mosses. The path is dry and sandy.

1 hr 34 min At the junction, take the right fork. The sandy path is sheltered and mosses and sheep laurel grow in abundance. In mid-June the pretty, pink-purple flowers of the sheep laurel blossom on the shrubs. The old-man's beard is almost black and drapes over the tops of the spruces like a widow's veil. Ignore any small tracks to the left and continue downhill along the sandy path until it enters the forest. A fire access road runs behind the trees on the left.

1 hr 46 min Descend through a wet, grassy hollow of alders and pass into the stands of tall, dry trunks. Lots of fallen trees lie in the long grass, and clumps of alder are growing profusely. A short boardwalk leads to a second similar stand from where the path meanders through the alders and crosses a grassy cutline. The suspension bridge over Big Brook comes into view.

1 hr 52 min Cross the bridge (if you are returning to Ochre Hill I suggest you stop here and rest before turning back, rather than continuing crossroads), and walk along the sandy path between the dry trunks and alders until it reaches a crossroads.

1 hr 53 min At the crossroads there is a signpost with a hiker. Turn left along the wide grass road for the quickest route to the campground; bear right around the bend and walk to the barrier. (If you go straight at the crossroads with the hiker you follow the Newman Sound Campground trail, which, in turn, connects with the Inner Newman Sound trail to HQ Wharf and Saltons Brook; see maps 19, 20, 21 and 22).

1 hr 55 min Go around the barrier and enter the campground by site 253 (you can leave a second car there). Turn left and follow the gravel road and the green arrows to the exit.

Background Notes:

Like the moose and the beaver, the snowshoe hare is another animal found in Terra Nova National Park that is not native to Newfoundland. Since its introduction in the late 1800s, it has thrived on the island. Its population growth peaks in ten-year cycles which scientists believe is due to overcrowding. This leads to an increase in diseases and a drop in the population. One of its main predators is the lynx, which can also be found in the park.

OCHRE HILL
(map 23)

Time: 2 hr
Distance: 8.25 km
(5 mi) loop
Difficulty: moderate;
good for older children

Condition: maintained;
some steep sections

Summary of Trail:
This trail starts from the Ochre Hill fire lookout. After the first 25 minutes a spur forks away from the main trail and passes over two sparse rock outcrops with spectacular views over Bread Cove Pond, Clode Sound and the abandoned community of Bread Cove. Returning to the main loop, the trail meanders down to the Ochre Hill Ponds. These are not marked as fishing holes, but nevertheless are popular with anglers. Loop around the ponds and hike up the hill to the tower. Should you want a shorter walk but still want to return to the tower, a shortcut runs up the hill from the ponds.

How to Get There:
- Take the Trans-Canada Highway south from the Newman Sound turning.
- After 6 km (3.6 mi) at the crossroads turn left for Ochre Hill (right for Sandy Pond). No trailers allowed.
- Continue up the gravel road for 5.3 km (3.2 mi) and park beneath the fire tower (the parking lot for Ochre Hill Ponds is after the first 2.2 km [1.3 mi]).

Trail Directions:
Facing the tower, take the long bank of steps up the hill on the left and walk around the rock outcrop. Enjoy the view towards Newman Sound with Rocky Pond in the foreground and Puzzle Pond further right. Continue right around the outcrop. There are steep rocks, so small children should be watched carefully.

5 min At the viewing platform you may wish to read the interpretive boards about glaciers, and look through the telescope. Continue down the steps and along the boardwalk towards the firetower (if the gates are not shut you can climb up to the observation galleries). Pass the shed and beacon and follow the path marked by stones. At the first junction (1 on map 23), turn left for Ochre Hill (straight returns to the parking lot via a long bank of steps). Follow the gravel path gently downhill around the small spruce clumps, lichen-covered boulders and erratics (large rocks left by glaciers). The evergreen forests blanket the lower hills towards Bread Cove Pond and Clode Sound.

10 min A short bank of steps leads off the exposed outcrop into the forest, and a rough rocky path continues downhill to the second junction (2 on map 23) and signpost. Turn left and continue steeply downhill (straight leads to the Ochre Hill Ponds). The trail is rough and awkward underfoot and hiking boots are an advantage. Walking on the moss-covered bank on the side of the path is much easier than the dry streambed it follows. Spruces hung with old-man's beard partially obscure the views towards Ochre Hill.

14 min The trail levels and continues through the forest of spruces and birches, carpets of moss and sheep laurel shrubs. The path crosses short boardwalks. They assist walking along the undulating terrain and over the bogs and mud patches. The view is obliterated by the dense forest, and although the path can be wet in places, it is largely flat and has a good sand and gravel surface.

25 min At the next junction (3 on map 23), take the spur left signposted to Ochre Hill and the viewpoint (right is the main loop towards to the lower parking lot and is signposted to Ochre Hill Ponds). The trees have become scraggly and sparse and the path runs through dense, thigh-high sheep laurel. Caribou and reindeer mosses grow beneath in the dry sandy soil. In the distance on the right the Ochre Hill Ponds lie below the hill while ahead rises the first rock outcrop. The trail levels and then enters the denser forest and ascends up the hill.

30 min As the trail ascends up the rough timber steps, across the ochre-coloured rocks, and turns a sharp bend, the view creeps up over the tree-tops. On the hill behind you the fire lookout towers above the forest, and all around you long views of the forested hills are punctuated with ponds and rock outcrops. Rock stones mark the trail, and mosses and lichens survive on the thin soil under the exposed, windy conditions.

35 min At the fork, walk left along the short spur to the viewpoint over Bread Cove and Clode Sound, and then return to the trail and take the right fork. This rounds the summit and descends steeply towards the next hill. Where there is no soil, the trail is marked by stones. Scattered clumps of small spruces struggle against the strong winds and inadequate soils. Mosses thrive on the warm rocks between the leggy sheep laurel. The only signs of civilization are the fire lookout, the communities on the far side of Clode Sound and the Trans-Canada Highway winding its way over the forested hills. The rest looks wild and untouched.

42 min At the fork, turn either right or left. This is a small loop at the end of the trail. Be careful of the very steep drop to the plateau as there are no barriers. On the plateau a small pond feeds into the larger Bread Cove Pond. These were part of the route for transporting logs from the far slopes of Dunphys Pond to the sawmills at Bread Cove. At this distance the ruined dam and mill sites are indistinguishable, but at one time the park considered cutting a trail into Bread Cove to the site of what was once the largest community in the area. Unfortunately, nothing has materialized and the cove is still only accessible by boat or along an unmarked, overgrown trail. After a suitable rest, return to junction 3.

1 hr Back at junction 3, turn left towards the ponds and parking.

1 hr 5 min Pass within 10 m/yd of the pond that has been on the left for a while. Sheep laurel and reindeer and caribou mosses grow on either side of the path, and past the short boardwalk the spruces become denser.

1 hr 7 min The path hugs the pond and continues through the sheep laurel along the edge. Even with the short boardwalks, some sections can remain muddy. Pass the tiny rock island with a solitary tree and follow the path away from the pond.

1 hr 15 min At the junction (4 on map 23), turn left and cross the railed bridge over the stream linking the two ponds (if you want to exclude the second pond and cut the hike short by about 25 minutes, turn right at this junction, right at the next junction [6 on map 23] and follow the log from the 1 hr 38 min point below).

1 hr 20 min Cross another railed bridge and boardwalk. On the right, the pond is visible through the trees. On the left, the open bog may have once been a pond. Under the spruces and birches the green moss grows indiscriminately over fallen trees, boulders and earth.

1 hr 27 min Cross the small boardwalk over the stream from the elongated pond on the right and continue parallel with the gravel road behind the trees on the left. You may see bear tracks.

1 hr 30 min At the junction (5 on map 23), turn right and continue along the meandering gravel path through the sheep laurel, moss and spruce trees (left leads to the lower parking lot). As the trail descends gently, the long, narrow pond ahead looks like a river. Cross the boardwalk bridge. Pitcher plants grow between the sphagnum moss and sheep laurel. Old-man's beard drapes over the trees like garlands on Christmas trees. By the water, the path bends to the left, crosses a small boardwalk and bends left again away from the pond.

1 hr 35 min Cross the brown bridge with two rails.

1 hr 38 min At the junction (6 on map 23), follow the signpost left towards the scenic viewpoint (straight connects to junction 4 on map 23, from where the short-cut comes). Old-man's beard hangs on the trunks and branches of the spruce. Green moss covers the ground around the trail as it winds uphill through the forest. Smooth-leaved bluebead lilies and shiny crackerberries make their appearance. Pass the big uprooted tree on the right and cross the tiny boardwalk beside the wet patch. Boardwalks cross over small brooks and wet areas as the path continues uphill. Pass the tiny pond in the small open bog on the right. On the right, a big erratic has been stranded by retreating glaciers.

1 hr 47 min Turn left and climb over the rock outcrop where the trail is marked with small stones. Before taking the steps down the far side of the outcrop and continuing in the trees, enjoy the unbroken view from the outcrop to the lookout on Ochre Hill and to distant Clode Sound. In the woods, the path gently ascends as views of Clode Sound are glimpsed through the trees. Old-man's beard drapes over the trunks and lower branches of the trees in a sea of grey-green.

1 hr 53 min The path continues through the forest, first gently descending along a rocky path and then rising slowly towards the lookout. The blue waters of Clode Sound are a welcome contrast to the evergreen hills.

1 hr 55 min Back at junction 2 the loop is complete. Continue straight up the steep hill. The rocky up-hill path to the steps is mercifully short.

1 hr 56 min Climb up the steps and emerge from the woods onto the rock outcrop. The path meanders around the rocks towards the lookout.

2 hr At the junction (1 on map 23), turn left and go down the long bank of steps to the parking lot.

Background Notes:

The wind blows around your ears as you stand on the rock outcrop. In the distance the icebergs slowly move across the horizon. Sometimes the currents bring them into the fjord of Clode Sound where they grind to a temporary halt, but mostly it is the pack ice that paralyses the cove for months of the year. At the foot of the vertical cliff lies Bread Cove Pond. A stream flows in from the west, exits in the east and flows down the hill into Clode Sound. A few logs lie around the pond outlet, and through binoculars you may just discern the remains of a dam. If you could get down to the cove, you might find a rusting pis-ton and cylinder lying in the salt water near the brook mouth. You might find some overgrown trails and some root cellars, for between the early 1910s and the late 1950s anywhere from 15 to 34 families lived in log houses scattered around the now-deserted cove. The *Bread Cove Story Area Document,* prepared by Michael Rosen in 1977, charts the history of the cove beginning in 1910 with the opening of the first mill. In addition to this mill and three others that operated from the cove until the 1940s and 1950s, a merchant from Port Blandford ran a pit prop operation from the cove. In the winter Bread Cove was cut off from the outside world by ice. However, at times horse and dog sleds moved back and forth across the sound. Life was simple yet comfortable, and Bread Cove even had a small school that functioned for a few years before the teacher moved away.

SANDY POND
(map 24)

Time: 45 min   **Condition:** maintained
Distance: 3 km
(1.8 mi) loop
Difficulty: easy;
good for children

Summary of Trail:
This pretty trail circumnavigates the pond, passing under spruces heavy with old-man's beard, and cuts through large areas covered in the sheep laurel shrub. The pond is clear and blue through the trees, and at the far end a bridge spans the brook that links Sandy Pond to Beachy Pond. In many places the trail runs along the banks of the pond. This popular corner of the park boasts a white, sandy beach, supervised swimming and boats for rent. Interpretive boards are planned for the trail.

How to Get There:
- Take the Trans-Canada Highway south from the Newman Sound turning.
- After 6 km (3.5 mi) turn right for Sandy Pond (left for Ochre Hill).
- Follow the paved road for 2.4 km (1.4 mi), pass the overflow parking lot and park by the Weston's concessionary hut.

Map 24: SANDY POND

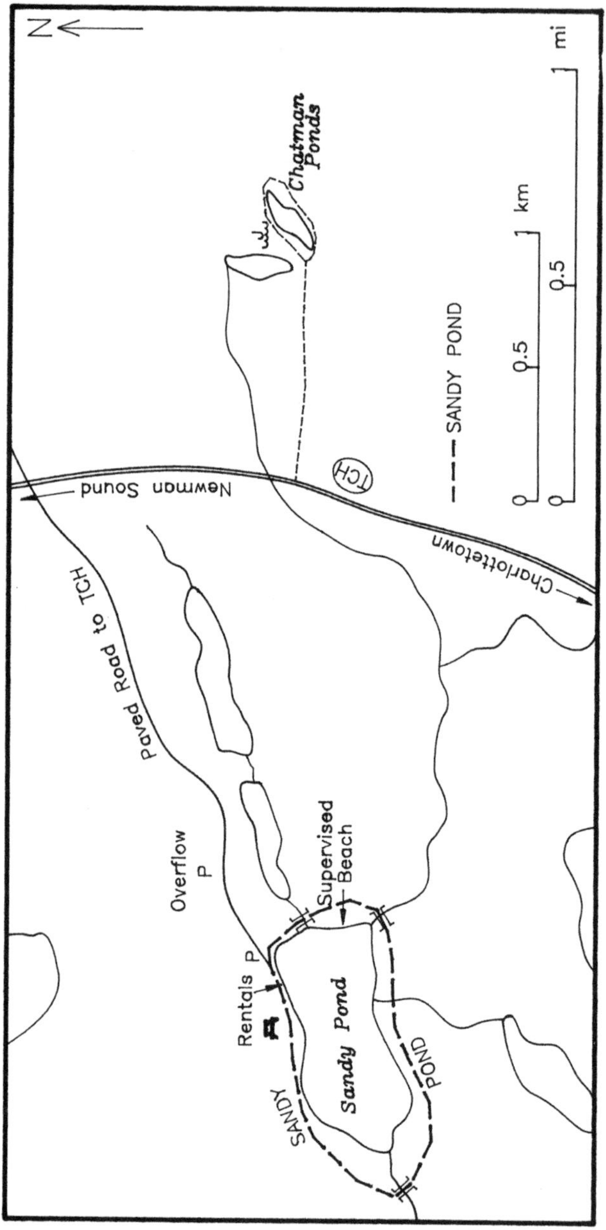

N

Chatman Ponds

Newman Sound

TCH

Paved Road to TCH

Overflow P

Rentals P

Supervised Beach

Sandy Pond

SANDY POND

Charlottetown

—·— SANDY POND

mi

km

0.5   0.5   1

Trail Directions:

Take the trail by the signposts (one of a hiker and the other of a picnic table) at the far end of the parking lot. Ignore the boardwalk and paths on the left that lead to the picnic sites by the pond and follow the gravel path through the spruce forest. In areas not dominated by sheep laurel, carpets of green moss spread across the forest floor. The pond lurks beyond the trees on the left as the trail continues around the pond. Although there are many short boardwalks, in early summer there may be some minor muddy patches.

12 min Cross the bridge with rails over the stream. The pond is not visible for a short while, then the trail follows a long curved boardwalk over an open area. On the left, the pond is silting up and being choked by long grasses.

18 min Cross the big bridge over the river at the far end of the pond. This is the link to Beachy Pond and Dunphys Pond and is part of the main canoe route through the park. The trail meanders through the spruce forests and dense sheep laurel on the south bank of the pond. At times the pond is visible through the trees, at times it is lost in the distance.

32 min The path comes close to the water's edge directly across from the canoe rental and launch.

35 min The rush of water echoes through the forest. Pass over the open area and cross the bridge over the large brook. The water spills over the remains of a dam that was once part of the logging route. Continue around the pond and then behind the sandy beach and supervised swimming area.

40 min Walk along the wide boardwalk behind the main beach area on the left. On the right, a beaver dam blocks a small stream, forming a small pond. Steps lead down to the beach and the right fork in the boardwalk leads to the kitchen shelter and

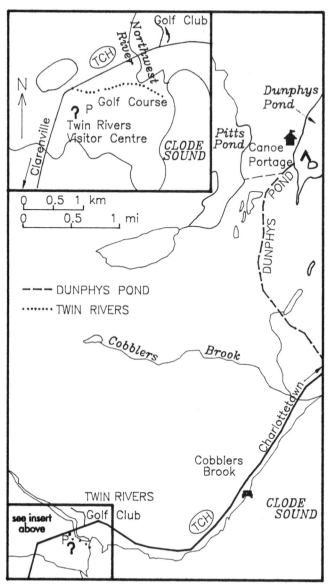

Map 25: DUNPHYS POND & TWIN RIVERS

parking lot. The left fork continues to the concessions and washrooms.

42 min Continuing along the wide boardwalk, pass the notice board on the left and another set of steps to the beach. The second fork on the right also leads to the kitchen shelter and parking lot. Bear left and pass the change cabin, washrooms and the water tap (boil before drinking) on the right. At the last fork in the boardwalk, bear right to return to the parking lot (the left fork leads to the beach and boat rentals).

45 min Back at the second parking lot.

DUNPHYS POND
(map 25)

Time: 1 hr 15 min
Distance: 4.75 km
(2.9 mi) one way
Difficulty: easy;
good for children

Condition: maintained;
some wet patches

Summary of Trail:

The trail to Dunphys Pond passes through spruce and birch forests with some views across the hills and towards the pond. Cycling is allowed, but the cobble surface of the old fire access road is not very comfortable and the wet patches may be a problem. At the end of the trail there is a small picnic shelter, a canoe rack and a warden's cabin, but there is no good place to sit and look out over the pond and the island campground. A shame, for this is a peaceful and picturesque spot.

How to Get There:

- Take the Trans-Canada Highway south from the Newman Sound turning.
- Continue for 23 km (14 mi) passing the turning to the community of Terra Nova, the crossroads to Ochre Hill and Sandy Pond, and the turning to Charlottetown, then turn right into the track signposted Dunphys Pond and park.

Trail Directions:

Take the track past the barrier and walk up the gentle hill through the forest.

10 min The road is made of cobbles, gravel and sand and can be uncomfortable for walking. However, it is largely flat with only short gentle uphill sections. Old-man's beard hangs on the stands of spruces.

20 min When the pond behind the trees on the right ends, alders swamp the path.

23 min The pond behind the trees drains through a wet scrub of scraggly trees and through the culvert under the path. The trail continues up the hill.

25 min On the right, there is a widening, like a passing area. Reindeer mosses grow under the sheep laurel shrubs and the black spruces and moose prints mark the soft gravel. The centre of the road is overgrown with small shrubbery. Continue up the hill to the crest where the trail levels.

30 min Follow the bend to the left. It can be wet.

35 min Follow the bend to the right, and then walk over the stream in the culvert. Continuing gently uphill, there may be some wet patches.

42 min Although there is a culvert in the road, in late spring streams flow along the surface, leaving it soft and muddy. Behind the alders on the left an open area stretches up the hill.

45 min On the right, the hill slopes away, exposing a sea of undulating evergreen forest.

47 min The bog on the left drains through the culvert under the road. A flush of young trees on the left represents a forest reviving, while on the right ghostly stumps project above the sheep laurel like frail skeletons.

55 min In the far distance Dunphys Pond nestles comfortably between the undulating hills of trees, like an oasis of water. The road starts its gentle decline.

1 hr Beware of the two large holes in the middle of the road. In recent years someone has placed a stick in one and covered the other with a board, but they are still dangerous if not noticed. As the road descends through the tall, dry spruces covered in old-man's beard, sections are overgrown with alders. The pond beckons from the distance.

1 hr 5 min Pass the portage to Pitts Pond on the left. Further along, a culvert does not prevent the road from becoming muddy.

1 hr 8 min Follow the road around the bend to the right and see the pond ahead through trees.

1 hr 10 min Pass the small shelter and picnic table and walk around the mud to get to the pond.

1 hr 15 min Pass the warden's cabin on the left and walk down to the pond. If it is not too wet or the blackflies and mosquitoes are not too bad, rest awhile on the banks and look out across the still and silent pond. Listen for the voices of the men, the chopping of their axes and the rasping of their saws.

Background Notes:

Men from the pit prop and pulpwood operation at Bread Cove worked as far back as Dunphys Pond. Unlike the men who worked at the sawmills, these men (called Pelly men after their boss, Daniel Pelly) spent the winter months living and working in small cabins in the woods. They were called "Planters" and were paid in advance, agreeing to supply a quota of logs by the end of the season. Throughout the area signs still remain of the log booming and towing, and of the dams built for the spring log drives. Once in Bread Cove the logs were shipped around the island and to Europe.

TWIN RIVERS
(map 25)

Time: 10 min   **Condition:** maintained
Distance: 800 m/yd
one way
Difficulty: easy;
good for children

Summary of Trail:
This short trail from the Twin Rivers Visitor Centre leads to the Northwest River by the side of the Twin Rivers golf course. Although this is one of New-foundland's scheduled salmon rivers, at the time of writing the river was closed to fishing to allow the decreasing stocks of salmon to recover. In late summer you may see salmon jumping up the rapids from the steep banks, and there are a few rough paths down to the water for better viewing.

How to Get There:
- Take the Trans-Canada Highway to the Twin Rivers Visitor Centre at the south entrance to the park (approximately 30 km [18 mi] from Newman Sound turning) and park in front of the building.

Trail Directions:

Take the path behind the viewing area and interpretive board left of the Visitor Centre. Descend the long bank of steps and follow the boardwalk over the silted pond, overgrown with Labrador tea, small conifers and an assortment of wildflowers. Pass the widening in the boardwalk which may contain another interpretive board. The boardwalk narrows and enters into the dark forest bare of undergrowth.

2 min When the boardwalk ends, the gravel path narrows even more as it passes through a large clump of sheep laurel and enters the dark forest once more. Since the trail runs close to the Trans-Canada Highway, the intermittent rumble of traffic cannot be avoided.

3 min Through the trees on the right you can spy on the golf course, but please stay off the green.

5 min Pass across the track between the Trans-Canada Highway and the golf course (access for golfers only), and pick up the narrow path through the trees. Turn left onto the dirt road and then right at the signpost with a hiker and fishing symbols (before the tunnel under the highway). Although there is easy access to the golf course throughout the trail, please remain on the path. At the small viewing area an interpretive board gives information about salmon, and you can see the formidable obstacle they face on their way upstream to spawn. Turn right and continue between the river and the golf course. There is a fence on the left, for the drop to the river is steep and a few rough paths descend to the river. Take heed of any notices about fishing bans.

10 min A boardwalk cuts through the bushes at the side of golf course and then continues alongside the golf course before fizzling into nothing. Turn around and return.

L'ANSE AUX MEADOWS:
Replica Viking Huts. BM

NATIONAL
HISTORIC SITES

NATIONAL HISTORIC SITES - Trails at a Glance

Name	Time* hr:min	Distance* (approx)	Difficulty
Signal Hill (map 26)			
Queens Battery	0:10	750 m/yd	moderate
Gibbet Hill (detour)	0:05	400 m/yd	moderate
Ladies Lookout	1:10	4.5 km (2.7 mi) loop	moderate
Cuckold Head (detour)	0:15	800 m/yd	very strenuous
North Head	1:10	3.2 km (1.9 mi) loop	moderate
Cape Spear (map 27)			
Restored Lighthouse	0:07	500 m/yd	moderate
Most Easterly Point	0:10	750 m/yd loop	easy
WWII Battery	0:25	1.5 km (.9 mi) loop	moderate
Coast	3:20	9.5 km (5.7 mi)	moderate
Castle Hill (map 28)			
Hilltop	0:45	2 km (1.2 mi) loop	moderate
Port au Choix (map 29)			
Phillips Garden & Pointe Riche	1:10 (2.7 mi)	4 km	easy
L'Anse aux Meadows (map 30)			
Viking Village	0:30	1.8 km (1.1 mi) loop	easy

*unless stated otherwise times and distances are one way

SIGNAL HILL NATIONAL HISTORIC SITE

Situated on a rocky ridge between the sheltered harbour of St. John's and the open Atlantic Ocean, Signal Hill stands as a buffer between the city and the sea. Stark cliffs plunge into the still waters of the harbour on one side, and the ocean pounds incessantly against the other. Cabot Tower dominates the bare hill like a beacon. Together, the hill and the tower are an invaluable visual aid in navigating the streets of St. John's where the lack of road signs, abundance of one-way systems and outdated street maps have caused havoc to many a visitor. Called the Lookout until 1762, Signal Hill's rugged summit is a favourite haunt for residents of St. John's, even though its windswept beauty was not always remembered with affection. Soldiers stationed on its blustery heights in the 19th century considered it among the most miserable postings in the British Empire.

Signal Hill's rich human history led to these 648 hectares of dramatic landscape being declared a National Historic Park in 1958 (now renamed a National Historic Site). The exhibits at the Visitor Centre and around Cabot Tower provide a good overview of Newfoundland and its capital, and any visitor to the island should consider a visit there mandatory. The tower is open to the public and offers a welcome refuge from the winds that buffet the hillside. After browsing through the souvenir and book shop, visitors can climb the spiral staircase to the amateur radio station (operated by the Society of Newfoundland Radio Amateurs) and onto the roof deck where flag signalling took place until 1958. The views of the city and coastline are spectacular from all around the hill, but nowhere are they as good as from the roof of the tower. Visitors can also walk the windy trails, watch icebergs drift by, look for whales frolicking in the frigid waters, enjoy the colourful Military Tattoo on the parade ground outside the Queen's Battery, and draw in the abundant fresh air. (Icebergs can be viewed from April to mid-July. The main season for watching whales is late June to mid-August, although they can be sighted year round. See Useful Information below for Tattoo times.)

History: With John Cabot's discovery of the rich fishing grounds off the coast of Newfoundland in 1497, St. John's Harbour became a seasonal base for the English fishery. The British had limited salt supplies for preserving fish and consequently they practised a "dry fishing" that relied on a land base. St. John's became a base where the fish were cleaned, dried on the beaches and on wooden platforms called flakes, and lightly salted before transportation to England. The French, Spanish and Portuguese, who also fished the rich grounds, had native supplies of salt and practised "green fishing." This enabled them to clean, heavily salt and store fish in the ship's hold without the need for a land base. Every year in May migratory fishermen arrived in St. John's from England. The captains took possession of the stages and flakes left from the previous year, and fishing would commence under the rule of the "fishing admiral." This self-appointed ruler was the captain of the first ship to reach the harbour that season. He would lay down his own laws, often making the lives of the fishermen intolerable during the six-month season.

After the ascension of Louis XIV to the French throne, France changed its fishing policy and French fishermen began to settle on the island near the rich cod banks. In 1660 they chose Plaisance (present-day Placentia, see Castle Hill National Historic Site) for the site of their first royal colony in Newfoundland. Friction between the two empires was rife, but the English government resisted efforts to colonize the island. They feared that building fortified colonies would attract men out of the migratory fishery and deplete the stocks of skilled seamen upon whom they could call during wartime. Their naval strategy was to blockade the enemy in his home waters, making fortifications unnecessary in the colonies. It is likely that the English West Country merchants may have also been working against settlement, believing the settlers would compete against the fishery.

In 1696, European conflicts spilled over into the New World and the French from Plaisance attacked St. John's; two sea attacks were repulsed from temporary works in the Narrows, but a third land attack was successful and St. John's was captured and razed. The British government finally realized the need for a permanent military presence in Newfoundland, or the island and the fishery would fall to the French. Three hundred and fifty men were sent to rebuild Fort William in St. John's and the batteries by the Narrows. The French attacked again in 1705 and 1709, coming overland both times. On each occasion they destroyed St. John's before returning to Plaisance, and in 1709 they also succeeded in capturing Fort William and the southside battery. In 1713 the War of Spanish Succession ended in Europe, and with the Treaty of Utrecht the French gave up Plaisance for concessions in other parts of Canada.

In the wake of peace the British garrison moved to Plaisance, which they renamed Placentia, and the defences in St. John's were allowed to go to ruin. War resumed in Europe in 1740, and concern was once again sparked for the defences in Newfoundland. Fort William and the batteries in the Narrows were hastily repaired and a new garrison arrived in St. John's. This time the only action in the New World was the fruitless British capture of Louisburg on Isle Royale (present day Cape Breton Island), which was promptly returned to the French by the Treaty of Aix-la-Chapelle in 1748.

War in Europe once more embraced the colonies when the Seven Years War began in 1756. Louisburg was again captured by the British, along with Quebec City. The French, having lost nearly all their possessions in America, retaliated by capturing St. John's on June 27, 1762. The British acted quickly and sent Colonel William Amherst with troops, and Admiral Lord Colville with a fleet, to take back the town. Using the French strategy of approaching overland, Amherst landed at Torbay, nine miles up the coast from St. John's, and attacked from Quidi Vidi to the rear. The French were defeated and the British recaptured their capital.

Much was learned from this battle about the defences of St. John's. As a result Fort Townshend was constructed out of firing range of Signal Hill, the Narrows batteries were strengthened, and in the late 1770s small batteries were added at Quidi Vidi, Cuckold Cove, Torbay and Bay Bulls to protect the notoriously weak rear.

In the 1790s, with the dual threats from Europe and the United States, the strategic importance of Signal Hill was realized, and decisions were made to develop the site to its full potential. The batteries guarding the harbour were strengthened, and the summits and valleys of the hill became a scene of ambitious construction. Blockhouses, officers' barracks, storehouses, new batteries and a masonry and wood stockade were constructed. Spruce and fir trees were cut down and stone quarried from the base of Gibbet Hill. Stone was also brought from the dismantled French fortress of Louisburg on Cape Breton Island (which the English had captured again in 1760) and used for the fortifications built on Signal Hill between 1796 and 1815. Since there was no road up the hill until 1796, the artillery had to be parbuckled up the cliffs from the harbour below. These tremendous efforts were rewarded in July 1796 when the French were sighted approaching the harbour. Upon seeing the impressive defences, they aborted their mission and sailed away, leaving St. John's untouched.

In 1815 the war in Europe ended with a French defeat, and the defences were allowed to deteriorate once more. In 1827 Lieutenant Colonel Gustavus Nicholls drew up an elaborate plan to phase out Forts William and Townshend and make Signal Hill the ultimate retreat. His plan was too expensive to complete; however, new barracks and some other facilities were constructed, and by 1842 half the garrison was housed on Signal Hill.

The new barracks proved uninhabitable due to the cold, the dampness and inadequate ventilation, and conditions for the garrison were intolerable. Shortages of everything plagued the soldiers' lives. There was never enough firewood, coal, candles, bedding or eating utensils. No other clothing was provided besides the soldiers' uniforms. There were chronic shortages of food, with the situation becoming so desperate that the allowance for wives and children was withdrawn. Up to 192 men lived miserably in damp, smoky barracks on the eastern extreme of Signal Hill, where it was not unheard of to find the sentinel frozen to death. The only reasonable barrack was the one by Georges Pond which had been built as a military hospital. With the failure of the barracks at the top of the hill, the hospital at Georges Pond was converted and the soldiers moved there and to Forts William and Townsend. The officers chose to live in the greater comfort of the town; their barrack at the top of the hill remained empty.

Nicholls's great scheme to centralize the defences on Signal Hill was never realized. Britain changed her policy to her colonies, requiring them to bear some of their own costs now that free trade had been introduced. As part of the new policy, the Royal Artillery was withdrawn from St. John's in 1852.

The steady withdrawal of British troops in North America was interrupted by the American Civil War. Fearing reprisals because of their open sympathy for the Confederacy, the British government returned the Royal Artillery to Signal Hill in 1862, and more improvements to the defences were carried out. With the end of the war in America, the threat to Newfoundland decreased, and by 1870 the last of the garrison was withdrawn.

Apart from building fortifications and defending St. John's, the garrison's duties included operating the flag-signalling system on Signal Hill. Records dating back to 1704 mention the firing of a small canon, hoisting of colours, and discharging of muskets whenever a sail approached the harbour. In 1795 a military blockhouse was built on Ladies Lookout and assumed the signalling functions. At first the signals were exclusively military, but as trade and the population grew they became increasingly mercantile. Each mercantile firm had its own house flag, and when spotters in the offices along the waterfront saw the colours raised, they hastened to the dock to prepare for the ship's arrival. Other flags warned the firm of ships in distress or those with disease on board. Customs officials were also alerted with flags, and harbour pilots knew from the flags if a ship needed assistance entering the Narrows. In the 1850s the colony took over the operating costs of the signal station, although the military continued to man it until 1870.

In 1854 the blockhouse on Ladies Lookout was replaced by one near the present Cabot Tower; when that one burnt down in 1894, it was succeeded by Cabot Tower. Built in the midst of controversy, the tower was supposed to serve as a 24-hour signal station and weather observatory, and commemorate the diamond jubilee of Queen Victoria and the quatercentenary of John Cabot's landing in Newfoundland. The cornerstone was laid on June 22, 1897, but construction did not start until more than a year later; even then, only one of the four planned turrets was ever built. The tower is constructed of red sandstone that is said to have come from the ruins of St. George's Hospital, which burned down in 1892. It is unlikely it was ever equipped with the "brilliant electric flashlight" for night-time communication with ships entering the harbour, and the meteorological observatory it was to house was never installed. However, the tower did become an integral part of the port's signalling strategy, which continued until 1958 when Signal Hill became a National Historic Park.

Cabot Tower is often erroneously identified with the world's first transatlantic wireless message, received by Marconi on December 12, 1901. It was received on Signal Hill, but in the military barrack that had caused the garrison so much misery, not in the tower. In 1870 the barrack had been converted into a fever hospital, but by the time Marconi arrived it was virtually empty. Signal Hill had not been Marconi's first choice for his transatlantic transmission, but after his station in Cape Cod, Massachusetts, was destroyed by a gale he chose St. John's to continue with his project. With everything set up for the transmission from Poldhu, in Cornwall, Marconi waited at the appointed time. "Three scant little clicks" were clearly heard by him and his assistant Kemp. Electro-magnetic radio waves had crossed the Atlantic, despite the sceptics' opinions that transmission would be prevented by the earth's curvature. Marconi applied to erect a permanent wireless station in Newfoundland, but his application was blocked by the Anglo-American Telegraph Company, which feared that the new system was a threat to its own transatlantic communications system of undersea cable links. He left for New York but was waylaid in Cape Breton, where in 1902 he set up the first North American wireless station.

This was not the last that Newfoundland saw of Marconi. In 1920, three engineers of the Canadian Marconi Company were temporarily based at Cabot Tower where they received the first wireless transmission of the human voice from a ship in the Atlantic. In 1933 Marconi's firm established a wireless telegraph station on the second floor of Cabot Tower to inform vessels of ice conditions, give directions for entering the harbour in fog, listen for distress signals, and receive messages from northern Newfoundland and Labrador. It closed in 1960.

Another function of the military stationed at Signal Hill was the firing of a gun to regulate daily activities. In 1832 the evening gun (which signalled the tattoo or return to barracks) was joined by the morning gun (which signalled reveille), and the earliest reference to a noonday gun (to signal lunch) dates from 1842. Civilians in St. John's observed the signals, too, and mariners set their chronometers by the noonday gun. In 1869 the morning and evening firings were dropped, and when the garrison withdrew in 1870 the colonial government took on responsibility for the noonday gun, along with the fog gun at Fort Amherst, the fire alarm gun at Queen's Battery and the flag-signalling service.

When the garrison withdrew from Signal Hill in 1870, the remaining wooden buildings were in ruins, but the colonial government found uses for the two stone barracks. The barracks at the converted military hospital by Georges Pond was refitted as a quarantine hospital for diphtheria and tuberculosis cases. When it burned down in the Great Fire of 1892, the facilities were moved to the barracks on top of Signal Hill, which then became Signal Hill Hospital. No less a problem than when soldiers had lived there, the weather continued to hamper efforts to put the ill-fated barracks to good use. In 1890 a savage gale unroofed the hospital and blew down some chimneys. When a defective chimney caught fire in 1920, the fire trucks could not get up the hill and the hospital was lost in a splendid blaze.

The only hospital to be built on the hill after the military withdrew in 1870 was a small cholera hospital in Ross's Valley below Cabot Tower. Military tradesmen had lived here with their families, kept animals and dug gardens in the 19th century. The small hospital was built in 1892 in response to a cholera epidemic in Europe. The idea was that victims could be landed at Chain Rock and brought to the building along an isolated track. The scare proved to be just that and Ross's Valley Hospital was only used twice for smallpox until it, too, succumbed to fire in 1911.

During both the First and Second World Wars, Newfoundland's security was vital to Canada because the island commanded both entrances to the Gulf of St. Lawrence. In 1916 Waldegrave Battery was reactivated as Fort Waldegrave and watches were maintained at Signal Hill and Cape Spear. During the Second World War, St. John's experienced the most extensive defence measures it had ever known. Newfoundland was thrust into the forefront of the North American defence strategy, and Canadian and American troops were stationed in St. John's.

Canada established coastal defence forts in the Narrows at Fort Amherst and Fort Chain Rock, and the United States placed coast artillery on Signal Hill to back up counterbombardment batteries at Cape Spear and Red Cliff Head. The Americans also built an anti-aircraft battery on the summit of Signal Hill. Although submarines lurked in the waters off Newfoundland's rugged coastline, Signal Hill did not see active service.

Signal Hill has survived as a strategic site for more than 300 years. Its story is largely of unrealized plans, shifting policies and neverending struggles against the elements. Fierce winds and vicious storms dominated the lives of those who tried to tame it. Sentries froze to death, engineers were foiled by the winds, and soldiers dreaded a posting there. However, in the hearts of the people of St. John's, Signal Hill has been the defender in their hour of need. Today it is held in deep affection and respect by all. There is a good paved road to the top, several walking trails and warm, dry buildings that offer shelter from the wind. Signal Hill's spirit has not been broken, but it has taken on a different role in its maturity. Once a landmark for the military, today it is an attraction for visitors, hikers, joggers and families taking the dog for a walk (dogs must be kept on a leash), as well as a navigational aid to motorists manoeuvring through the narrow, hilly streets of St. John's. Perhaps some of its wilderness has been tamed.

How to Get There:
- Follow Duckworth Street eastward from downtown St. John's until you pass the large white building of the Hotel Newfoundland on the left.
- At the Stop sign at the end of Duckworth Street, continue straight up the hill. Pass the Battery Hotel on the right and enter the park (1 km [.6 mi] from Hotel Newfoundland).
- For Queen's Battery and the Visitor Centre, turn right 100m/yd after the park entrance.
- For Ladies Lookout, North Head and Cabot Tower, continue up the hill for 800 m/yd.

Useful Information:
Signal Hill National Historic Site:
  Tel: (709) 772-5367
Visitor Centre and Cabot Tower are open daily year round. Hours are June to Labour Day, 08:30-20:00, the rest of the year, 08:30-16:30
Military Tattoo runs from mid-July to mid-August (not daily, check for days and times)
Quidi Vidi Battery: Tel: (709) 729-2463, open daily mid-June to end of October, 10:30-18:00

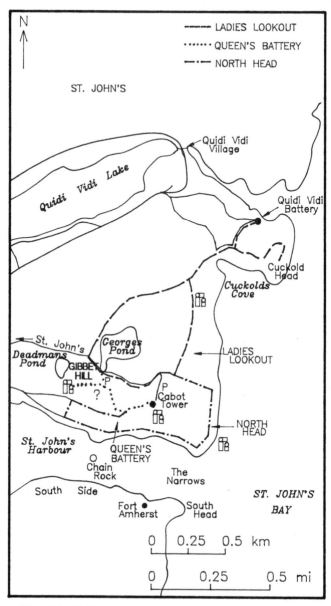

Map 26: SIGNAL HILL NATIONAL HISTORIC SITE

QUEEN'S BATTERY & GIBBET HILL
(map 26)

Visitor Centre to Cabot Tower via Queen's Battery:

Time: 10 min
Distance: 750 m/yd one way
Difficulty: moderate; good for children

Condition: maintained; gravel path uphill; steps up Gibbet Hill

DETOUR: Gibbet Hill
Time: 5 min
Distance: 400 m/yd one way

Summary of Trail:

From the Visitor Centre, take the path past the stone barrack of the Queen's Battery and on up the hill towards Cabot Tower where you will find interpretive boards about St. John's and the military. From the tower's roof are lofty views of St. John's, the harbour, the ocean and Cape Spear. To extend your walk, take the North Head trail or Ladies Lookout trail from the Cabot Tower parking lot. Once back at the Visitor Centre parking lot, clamber up Gibbet Hill for a more windy, lofty bird's-eye view.

How to Get There:

- See page 245 for directions to site.
- 100 m/yd after the park entrance, turn right for the Visitor Centre and leave your car in the parking lot.

Trail Directions:

Take the trail from the corner of the parking lot and follow the gravel path up the hill. The parking lot is near the site of St. George's Hospital, a small stone building that housed some of the British garrison until 1870. As inhospitable to patients as it was to soldiers, the red stone barrack certainly had plenty of the fresh air and isolation considered to be the primary treatment for tuberculosis and diphtheria. These qualities made it the ideal location for a fever and quarantine hospital. In 1892 St. George's fell victim to the Great Fire of St. John's after which the quarantine facility was moved to the equally cold and windy stone barracks at the top of Signal Hill.

2 min The stone barrack of the Queen's Battery was one of a dozen batteries and forts built in the 1760s to defend St. John's. When it was built there was no road up the hill, so the canons had to be hoisted up the cliffs. From 1939 until the park was established in 1958, a caretaker lived in the building with his family. At that time the stone was covered in clapboard, but in 1961 the building was totally destroyed by fire. Turn left onto the gravel path before the building and walk past the canons on the edge of the grass parade ground. Continue up the gravel easy risers towards Cabot Tower.

10 min Cabot Tower was officially opened on June 20, 1900, to commemorate the diamond jubilee of Queen Victoria and the quatercentenary of the landing of John Cabot.

Detour: Gibbet Hill

Back at the Visitor Centre, take the gravel path from the parking lot to the road and turn at the signpost to Gibbet Hill. Take the banks of steps and the rocky path to the top. Below on the right lies Deadmans Pond. According to local folklore, bodies removed from the gibbet were stuffed into weighted barrels and rolled down the side of the hill into the pond. However, history speaks only of the drowning of Frederick Weston Carter and two young women on December 26, 1869. The top of the hill marks the location of Wallace Battery, with the concrete base marking the position of a Second World War anti-aircraft gun mount. The gibbet was erected in the 1750s, but it was more of a symbol than an actual instrument. There is only one known eye-witness account of a body on the gibbet. If the wind doesn't chase you back down the hill, enjoy the panoramic bird's-eye view.

LADIES LOOKOUT TO QUIDI VIDI BATTERY
(map 26)

Ladies Lookout to Quidi Vidi Battery
Time: 1 hr 10 min
Distance: 4.5 km (2.7 mi) loop
Difficulty: moderate; very strenuous spur; good for children (except for spur)
Condition: partly maintained; rocky path downhill; spur very steep

DETOUR: Cuckold Head Spur
Time: 15 min
Distance: 800 m/yd one way

Summary of Trail:
The first part of the trail runs up to Ladies Lookout and then down to the ridge to join the old road that

links Georges Pond to Quidi Vidi Battery. From the Battery, climb the steep trail up Cuckold Head for spectacular views of the coastline. On the way back, turn off the outward-going path and take the Burma Road to Georges Pond (not signposted). Once at the pond, the quickest way back to the tower is to walk up the road. A more interesting route is to head for the Visitor Centre and take the trail via the Queen's Battery.

How to Get There:

- See page 245 for directions to the site.
- Once in the park, drive 800 m/yd up the paved road to Cabot Tower and leave your car in the parking lot.

Trail Directions:

Start at the north end of the parking lot at the sign-post for Ladies Lookout and North Head. Follow the gravel path for 15 m/yd and take the badly defined fork left to the top of the ridge.

3 min At 169 metres above sea level, Ladies Lookout is the highest point in the park. Nearly 300 years ago, information received from ships at sea was transmitted from this head by gun and musket fire to the St. John's Harbour authorities. The lookout was the site of the first military blockhouse to assume signalling functions on the hill. Constructed in 1795, it may have replaced an earlier crude signal tower, and in 1815 it was superseded by the Signal Hill blockhouse built in the Cabot Tower vicinity. This burned down in 1894 and was replaced by the Cabot Tower which was officially opened in 1900. According to legend, sailors' wives came to the lookout to await their husbands' return, hence the name Ladies Lookout. Enjoy the views of the wild, rugged coastline on one side and the barren, rocky landscape on the other side. The 20th-century city of St. John's sprawls in the distance in a tapestry of colours. With your back to Cabot Tower, walk by the mast and pick up the narrow, rocky path down the hill.

8 min There is a sharp left bend as the path continues steeply downhill through dense shrubbery. The sea remains in view as the trail crosses the bald rocks.

10 min Take the bank of rough, open timber steps. Ignore any tracks that cross the narrow path and continue downhill.

15 min Take the steps out onto the gravel road. Turn right and proceed downhill along the rocky cart track (left along the gravel road leads to the paved road by Georges Pond opposite the Visitor Centre).

20 min Look out over the sea from the new viewing platform. The path bends to the left and passes between a row of boulders which block the track to cars. Continue downhill and come out onto a wide gravel road by a sign for Signal Hill National Historic Site.

23 min Turn right onto the gravel road *.

28 min Pass close to a house on the right and enter through the gates to Quidi Vidi Battery. Visit the tiny white clapboard barrack and talk to the "soldiers" about their lives in the 18th and 19th centuries. Built during the period of the American Revolution, Quidi Vidi Battery protected the vulnerable rear of Signal Hill, which had previously been susceptible to land attacks. After visiting the barrack, turn back and return along the gravel road.

35 min Turn left at the Signal Hill National Historic Site sign and return up the path.

45 min At the gravel road (the Burma Road), turn right towards the red and white mast (or return to Cabot Tower as you came along the narrow path up the hill). Pass between two hills, after which Cabot Tower appears on the far left and St. John's sprawls on the right.

50 min Ignore the gravel road on the left to the beacon and hut. Round the bend and see Gibbet Hill ahead.

53 min Ignore the gravel road on the left to a bomb shelter set in the hillside. Continue by Georges Pond and pass a boarded-up, concrete kiosk with a cone-shaped roof that looks like it belongs in a park in Paris rather than a park in Newfoundland. This is a monument to the first piped water system in St. John's. The main pipe was constructed around 1846 and ran from Georges Pond down the hill and along Water Street.

I hr Pass through the gate across the gravel road and turn left onto the paved road to the tower. Pass the Visitor Centre on the right.

I hr 6 min Ignore the gravel road on the right to Queen's Battery.

I hr 10 min Back at the parking lot.

Detour: Cuckold Head Spur

After turning onto the gravel road to Quidi Vidi Battery, on the first bend take the rough path up the hill on the right. Cuckold Cove, at one-time a landing point for the transatlantic cable and the location of a small cable station, lies on the right before the path. Follow the numerous spidery paths which eventually come together and continue as one.

5 min Pass a huge boulder and take the right fork.

8 min Start the steep, tough climb up the loose scree and gravel. The path is badly defined, with one short, nearly vertical section.

15 min The grass and rock summit is strewn with bones brought by gulls from the Robin Hood Dump. From this summit Cabot Tower looks like a sentinel on Signal Hill, waves crash against the rocks in Cuckold Cove, the lighthouse at distant Cape Spear marks the most easterly promontory in North America and Quidi Vidi Village lies snug in its cosy harbour. Although only a stone's throw from the suburban malls and city lights, even here the strange austere beauty that is so typical of rural Newfoundland surrounds you. There have been several suggestions concerning the origins of the name Cuckold Head. I like the one that brands a cuckold as the weak husband of an unfaithful wife, but what this has to do with the head I'm not sure.

30 min Back at the bottom of the hill, turn left onto the gravel road.

NORTH HEAD
(map 26)

Time: 1 hr 10 min
Distance: 3.2 km (1.9 mi) loop
Difficulty: moderate; not recommended for young children

Condition: maintained within the park boundary; steep descent with steps; bare rock and gravel path; narrow ledge clinging to rock face

Summary of Trail:
The first part of the North Head trail crosses stark rocks to a narrow ledge with a steep drop to the sea. Then it passes through two small Second World War gun batteries and enters the ramshackle world of The Battery neighbourhood of St. John's, where the

park ends. Turning into an alley that climbs up the steep hillside of clapboard houses, the trail doubles back on itself to re-enter the park behind the Queen's Battery. To return to Cabot Tower, continue up the grassy slope, or first take the path to the Visitor Centre for a brief outline of St. John's history.

How to Get There:
- See page 245 for directions to the site.
- Once in the park, drive 800 m/yd up the paved road to the parking lot by Cabot Tower.

Trail Directions:
Take the path signposted to North Head by the entrance to the parking lot. Almost immediately, the trail descends steeply over numerous long banks of steps down the side of the hill. The trail is rough and rocky between the steps, but the view across St. John's Bay to Cape Spear, the Atlantic and the harbour is adequate compensation for any discomfort.

5 min Take the bank of steps up. The Narrows marks the entrance into the harbour. On the rocks on the south side, a small lighthouse and the ruins of a gun battery mark the location of Fort Amherst. Note the sign: Attention, Hazardous Coastline — Stay on Walking Trail. More steps lead down into Ross's Valley where an isolation hospital was built in 1892. Only used twice in 1911, it was set on fire by vandals and destroyed. Steep cliffs loom up on the right with Cabot Tower perched at the top, and there are more steps up as the path makes its way across the bare rocks.

13 min At the fork in the trail, ignore the short left spur and take the right path down the gravel steps. The Narrows are now on the left and the harbour is ahead. Continue down the banks of steps which are interspersed with sections of rough gravel and rock path.

20 min Walk up the bank of rough timber steps on the edge of the cliff. Proceed along the narrow path up and down several banks of steps. There are rails along the banks of steps, but none along the narrow gravel path, even where the sides fall away steeply.

25 min Pass across the timber ledge where the churning sea resonates up a long cleft in the rocks. The banks of steps continue and the very narrow path continues around the cliffs.

30 min Continue over the narrowest ledge of the trail; there is a very welcome chain handrail embedded in the cliff face on the right, and a-not-so-very-welcome vertical drop on the left. After the narrow ledge, approach the Second World War fortifications. With the Narrows to your back, the sheltered harbour opens out ahead and the city stretches up the hill beyond.

32 min Pass Fort Chain Rock in the harbour and the two gun batteries. Chain Rock was used to attach booms, chains and nets to block the harbour entrance during attacks. Records indicate the use of a chain as early as 1770; it was lowered and raised by a capstan located on Pancake Rock on the south side of the Narrows. Past the second fortification, the trail continues towards the small clapboard houses of The Battery, named after the Waldegrave Battery, which was built on this site in 1798.

37 min Cross the deck of a small white house with green trim. The trail leaves the park and squeezes through the narrow lane between the colourful, ramshackle fishermen's houses.

40 min About 300 m/yd down the lane, turn right into a narrow alley opposite the fire hydrant. A red handrail on the right assists the climb up the steps between the houses.

45 min The alley comes out onto a lane. Turn right, walk to the end and take the path above the houses on the right. Ignore the steps going down to the houses. Just after the last steps, the path forks into two trodden trails. Take the left one up the hill towards the chimney of the Queen's Battery. Continue along the trodden grass path, pass some house foundations on the right and clamber up the hill. The path is badly defined as it heads towards a scree slope and a trickling stream. There is no obvious point where you enter back into the park. Continue steeply over the top edge of a red sandstone cliff and join a thin, trodden path from the back of the Visitor Centre on the left. Turn right and continue up the hill towards the stone barrack of Queen's Battery.

55 min At Queen's Battery the cannons point across the Narrows. Cross the gravel road by the barrack (turn left for the Visitor Centre) and take the gravel path between the second bank of canons and the open grassy parade ground where the Tattoo takes place. Follow the gravel path up the grassy hill towards Cabot Tower.

I hr 5 min Arrive at Cabot Tower. Outside there are several exhibit boards about St. John's. Inside, browse through the souvenir/bookshop, see the exhibit about Marconi and watch the operator of the amateur radio station. If the weather is not too blustery, climb out onto the roof and take in the magnificent view of the city and coastline. Outside the tower stands the noonday gun, the last active remnant of signalling on Signal Hill.

I hr 10 min Back at the parking lot.

CAPE SPEAR NATIONAL HISTORIC SITE

Cape Spear is a beautiful, windy promontory located 15 km (9 mi) from downtown St. John's and has the added distinction of being the most easterly point in North America. On sunny days from late June to mid-August, it is a good spot for whale watching. Although this is the main whale watching season, whales can be seen from the cape throughout most of the year. From March or April until mid-July, icebergs are routinely sighted off its rocky shore, and in the fall it is the place to watch enormous waves crashing over the rocks. The site's claim to historical fame is supported by the old lighthouse, which has been operational since 1835. Below it stands the present-day automated light tower (not open to the public), a small house (the lighthouse keeper's residence after the dwelling in the old lighthouse was vacated in 1955), a tiny interpretive centre (formerly the assistant lighthouse keeper's house), and Second World War fortifications constructed in defence of St. John's Harbour. Behind the lighthouse a long trail runs around the North Head and along the coastline to Maddox Cove. There are also a couple of shorter trails from the car park to the Most Easterly Point in North America and around the Second World War fortifications.

History: In 1832 representative government was granted to Newfoundland. The first public project the new government legislated was the building of more lighthouses around the island's rugged coastline in order to improve coastal navigation. Although the British military had operated a light at Fort Amherst (at the entrance to St. John's Harbour) since 1810, the first of the new publicly built lighthouses was to be constructed at Cape Spear to aid navigation to St. John's. Construction of the lighthouse began in late 1834 on a promontory 75 metres above sea level, overlooking the approaches to St. John's.

The plans for the lighthouse have disappeared (probably lost in the Great Fire of 1892), but the original structure consisted of a two-storey, square wooden residence surrounding a central stone core. A lighting apparatus was mounted at the top of the tower on a seven-sided metal frame which was made to slowly rotate by a weight-operated clockwork mechanism. This produced a 17-second flash of white light followed by 43 seconds of darkness. Seven parabolic reflectors collected and reflected the light rays from Argand lamps (named after their Swiss inventor). These lamps were similar to those found in Canadian homes in the 19th century with the exception that they had a circular hollow wick rather than a flat one. This improved the air flow, helped prevent deposits of soot on the inside of the glass chimneys and produced a brighter light.

The lighting apparatus was brought to Newfoundland from a Scottish lighthouse at Inchkeith, near Edinburgh. It was shipped to Newfoundland in the spring of 1836 and put into operation on September 1 of the same year. At first the lighting fuel was whale oil, but due to cost and availability it was later changed to seal oil. By 1874 the lamps were converted to kerosene, and in 1912 the old system of reflectors became obsolete and a new diatropic system using a series of highly polished prisms was installed. Acetylene gas was introduced in 1916 and electricity in 1930.

After Newfoundland's entry into Confederation in 1949, all lighthouses fell under the jurisdiction of the federal Department of Transport and a programme of modernization was begun. A new tower was built lower down the hill, the diatropic system was moved, a new lighthouse keeper's residence was constructed, and the old lighthouse was abandoned in 1955.

The first lighthouse keeper, Emanuel Warre, tended the light from 1836 until his death in 1846. At that time James Cantwell, a St. John's Harbour pilot, was appointed keeper, supposedly through the influence of a Dutch prince whose ship he had guided into the harbour. The Cantwell family continue to tend the light today.

The lighthouse keeper occupied a position of importance and prestige in 19th-century Newfoundland communities. In a society that was to remain largely cashless for another century, his annual salary of 95 pounds sterling, plus a fuel allowance of 15 pounds (later raised to 28 pounds) and extra pay for work not considered part of the regular duties, brought him up to the level of middle-range civil servants. In addition, the need to keep records made literacy a prerequisite for the job and set the keeper and his family apart from most of their neighbours.

The lighthouse keeper was obliged to pay an assistant from his own annual salary, although in many cases this role was played by his son or wife, which meant the salary remained as part of the family income. A son who was adequately qualified could inherit the position of head keeper upon his father's death, and was more likely to do so than any equally qualified widow. In Europe and the

United States it was not unheard of to have a female lighthouse keeper, but when the wife of the lighthouse keeper at Pointe Riche applied to continue tending the light after her husband's death, she was rejected on grounds that the work was too heavy for a woman.

The light operated during the night in accordance with the British lighthouse procedure under which Newfoundland lighthouses were run. The keeper's responsibilities included winding the clockwork rotary mechanism every three hours, ensuring that the wicks were not smoking, checking that there was sufficient oil in the lamps and making sure the speed of rotation did not alter. If repairs could not be immediately implemented, the keeper and his assistant were obliged to turn the light by hand. And the job did not end with daylight. Regular daily activities included polishing the reflectors, cleaning the windows of the tower, keeping a regular watch and maintaining the building. Maintenance of the building at Cape Spear was very time consuming because of the damp conditions. It continues to be a problem today, with the entire structure needing repainting every two years. The keeper was also responsible for recording the temperature, weather conditions, tides, and the times of sunrise and sunset. When a flag staff was added in 1839, it was the lighthouse keeper's job to notify Signal Hill by flag code of ships coming up the coast.

Before the 1860s there was no road from the lighthouse to St. John's, so the keeper and his family were effectively isolated from the outside world. Provisions and supplies were brought in by boat to one of the nearby coves and at first rolled up the hill in barrels, and in time carted, to the lighthouse. Stores were kept originally in the main building, but a number of small storehouses were later constructed for the storage of oil and general supplies. The family had what is now referred to as a small sustenance garden where they grew potatoes, turnips and cabbage for year-round use. They may have also grown hops for making bread and probably had a few animals at pasture.

In 1839 the signal staff was erected outside the building and the keeper took on the signalling duties that were a part of the St. John's Code of Signals relayed through the signal station on Signal Hill. In 1878 a steam-powered fog alarm was built. Water for the "Booth trumpet," as it was called, had to be collected from ditches, and the anthracite coal that was burned to produce the steam had to be brought in by boat. A second boiler was installed in 1882, and in 1896 another system was added in response to complaints that the alarm was inaudible from the southern approaches to the harbour. In 1910 a new alarm was installed.

During the Second World War, Newfoundland became a base for naval and air patrols across the Atlantic, and St. John's was designated an advance naval port and ordered to build fortifications. Heavy coastal artillery was installed to protect the approaches to the harbour. Smaller guns were positioned at Fort Amherst and Fort Chain Rock at the harbour mouth. The construction of mess halls, barracks and administration buildings began in July 1941. By the end of September the guns were in place, and by February 1942 they were in service. Two gun emplacements were constructed on the tip of the cape along with a series of underground passages connecting the gun sites to magazines and equipment rooms. Although these guns had a range of nearly 13 kilometres and a calibre of 10 inches, they had been built in 1895/96 and were not modern weapons. "A" Troop of the 103rd Coast Defence Battery of the Royal Canadian Artillery arrived to man the guns, and a small detachment of American troops was sent to man the anti-aircraft searchlight set up on the bluff above them. There were many submarine attacks in nearby waters, but Fort Cape Spear, as it came to be known, never saw action. After the war, the disappearing carriages that had enabled the guns to be lowered behind the protecting parapet for loading and maintenance were disassembled and removed. However, the cost of removing the 30-ton gun barrels was higher than their salvage value, so they have remained.

In 1962 the lighthouse was saved from demolition and declared of national historic importance. In the late 1970s Parks Canada (now the Canadian Parks Service) began restoration work on Newfoundland's oldest surviving lighthouse. Today we see it how it looked in 1839 during the early years of Emanuel Warre's service, before major architectural changes were made — and before it was painted red and white in 1841, after the British Admiralty complained that it was difficult to see against the snow. During the restoration, any additions and changes were removed with great care, and surprising discoveries were made as the original structure began to appear. The most interesting find was the presence of false windows which had been installed in an attempt to maintain a symmetry in the external appearance of the residential structure without creating the problem of heat loss that comes with real windows. Layers of wallpaper and newspaper were removed and carefully matched, and period pieces of furniture were brought in to complement the decor. In the summer of 1982 the lighthouse was ready for its first visitors, although the site was officially opened in June 1983 by the Prince and Princess of Wales.

How to Get There:

- From St. John's drive west along Water Street and leave the shopping area. Pass the container depot on the left, and go under the overpass to the first set of lights (this is a new junction and at the time of writing there were no signposts).
- Turn left across the bridge, and at the junction go straight up Blackhead Road (a signpost at the junction indicates Cape Spear, straight, and Fort Amherst, left). Stay on Blackhead Road, ignoring all turnings into the subdivision, and then pass into the wooded countryside. Approximately 7 km (4.2 mi) after the bridge, pass the turning on the right (signposted Maddox Cove and Petty Harbour, right, Cape Spear and Blackhead, straight).
- For the National Historic Site continue straight for a further 7 km (4.2 mi) to the parking lot at Cape Spear. (If you want to leave a second car at Maddox Cove so as to walk the Coastal trail one way, turn right and continue for 4 km [2.4 mi] until the road reaches the sea at Maddox Cove. There is no sign indicating you are at Maddox Cove. As the road turns right at the waterfront, turn left onto the small bridge. Park by the gravel track on the right by a house as the road bends to the left).

Useful Information:

Cape Spear National Historic Site:
  Tel: (709) 772-4862 or 772-5367

The restored lighthouse and Visitor Centre are open daily from early June to Labour Day, 10:00-18:00 (they are sometimes open for a few hours daily until mid-October, so check with the park).

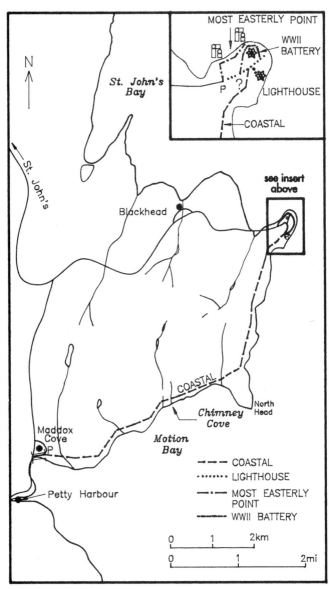

Map 27: CAPE SPEAR NATIONAL HISTORIC SITE

RESTORED LIGHTHOUSE
(map 27)

Time: 7 min
Distance: 500 m/yd
one way
Difficulty: moderate;
good for children

Condition: maintained;
steps uphill and rocky
path

Summary of Trail:

This short trail leads from the parking lot to the old lighthouse on the rock bluff. There are steps up the hill and a few benches for the weary as far as the Visitor Centre. The short remaining section up to the lighthouse has been left as a rough trail, just as it was in the 1830s. The windy cape is hilly, rocky and largely bare of trees, but the view of the coastline is tremendous. The lighthouse is open to the public during the summer season. Inside the building, interpreters show you around the residence of the lighthouse keeper, which is preserved as it was in the days of the first keeper, Emanuel Warre.

How to Get There:

- See page 263 for directions to the site.

Trail Directions:

From the parking lot, walk up the step towards the modern light station, Visitor Centre and restored lighthouse.

7 min Pass the Visitor Centre and take the rough path uphill to the lighthouse.

12 min At the restored lighthouse, visit the home of the lighthouse keeper.

MOST EASTERLY POINT IN NORTH AMERICA
(map 27)

Time: 10 min

Distance: 750 m/yd loop

Difficulty: easy; good for children

Condition: maintained; paved path and gravel path; boardwalk

Summary of Trail:

From the parking lot, the trail continues below the viewpoint along the grassy terrace before the rocks. There is no barrier, but please do not walk out on the rocks. The sea is very unpredictable and dangerous. Follow the boardwalk to the second viewing area and then return to the parking lot. It is usually windy at Cape Spear, but the view is well worth the cold ears.

How to Get There:

- See page 263 for directions to the site.

Trail Directions:

From the parking lot, take the paved path left of the steps to the lighthouse (signposted Most Easterly Point in North America and WW II Gun Battery). Walk towards the sea and enjoy the beautiful view. On the right, small batteries and observation posts peer out of the hill. These are reminders of Cape Spear's important wartime function in the defence of St. John's.

5 min Continue to the viewing point at the end of the paved path and look out over St. John's Bay (ignore the gravel path on the right before the viewing point). Return to the gravel path you previously ignored and turn towards the huge gun barrels ahead. Turn left immediately and follow the trail as it leads below the first viewing platform. Stay away from the rocks. Take the boardwalk to the second viewing platform (with bench) and enjoy more of the spectacular scenery. From this point the path loops inland, passes up a few steps and ends at the parking lot.

10 min Back at the parking lot.

WORLD WAR II BATTERY
AND RESTORED LIGHTHOUSE
(map 27)

Time: 25 min
Distance: 1.5 km (.9 mi) loop
Difficulty: moderate; good for older children

Condition: maintained; steps uphill and rough trail

Summary of Trail:

Sharing the same first section as the trail to the Most Easterly Point, this trail turns off into the World War II Battery at the tip of the cape. The hillside is scarred with rooms and underground passages built in the defence of St. John's. The trail passes through the battery and continues across the bare rocks below the present light station. Several banks of steep steps lead up the cliffs to emerge near the Visitor Centre. From there the trail joins the short Restored Lighthouse trail, which climbs uphill from the parking lot to the lighthouse.

How to Get There:
- See page 263 for directions to the site.

Trail Directions:

Start as for the Most Easterly Point and turn right before the first viewing point.

5 min Follow the gravel path through the battery (ignore the path on the left for the Most Easterly Point). Pick up the trail on the far side (signposted for the Visitor Centre and 1835 Lighthouse) and continue over the rocks below the light station. Climb up the banks of steps and emerge onto the gravel road near the Visitor Centre (there is a signpost indicating the WW II Gun Battery back from where you came).

15 min Once at the top of the stairs, turn left to the Visitor Centre and continue up the hill to the restored lighthouse.

18 min Visit the restored lighthouse. Built in 1834/35 and in service since 1836, this is Newfoundland's oldest surviving lighthouse. During the summer it is open to the public.

25 min Back at the parking lot.

COASTAL TRAIL
(map 27)

Time: 3 hr 20 min
Distance: 9.5 km (5.7 mi) one way
Difficulty: moderate; good for older children

Condition: not maintained; very wet in parts; badly defined in parts; uneven, with rocks and boulders

Summary of Trail:

Starting at the gravel road below the restored lighthouse, the first section of the trail cuts through low vegetation and meanders around outcrops of rocks.

Cutting across the bog at the neck of North Head, the trail becomes difficult to follow and very wet. It continues close to the edge of the low cliffs on the west side of the head. The terrain here is open and boggy. Once out of the bog, the trail passes between coastal forests and open terraces with streams and rocks. In the forest there are some steep gullies down which you have to scramble. The trail is overgrown and wet, and hard to follow in parts, although by keeping parallel with the coast you soon pick it up again to Maddox Cove. Although the trail is difficult and takes time, the stunning coastline makes it worthwhile. Allow a full day for the return trip. In late winter and early summer, polar bears have been coming off the pack ice in this area. They are extremely dangerous, so please check with the park for any sightings.

How to Get There:
- See page 263 for directions to the site, including where to park if you walk the trail one way only.

Trail Directions:
From the parking lot, take the long bank of steps up to the Visitor Centre. Once past the buildings, continue along the gravel road that leads below the restored lighthouse.

5 min At the fork, take the left track uphill. The path narrows as it runs along the ridge behind the lighthouse. The sea crashes beneath the cliffs on the left and a bog, reputedly excellent bakeapple-picking ground, fills the low land on the right. Foxes live amongst the rocks and the low cover of blueberries, junipers, dwarf birches and alders. The uneven path has a few wet patches and keeps dividing. Stay on the ridge and continue towards the head.

55 min The path runs down the side of the ridge through the trees.

58 min Scramble down a short rocky section and proceed close to the top edge of the steep cliffs that drop to a small cove below.

I hr Pass a second cove on the left as the path clips the top of the vertical cliffs, plummeting to the water. The trail then bears right, cutting across the lower ground in front of the North Head. Continue across the open grassy bog towards the sea on the west (right) side of the head. The sphagnum moss makes this section very wet and the trail hard to see.

I hr 10 min The trail reaches the sea, crosses a small stream and continues over the grassy, treeless bog close to the edge of the low cliffs. The ground is level, but rocks and small boulders protrude everywhere out of the bog, and several small streams run off into the sea.

I hr 20 min Cross the small stream and pass a solitary cluster of spruce trees along the edge of the cliffs on the left. The trail continues to be rocky.

I hr 26 min A stream runs into a small cove.

I hr 30 min Pass Chimney Cove.

I hr 35 min The path passes between two huge boulders.

I hr 37 min Cross two streams and continue downhill through low vegetation and clumps of spruce trees. Cross a wide stream by a small cabin. The trail is wet in places; it pushes through tight shrubbery and then stumbles into a grove of trees before turning away from the coast. The surface is uneven with numerous rocks and wet patches.

I hr 50 min The path ends abruptly at the rocky beach. Cross the stream, walk a few metres across the rocks and scramble back up onto the terrace well before the two huge boulders on the beach. The trail resumes along the terrace and passes a huge boulder.

2 hr 7 min The path again clips the top of the steep cliffs where a stream plunges to a small cove. Ignore any tracks going off to the left and continue uphill. Once more, the path comes very close to the steep edge and it continues to be very wet.

2 hr 12 min Scramble steeply downhill through the trees, over the rocks and across a stream, and continue sharply down the rocks.

2 hr 22 min Come out of the trees and continue along the more open trail. It is wet and runs very close to the cliff edge before continuing down another steep rocky section through trees.

2 hr 37 min Emerge out of the trees and continue over the rocks and puddles. Cross a stream.

2 hr 40 min You should be able to see Petty Harbour ahead (Maddox Cove only has a few houses and it is still hidden by the headland).

2 hr 48 min Go back into the trees where the trail is very wet and uneven.

2 hr 55 min Scramble down to a stream.

2 hr 58 min Pass close to the back of the house that appears through the trees on the right; the path turns left by a power post. Very wet patches.

3 hr 8 min There is a rail on the left, followed by second, longer railing. A very wet, open grassy section leads into an old cart track where at last there is a dry, flat surface. A track from the house joins from the right.

3 hr 18 min Pass another house on the left and walk out onto the gravel track.

3 hr 20 min The trail ends on the side road at Maddox Cove.

CASTLE HILL NATIONAL HISTORIC SITE

Castle Hill is situated on the western side of the Avalon Peninsula, only minutes from the ferry terminal at Argentia and less than a 90-minute drive from St. John's. The site encompasses the ruins of fortifications built at the end of the 17th century in defence of the French colony and fishery at Plaisance (now called Placentia). From its hilltop vantage the fort commands beautiful views over the gut (the narrow mouth), the roadstead (the harbour approaches), the large stone beach (called the Great Beach, this is where most colonists first settled) on which the town of Placentia has grown up, the surrounding hills and distant Placentia Bay. The French chose the site for their colony with foresight. The harbour was very deep, readily defensible, ice-free year round and sheltered from storms by the surrounding hills (in contrast to the British capital at St. John's, which was extremely windy and where the harbour froze regularly). In addition, Plaisance was on the route between French territories in Quebec, Acadia and France, was close to extensive fishing grounds and had a large stone beach suitable for drying fish. Today there is a Visitor Centre on the hill and short trails between the fortifications which demonstrate the strategic value of the location. Originally built for a military purpose, the beauty of the setting can today be enjoyed by visitors.

History: By the mid-17th century French, Spanish, Portuguese and Basque fishermen hooked, split and stored their catches of cod directly from their vessels before returning to Europe. They had very little need for the ports of Newfoundland. The English, however, were unable to pursue this kind of "bank" or "green" fishery because of the scarce supply of salt. They therefore developed a land-based or "dry" fishery, which required stone beaches for the drying of their catches.

The Newfoundland fishery was originally seasonal, with vessels arriving in mid-June and remaining until mid-September. But by 1650, approximately 350 English families were well established on the Avalon Peninsula and St. John's was evolving into the largest centre for the developing fishery. In contrast, the French fishery was largely in the hands of private shipowners who had not attempted to establish permanent settlements on the island. In 1643, with the ascension of Louis XIV to the French throne, France announced its intention to compete with the British fishing industry. In the pursuance of this policy, Plaisance was chosen in 1660 to be the site for the first royal colony.

The English and French had different strategies for the defence of their respective colonies. England relied on naval power to protect its territories and avoided investing in land fortifications. France, on the other hand, built strong land defences to protect its colonies. However, Plaisance got off to a faltering start, and 30 years were to pass before the colony was adequately defended. The first two governors, appointed in 1655 and 1660, never even reached their new seat of office because of the loud protests of merchants who until then had regulated the fishery to their own liking and did not like the idea of government interference. The third governor, appointed in 1662, did manage to reach Plaisance with a handful of settlers, but he was murdered soon afterwards in a garrison rebellion. A year later, in 1663, 50 more families arrived, but the colony continued to struggle. The fourth governor was recalled in 1666 because of charges of corruption, and it was not until the fifth and sixth governors (La Palme in 1667, and La Pioppe in 1670-85) that the colony achieved some stability.

The slow growth of the colony was due to the impossible economic position in which the settlers found themselves. In 1671 the population stood at 73 men or heads of households, in 1691 it was still only 83, but by 1710 it reached its peak of 260. Efforts to establish farming, trapping, forestry and animal husbandry all failed, and the settlers found themselves totally dependent on the fishery. The fishery was in turn dominated by the merchants, who supplied equipment and food in exchange for dry fish. This method of barter, called the mercantile system, was meant to benefit both the settlers and the mother country. In its ideal form it was supposed to provide a market for products from the colony while giving French merchants a closed market for manufactured goods that the colonists could not produce themselves. However, in practice it did not work this way because the French royal policy of colonization seems to have been at odds with the mercantile policy. The crown was slow in sending supplies for the settlers and the system heavily favoured the merchants, leaving the colonists impoverished and bitter. Although the colony never became self-sufficient and tensions were constantly high, the fishery was nevertheless very successful. After the English took over Plaisance in 1714, it took them 40 years to build the fishery back up to what it had been in the days of the French.

The building of the fortifications also got off to a slow start. Despite the king's intention to establish a military presence in Newfoundland, supplies and funds were not forthcoming. Before the arrival of the king's representatives, a defence structure of sorts had been erected by the fishermen and the first governors tried to maintain the wooden structure, but by 1686 it was a ruin. For the next ten years Plaisance was an easy target for Dutch buccaneers and English raiding parties. Although some soldiers and weapons were sent from France, there were never sufficient funds to initiate large-scale fortifications, and what was built was privately funded and inadequate. In 1690 war broke out in Europe and Plaisance was attacked twice, once by English freebooters and once by Basque fishermen. Its vulnerability was pitifully obvious. Nearly 30 years after its establishment, the colony was still virtually defenceless.

With the removal of Governor Parat in 1690 on charges of corruption, Plaisance received the first of two governors who put great energy and effort into providing defences for the colony. Louis de Pastour de Costebelle constructed a log palisade around the town on the south side of the gut. It seems that even this flimsy structure was enough to deter freebooters in search of easy prey, for an English raiding party that arrived in October 1690 left without attacking. In 1691, with the arrival of Governor Sieur de Saint-Ovide de Brouillan, Plaisance's first real fort was begun. Fort Louis was built at sea level on the north side of the gut and consisted of a large, earthen-walled enclosure that contained the governor's headquarters, barracks and eventually a stone powder magazine. On its walls, overlooking the roadstead and the gut, were 26 guns.

The energetic de Brouillan did not stop with the construction of Fort Louis. The following year a picket enclosure, christened "Le Gaillardin," meaning the strongpoint, was built atop Gaillardin Mountain to protect the landward approaches to Plaisance, and a battery of four cannons was mounted on the south beach to provide crossfire across the gut. In the autumn of 1693, the new defences were put to the test when five Royal Navy warships entered the harbour. A chain was drawn across the gut and the guns were prepared. For nine days the English bombarded the town and tried to land, but they eventually withdrew without fulfilling their mission. The town had been severely damaged, but with their new defences the French had managed to stave off the attack.

De Brouillan was not satisfied and continued work on the fortifications by beginning the construction of a small masonry fort on the hill overlooking Fort Louis and the outer harbour. The new Fort Royal was a square, stone structure with demi-bastions on each corner and surrounded by low parapets or breastworks. Although it was not completed when the English attacked in the summer of 1694, guns mounted on the hilltop near the new fort prevented the enemy from getting close enough to bombard the town and Fort Louis. By 1697 the entire defence complex was in place, if in a rudimentary form. The picket enclosure of Le Gaillardin was replaced by a small stone structure surrounded by breastworks, detached batteries containing heavy guns were built on the mountain and on the shore below the fort, and another battery was located on the opposite side of the harbour. The network of interlocking defences protected the roadstead and prevented ships from getting close enough to bombard the town, beach, gut and Fort Louis. Although the fortifications were crude by European standards, their location gave them great strength.

With the defence complex secure, the French king ordered d'Iberville to hasten to Newfoundland and destroy all the English outposts on the island.

A ten-year veteran of the king's army, d'Iberville had already made a name for himself because of his attacks against the English in the Hudson Bay area and in New England. Starting from Plaisance, he led his troops across the Avalon Peninsula to Ferryland, south of St. John's, in the autumn of 1696. In Ferryland he joined forces with de Brouillan, who had made his way from Plaisance by sea, and the combined forces set out to capture St. John's. The English settlers took refuge in Fort William in St. John's, but they were unable to withstand a long siege and surrendered to the French on November 30. After destroying St. John's and Fort William, d'Iberville continued his rampage around the English outposts of Conception and Trinity bays. He destroyed all the settlements with the exception of Carbonear Island, where the English settlers held out, and Bonavista, which he had not yet reached before he was ordered by the king to leave Newfoundland and resume attacks on British outposts around Hudson Bay. Disgusted that he had not been allowed to complete the total destruction of the English colonies, d'Iberville left Newfoundland. For their part, the English realized the vulnerability of their position and sent out 2,000 troops and 12 ships to retake St. John's. By the time they arrived, d'Iberville had long gone. The English rebuilt Fort William, and by the time the war ended with the Treaty of Ryswick in the spring of 1697, they had reoccupied all the outposts d'Iberville had destroyed.

With the Treaty of Ryswick, the War of the League of Augsburg (1690-97) was over and there was a temporary lull in hostilities in Newfoundland. Plaisance returned to a state of peace. The fortifications were left to deteriorate, and by 1702, when the War of Spanish Succession brought out the old hostilities between England and France, the defences were once more badly in need of repair. Fortunately for the settlers in Plaisance, a potential attack by the English in 1702 was staved off by the presence of French warships, but with its defences in ruins the colony was once more vulnerable to attack.

In the absence of resources to repair his fortifications, the governor of Plaisance, Daniel Auger de Subercase, used a strong offence as his means of defence. In the summer of 1705, Subercase followed d'Iberville's route overland and once more attacked St. John's from the rear, pre-empting a large-scale attack the English were planning on Plaisance. This time the French were unable to take Fort William, but they destroyed St. John's nevertheless and went on to ransack nearly all the English outposts in Newfoundland.

When the English retaliated in 1708, it soon became evident that they had changed their tactics. Seven warships imposed a naval blockade on Plaisance, causing much distress within the colony. If it were not for one ship that managed to slip through the blockade, the settlers would have been in danger of starvation. With the blockade restricting sea mobility, the colony suffered greatly. The fortifications could not be repaired due to a lack of materials, trade with France was curtailed and conditions became very difficult. The French made another attack on St. John's, in 1709, in an effort to relieve Plaisance, but the English ships remained, and the blockade continued until the war ended in 1713.

With the Treaty of Utrecht, the French ceded Plaisance to the English in exchange for fishing rights elsewhere, and the French colonists left to build a new colony and massive fort at Louisburg on Isle Royale (present-day Cape Breton Island).

The English moved their garrison from St. John's to Plaisance in 1714 and immediately renamed the settlement Placentia. Placentia actually supplanted St. John's in importance for a short time. However, in accordance with the English colonial policy of establishing naval power as opposed to maintaining forts, the defences were allowed to fall into even greater ruin. In the early 1720s, the English were forced to build Fort Frederick on the south side of the gut in order to convince the fishermen of the safety of the harbour. The fort was poorly maintained and was considered to be more of a ploy to satisfy the fishermen than a major defence. In 1740 a garrison was re-established at St. John's and Placentia declined in military importance. By the early 1740s, Fort Frederick and all the other defences were in ruins, and with the start of the War of Austrian Succession the English constructed a new fort on the site of Fort Louis. Like its predecessor, it was quickly destroyed by the undermining action of the sea and the harsh climate.

By the time the Seven Years War erupted in Europe in 1756, the English finally realized the military importance of Fort Royal. With the French capture of St. John's in 1762, the English governor ordered the restoration of Fort Royal and the other hilltop defences. Renamed Castle Graves, the new fort was never tested, and with peace returning in 1763, the rebuilding of the defences was never completed.

Placentia slowly prospered and by the mid-18th century about one-fifth of the total fishing in Newfoundland was based there. However, the garrison was not so lucky. Placentia's decline in military importance meant that the soldiers were often without arms or adequate clothing, and by 1811 the last of the garrison was removed and the fort fell into ruins.

How to Get There:
- Take the Trans-Canada Highway to Route 100 to

Map 28: CASTLE HILL NATIONAL HISTORIC SITE

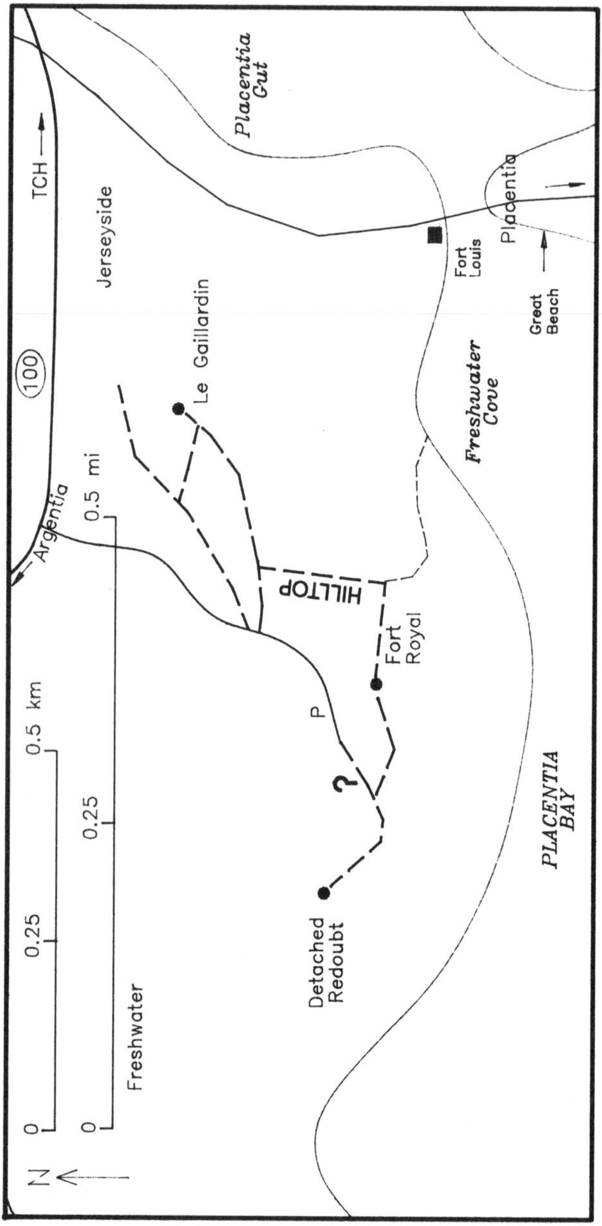

Argentia, Castle Hill and the Nova Scotia Ferry (approximately 80 km [48 mi] from St. John's city limits).

- Take Route 100 and continue for approximately 43 km (26 mi) before turning left for Freshwater, Placentia and Castle Hill (for Nova Scotia ferry continue straight).
- After 2 km (1.2 mi) turn right into Castle Hill National Historic Site and drive 1 km (.6 mi) up the hill to the parking lot by the Visitor Centre.

Useful Information:

Castle Hill National Historic Site: Tel: (709) 227-2401
The Visitor Centre is open daily year round. From mid-June to Labour Day the hours are 08:30-20:00, the rest of the year the hours are 08:30-16:30.

HILLTOP
(map 28)

Time: 45 min
Distance: 2 km
(1.2 mi) loop
Difficulty: moderate;
good for children

Condition: maintained;
gravel path with some
steps

Summary of Trail:

The Hilltop trail is the name I give to the paths that run around the French fortifications at Plaisance.

Today's Castle Hill National Historic Site encompasses the main defences of the colony. The suitability of this hilltop as a base from which to defend the town and harbour is apparent. The view across the harbour and out to Placentia Bay is long and clear.

The trail passes uphill and downhill but can be enjoyed by all levels of hikers.

How to Get There:
- See page 279-281 for directions to the site.

Trail Directions:
After walking around the Visitor Centre and viewing the film about an 18th-century soldier's life in Louisburg (although set in Louisburg, a soldier's life would have been very similar in Plaisance), come out of the building, turn right immediately and follow the path around the back of the building (for the time being ignore the path on the left up the hill). Pass the four plywood figures and follow the steps uphill to the Detached Redoubt.

2 min Sit down on the bench by the low stone walls of the fortifications and take in the breathtaking view across Placentia Bay in one direction, and the Great Beach (where most of the colonists first settled and on which the town of Placentia now stands) in the other. Built in 1697, the Redoubt's function was to prevent the enemy from occupying the hill and thus obtaining access to Fort Royal. The guns in the Redoubt also served to defend L'Anse Lafontaine (present-day Freshwater), which the guns at Fort Royal could not reach. After taking in the view, retrace your steps to the Visitor Centre and take the path uphill on your right (the one you ignored previously).

10 min Cross the small drawbridge across the dry moat and enter the confines of Fort Royal. The first wall served to protect movement around the fort, and the second wall (lower down the hill) was designed to protect the base of the hill. The fort was designed by the French architect Vauban, who, after the French left Plaisance in 1714, was responsible for the massive fortifications at the new colony of Louisburg on Isle Royale (now Cape Breton Island). The Fort Royal walls were constructed of stone and mortar, most of which was shipped from France. The walls were 5.5 metres high, 3-4 metres thick and were surrounded by a dry moat. Construction began in 1693 but was not completed until 1701.

15 min After walking around the fort, take the path signposted to Le Gaillardin and Placentia (directly downhill as you stand on the drawbridge with your back to the fort). Follow the gravel path through the trees and down the short banks of steps.

18 min Take a rest at the bench and enjoy the view of Placentia. After the second bank of steps, turn left (the right fork leads to Placentia but at the time of writing the trail was still under construction) and continue along the gravel path through the trees.

20 min Pass the bench and follow the trail up the hill.

21 min At the junction, turn right.

23 min Walk up the bank of steps and pass the bench. At the junction, turn right. Take the steps across the stone walls of Le Gaillardin.

24 min Le Gaillardin was the first fortification to be constructed on this hill. Built in 1692, it was originally a picket enclosure which was replaced by low stone walls in 1697. After the British took possession of the fortifications, it was abandoned and fell into ruin.

30 min After enjoying the view of Placentia and investigating the small fortifications, return to the last junction and take the right fork downhill through the trees.

37 min The narrow gravel path comes out onto an

overgrown road cutting. Turn left and continue downhill to the fenced enclosure.

40 min Walk around the enclosure and turn left onto the paved road leading to the Visitor Centre (on the right of the enclosure there is a short path back to Le Gaillardin).

43 min Back at the parking lot by the Visitor Centre (from the parking lot there are several paths leading to picnic tables).

PORT AU CHOIX NATIONAL HISTORIC SITE

Port au Choix National Historic Site lies on a small promontory halfway up the west coast of the Northern Peninsula. It is approximately 226 km (136 mi) along the Viking Trail (Route 430) north of the Trans-Canada Highway at Deer Lake. Situated in and around the community of Port au Choix, it sits about a third of the way between Gros Morne National Park and L'Anse aux Meadows National Historic Site at the tip of the peninsula. The park was established in 1974 after a major find of Maritime Archaic Indian burial sites. There is a modest Visitor Centre in the town and the nearby Phillips Garden trail runs over meadows that were at beach level at the time of the Dorset Eskimos. The centre is open from mid-June to Labour Day.

History: The residents of Port au Choix always knew there was something strange about the peninsula where they had built their homes. Every time they went to dig gardens or basements for new houses, they would come up with an assortment of small bones, chiselled stone points and shaped stones. Archaeologist Elmer Harp had done some excavations around the town in the late 1940s and early 1950s, but little did he or the residents know what they were sitting on. In the fall of 1967, when residents began excavating for a new theatre, skeletons began appearing everywhere. Memorial University was called in, and up came Dr. James Tuck to reconnoitre the site. The following year he returned with Dr. William Ritchie and a team of students, and excavations began in earnest. They uncovered three groups of graves totalling 90 skeletons. Radiocarbon dating produced a reading of 2340 BC (plus or minus 110 years). The sites were between 3,200 and 4,300 years old.

So who were these people? Where had they come from? Why were they buried in graves that varied from a few inches to nearly six feet beneath the ground? Why were the heads, grave furnishings and in some instances the overlying earth covered in red ochre? Why were some bodies just a pile of disarticulated bones while others were loosely flexed or, in the case of children, fully extended? Why were there headless skeletons and double internments? What did the killer-whale effigy symbolize? Why could the archaeologists not find any dwellings?

Many of these questions still do not have answers, but very early along in the excavations it was obvious that this site was a major find. As a result of the find, a culture about which little had been previously known was named the Maritime Archaic Indians.

It has been speculated for many years that the first people to settle in North America came across the Bering Strait from Asia by a land bridge. Very little is known about these Paleo or Dawn Age Indians, but it is thought they were forced west towards Europe or east to North America by a huge cap of ice that descended southwards over Asia some 25,000 to 40,000 years ago. These Paleo Indian hunters probably evolved into the people known as Archaic with those living by the sea called Maritime Archaic Indians. They were a hardy, healthy race who spent their time sealing, catching fish, harpooning sea mammals and spearing salmon.

For a few thousand years they flourished along the coasts of Labrador, until about 4,000 years ago when another ancient people, the Paleo Eskimos, began expanding south. Exchanges undoubtedly took place between the two cultures, for it is likely that the Eskimos borrowed the idea of the toggling harpoon from the Archaic Indians, who in turn probably learned about bows and arrows from the Eskimos. At some point during this period of Paleo advancement south, groups of Maritime Archaic Indians found their way across the Strait of Belle Isle into Newfoundland.

In their new home they had many varied food sources, but none were available year round, so the Maritime Archaic people adapted by moving around. At certain times of the year they had to use the skills of Eskimo hunters capturing seals on pack ice; during other seasons they had to adopt the techniques of mainland salmon fishers, trappers and caribou hunters. However, with the sea being the most abundant and easily exploited resource, they seem to have relied mostly on sea mammals, with caribou being of secondary importance.

At least 11 Maritime Archaic sites have been found on the island, but the one at Port au Choix is the most informative and important because of its size, the amount of artefacts yielded, and the cultural reconstruction it has enabled. It was probably a sacred cemetery, with people being brought there for burial some time after they had died. The burial ground (behind the Visitor Centre) is on an ancient beach (six metres above and 60 metres inland from the present sea) facing the sheltered waters of the Back Arm. The numerous tools and household items excavated from the graves have given archaeologists insights into how the Maritime Archaic Indians lived.

Ground and polished slate spears or lances hafted to wooden shafts were used to finish sea mammals caught on the toggling or barbed harpoons. Fish were speared with barbed stone points attached to long shafts, scrapers were used for cleaning skins, awls for making holes in leather, and delicate sewing needles for needlework. Many amulets in the form of bird beaks, animal skulls, claws and teeth point to the Maritime Archaic Indians having some religious beliefs. These were probably related to the speed, cunning and courage of animals. The simple stone killer-whale effigy found next to the skeleton of a young boy was possibly of such significance. It has come to represent the Maritime Archaic tradition. Delicate combs, whistles, shell necklaces and pendants suggest the people were conscious of their personal hygiene and appearance, but the most striking find was the extensive use of red ochre, which again probably had some religious significance. Red ochre was later used by the Beothuk Indians, the last native people of Newfoundland.

The Maritime Archaic Indians probably had Newfoundland to themselves for about 1,000 years, until the Paleo Eskimos followed them across the Strait of Belle Isle about 3,500 years ago. It is known that by 2,000 to 1,500 years ago a later group of Paleo Eskimos called the Dorset were occupying sites in Newfoundland previously used by the Maritime Archaic Indians, who seem to have disappeared. It is not known what happened to this people, for there is no evidence of conflict. Archaeologists now think that they were pushed inland by the arrival of the newcomers. At a time when the weather turned colder, the Dorset were better able to hunt in the sub-arctic conditions, using skills they had brought with them from Labrador. The Maritime Archaic Indians, unable to compete for prized coastal camps, may have withdrawn to hunting grounds in the interior. As yet, no camps have been found in the interior to support this theory.

The Dorset Eskimos adjusted to the conditions in Newfoundland and settled in all the well-chosen places where the Maritime Archaic Indians had lived. Even though the Maritime Archaic people did not live at Port au Choix (to date no living sites have been found), the Dorset did. Several of their sites have been discovered at Port au Choix with excavations of winter and summer dwellings and garbage dumps yielding tools, weapons, household goods and information about diet and culture. The artefacts also show how the Dorset had adapted some of their traditional possessions to suit life in Newfoundland. For example, in the Arctic they used seal-oil lamps to light and heat their dwellings whereas in Newfoundland these lamps are rare. With the luxury of wood on hand, they built fires in stone-lined hearths running down the middle of their houses. Soapstone storage and cooking vessels took on a different shape, and there were variations in their tools. The Newfoundland Dorset seem to have lost much of their complex religious trappings; there are few finely carved artefacts found on the island — in contrast with the wealth found on the mainland.

The Dorset were hunters and gatherers like the Maritime Archaic people and relied heavily on marine resources. Whether it was the warming of the climate, a change in resources or some other factors that caused their decline is unknown. As with the Maritime Archaic Indians, there is no conclusive evidence explaining what happened to them. When the Vikings arrived around 1000 AD, they encountered a people they called Skraelings who may have been the last of the Dorset Eskimos. Perhaps they returned to Labrador, where their traditions continued until 1300 AD. Maybe they ran into competition with inhabitants from the interior, who may have been descendants of the Maritime Archaic Indians. As yet nothing is known except that by 500 AD the Dorset culture in Newfoundland seems to have become extinct.

At Port au Choix, the Maritime Archaic Indian burial sites are located on the grassy area behind the Visitor Centre. Only a plaque marks the ancient beach that had such significance to these people. The Dorset Eskimo sites are located at Phillips Garden and elsewhere along the north side of the Pointe Riche Peninsula. At these sites archaeologists have also uncovered artefacts belonging to an early Paleo Eskimo group called the Groswater, after the site in Labrador where they were first discovered.

Port au Choix is one of the newer sites in the extensive system of historic sites managed by the Canadian Parks Service. These sites do not always crop up in the most convenient and accessible places. In the case of Port au Choix, the modern-day town surrounds the Archaic sites, detracting from the atmosphere, experience and significance of the burial grounds and separating them from the site at Phillips Garden. However, in 1991 a management plan was drawn up on how to develop the site so as to emphasize its significance. This included additional research into primarily the Dorset and Groswater sites, a new Visitor Centre on the road to Pointe Riche, improved and expanded trails, on-site interpretive programmes, the possible development of the Pointe Riche light station story, and the inclusion of the French Shore story. We look forward to these developments.

How to Get There:

- Take Route 430 (the Viking Trail) north from the Trans-Canada Highway at Deer Lake. After 212 km (127 mi) turn left for Port au Choix and Port Saunders. Continue for 14 km (8.5 mi) following the beaver symbols into the community of Port au Choix, and pass along the waterfront.
- At the large, grey FPI International fishplant on the right, turn left into the parking lot in front of a small, octagonal Visitor Centre by the Port au Choix National Historic Park sign.

Useful Information:

Port au Choix National Historic Site: Tel: (709) 861-3522 (summer) or (709) 623-2608 (off season)

The Visitor Centre is open daily from mid-June to Labour Day, 09:00-18:00 (it sometimes stays open until October, but check with the park)

PHILLIPS GARDEN AND POINTE RICHE
(map 29)

Parking lot to Pointe Riche (lighthouse):

Time: 1 hr 10 min   **Condition:** not maintained; undefined in parts; very open

Distance: 4.5 km (2.7 mi) one way

Difficulty: easy; good for children

(add **Time:** 1 hr 10 min; **Distance:** 4.4 km [2.6 mi] for Point Riche to the Visitor Centre, and add **Time:** 30 min, **Distance:** 1.3 km from the Visitor Centre to the parking, if you wish to do the loop)

Map 29: PORT AU CHOIX NATIONAL HISTORIC SITE

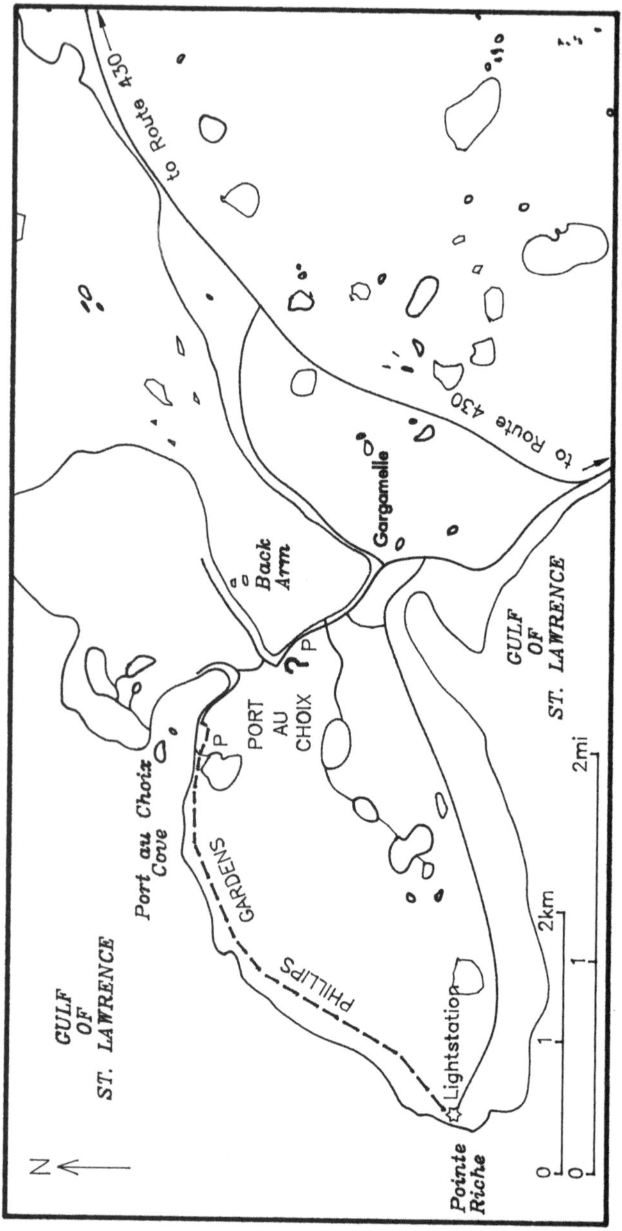

Summary of Trail:

The Phillips Garden trail along the north side of the Port au Choix Peninsula starts 1.5 km (.9 mi) outside the town at Port au Choix Cove. The elusive path first runs across the limestone rocks and open meadows where the remnants of Paleo Eskimo camps have been excavated, and then trudges over dark grey gravel and rocks to the lighthouse at Pointe Riche. From the lighthouse a gravel road runs back to the town and the Visitor Centre, so if you want to experience more of the rugged scenery on this side of the promontory, walk back this way. Then pass the Visitor Centre to complete the loop at the car.

How to Get There:

- See page 291 for directions to the site.
- For the Phillips Garden trail go past the Visitor Centre for 700 m/yd and continue straight to the junction before Port au Choix Cove.
- Turn left and continue for 600 m/yd. Pass a small park boundary sign, and park in a rough gravel clearing below the rock terrace on the left.

Trail Directions:

Take the rough trail (marked by a small hiking symbol) to the brick monument on the rock terrace.

2 min Read the plaque about the Phillips Garden trail on the brick monument. Take the trail along the flat, open coastal terrace.

4 min Cross the small brook. When the path divides, take the right fork through the low vegetation of Labrador tea, potentilla and dwarf spruce. Cross the huge, flat slabs of rocks pitted like a pock-marked face with tiny, shallow holes and depressions filled with water. Don't worry if you lose the path. Continue with the sea on your right and head towards the trail that cuts through the green meadows in the distance. There may be two small posts marking the trail. Ignore any tracks that join from the left.

20 min The path veers sharply left and arrives at a plaque about the Paleo Eskimos at Phillips Garden and the sites that have been discovered there. The clearing behind the plaque used to be the beach some 1,900 to 1,400 years ago. Seventy-one house depressions have been discovered there, and as part of a three-year excavation programme that ended in 1992, Dr. Priscilla Renouf and her team uncovered a Dorset Eskimo dwelling. In addition to this site, Dr. Renouf's team excavated a midden (garbage site) further along the trail and a third small site across the road from the Sea Echo Motel in the town of Port au Choix. After the seal bones found on the site have been examined in the laboratories, it will be possible to determine if the house was a winter or summer dwelling. Apart from bones, the team uncovered assorted projectile points and a sled runner made of whalebone.

35 min On the left, just before the path turns left and scrambles uphill, lies the second site worked on by Dr. Renouf. This midden dates back 2,400-2,100 years and is older than the first. Dr. Renouf's team has shown that the people who used this dump were an earlier group within the Paleo Eskimo tradition who have been called the Groswater. Delicate craftsmanship distinguishes their tools from those of the later Dorset Eskimos. Above the midden, the team has also excavated a few dwellings from the same period.

37 min Proceed along the coastal path past the midden. The path disappears by the coastal limestone rock formations sculpted by the sea. Continue with the sea on the right towards a small flat stack.

42 min Take the boardwalk section, which is followed by three more short boardwalks before the trail disappears yet again.

47 min The beacon and light tower rise up in the distance out of the dark grey gravel and rocks which cover this part of the peninsula. There is very little vegetation and the path is unclear, but keep walking towards the light tower and eventually you will pick up a cart track.

I hr 10 min Arrive at Pointe Riche. The lighthouse is not open to the public. (If you want to make a loop of the trail, take the road from the lighthouse along the south side of the peninsula for 3.7 km [2.2 mi]. Turn left by the Pointe Riche Lighthouse sign and walk to the junction. Turn left and return to the Visitor Centre along the road, and for this section add 1 hr 10 min/4.4 km [2.6 mi]. To complete the loop and return to your car at Port au Choix Cove, continue along the route you drove to the trailhead, adding a further 20 min/1.3 km [.8 mi]).

L'ANSE AUX MEADOWS NATIONAL HISTORIC SITE

You can't go much further north than L'Anse aux Meadows National Historic Site before falling off the tip of Newfoundland. Located 433 km (260 mi) from the Trans-Canada Highway at Deer Lake, the park marks the end of a long drive up Route 430 (the Viking Trail). It is a barren though strangely scenic spot 10 km (6 mi) north of the treeline on the eastern shore of the Strait of Belle Isle, 42 km (25 mi) from the town of St. Anthony, approximately 1,100 km (660 mi) from St. John's and 750 km (450 mi) from the ferry at Channel-Port aux Basques. It is also the only place in North America with incontestable evidence of Viking settlement. Dating back to 1000 AD, this site places the Vikings half a millenium ahead of Columbus in their arrival in North America. After the discovery of this isolated site in 1960, followed by several years of excavations, 80 square kilometres of "Lancey Meadows," as it was locally known, became a National Historic Park (now a National Historic Site). In 1978 the importance of the discovery was reflected by UNESCO's choice to make it the first site on their World Cultural List. From the back of the Visitor Centre, a short trail leads to the site of the archaeological remains of the Norse village and to a fenced enclosure containing three replica longhouses.

History: Bearded warfaring adventurers, sailing across the seas in sleek ships to plunder, pillage and raid — this is probably the definition most of us would give if asked to describe the Vikings. It certainly would have been a true description for the period between the 9th and 11th centuries when the Vikings were blazing a path of destruction from the Baltic to the Mediterranean, but it is not a true description of all Norse people. So what is the difference between Vikings and Norse, and who arrived in L'Anse aux Meadows?

The Norse were the Scandinavian people inhabiting the lands occupied today by Norway, Sweden (the island of Gotland), and Denmark. They were comparatively peaceful farmers and traders for whom land was all-important. When it became scarce, they sailed westwards in search of new homelands, crossing the ocean in heavy, seaworthy merchant vessels called *knarrs*, establishing new settlements and opening up the world of the North Atlantic to trade and commerce. The Norse were an intelligent, energetic and adaptable people. At a time when the English, French and Spanish hardly dared sail beyond sight of land, the Norse had sailed to the Faroes, Iceland and Greenland, conquered a good part of Ireland, invaded Normandy and Sicily, and were the first Europeans to land in North America. They also set up extensive trade routes along the rivers of Russia and traded far into the Byzantine Empire. Apart from their obvious shipbuilding and navigational skills, they left a legacy of literature in the form of the Eddas (a collection of poems) and sagas (prose writings) and their organization of the Duchy of Normandy led to a system of government adopted throughout the Anglo-Saxon world. These are the people who arrived in North America. The Vikings, in turn, were

Norse pirates and freebooters who raided and pillaged solely for their own interest. This marauding minority has given the Norse people an unjust label throughout history, overshadowing many of the extraordinary deeds they accomplished.

Land was not plentiful in the Norse homeland, but it was of great importance. As their own lands became overcrowded, the Norse sailed in search of similar places to settle. With the shipbuilding technology that had developed out of living in sheltered fjords and inlets, they had become skilled shipbuilders and had the means with which to make these journeys. Using the North Atlantic islands as stepping stones across the ocean, the Norse sailed westwards to Iceland and Greenland. From there they sailed to the shores of North America.

The Norse, and especially the Vikings, loved their ships and carved them on stones, wrote poems about them and buried their great men in them. They referred to them by such reverential epithets as "Deer of the Sea," "Wave Walker," "Sea Bird" or "Raven of the Wind." Without doubt the most remarkable relics of the Vikings are their ships. They were light and flexible, had a very shallow draught and were fitted with a keel to make them more stable. This meant the larger ships could be sailed in rough seas without breaking up whereas lighter ships could be sailed or rowed great distances up rivers in pursuit of trading. By running their ships onto the beach, they could land in places where there were no natural harbours, and they could portage the ships and boats from one watercourse to another to avoid waterfalls, rapids, dams and fortifications.

The journeys and explorations of these tough people in their strong, seaworthy vessels are recorded in the sagas that were passed down through history first by the spoken, and later the written, word. The Greenlander's Saga and Eric the Red's Saga tell of accidental landfalls only a few days' sail west of the Norse colonies in Iceland and later of journeys made from Greenland. There are some obvious fictitious incidents, but the descriptions of the countryside, natural resources and local inhabitants seem consistent with fact. Thus in the sagas we hear of the discovery of Vinland.

About 985 AD, after he was exiled from Iceland, Eric the Red sailed west in search of new farmland. Arriving in Greenland, he sailed south to Cape Farewell and west along the edge of the glacier-clad land. He found a gentle and comparatively fertile valley along a fjord which he named after himself. He built a farm for his family and started a successful colony that kept up regular trading with Norway until its demise in the 15th century.

Four years after Eric left Iceland, another sailor, Bjarni Herjolfsson, was blown off course by a storm while voyaging to Greenland. In trying to find his way, he sailed along an unfamiliar coastline where he saw low hills covered in trees. He did not land but undoubtedly had laid eyes on North America. He brought back news of his discovery to Greenland and years later Eric's son, Leif the Lucky, bought Bjarni's aging ship from him and set out to find the new land.

Lief Ericson sailed from Greenland across the Davis Strait, whereupon he sighted a land that is believed to be Baffin Island, which he named Helluland, or the land of flat stones. Next he cruised southwards for two days and nights along what was probably the low forested land of Labrador, which he named Markland, or woodland. From there he sailed on to another land where he and his men landed and built houses in which to overwinter.

The sagas speak of rivers full of salmon, a land covered in high grass and groves of trees. During the frost-free winter the sailors gathered timber and berries. They sailed home the following spring, having named the land Vinland. At least three expeditions returned to Vinland after Ericson's discovery. The most notable was led by Thorfinn Karlsefni, who hoped to form a permanent settlement. He brought three shiploads of people (there were probably in the region of 20-35 people per ship, although other sources quote the size of this expedition as being as large as 150-160 people), including some domestic animals. They settled into the houses left by Ericson and found the land to be as fertile as promised. However, with escalating attacks from the native "skraelings," they were forced to abandon their colony after three years and returned to Greenland.

So was Lief Ericson's Vinland our Newfoundland, or was it some other place? For more than a century, scholars have been arguing the matter. Much of the debate seems to centre on the words for grapes, berries and grazing lands that are mentioned in the sagas. Some scholars argue that the translation has been incorrect and that "vin" refers to berries for wine making (of which there was an abundance in Newfoundland) and not grapes, which do not grow further north than New Brunswick. Others say the word "vin" refers to grasslands, of which again there was plenty around L'Anse aux Meadows. The reference to frost-free winters is also a point of disagreement. Those supporting the Newfoundland site say it is quite possible that the weather was more temperate in Lief's time, while others are not swayed.

In 1960, Helge Ingstad began a systematic search for a Norse colony. Starting at Rhode Island, he worked north along the east coast of the United

States and Canada. He was rewarded for his efforts when at L'Anse aux Meadows (from the French L'Anse aux Meduses, meaning bay of jellyfish) George Decker led him to an ancient marine terrace covered in heather, willows and grass. There, almost level with the heather and grass, he "noted a number of indistinct overgrown elevations in the ground." He had found what he was looking for.

The digging began the following year when Ingstad returned with his colleague and wife, archaeologist Anne Stine, and a team of international experts. Slowly, the remains of one- to two-metre-thick sod walls began to emerge. Then, within the simple rectangular structures, they found several stone hearths and cooking pits. The absence of large stones suggested the houses were built of turf with timbers and a wooden framework to help support the sod construction. Platforms raised above the clay floors appeared to be sleeping platforms and seats. The largest house measured 21 by 17 metres. Artefacts included a bronze pin with a ring through the head (the type the Norse used to pin their capes), a bone needle and a small soapstone spindle whorl, used exclusively by women for spinning wool. Carbon dating placed the settlement at about 1000 AD, the approximate year Lief set sail for Vinland.

The excavators uncovered a total of eight buildings, three of which were large dwellings, the rest probably workshops and a smithy. Each longhouse sheltered several families and was divided into rooms. A smaller room was the residence of the chieftain and his family. The larger rooms were occupied by the remaining families, who cooked on a central fireplace and slept on platforms that ran along the length of the house. As one longhouse could accomodate 20 to 30 people, no more than 60 to 90 individuals would have lived in the settlement, suggesting that the references stating Karlsefni had as many as 160 people in his expedition could be mistaken.

L'Anse aux Meadows was a camp of settlers consisting of sailors, carpenters, blacksmiths, hired hands, serfs, slaves and women, and not Viking raiders. We know from the sagas that Karlsefni brought his wife Gudrid with him as well as four other women. The discovery of a spindle whorl, fragment of bone needle, and small whet stone for sharpening supports this story. The sagas also mention Gudrid giving birth to a son, Snorri, the first European to be born in America. Other items such as a stone oil lamp, cloak pin and bits of woodworking debris bear witness to the simple life the settlers led. Men and women lived and did much of their work in the dark, smoky longhouses, cooking, eating, sleeping and working together to ensure the settlement's survival.

Summer was the season for exploration. As many as two-thirds of the settlers might have left the camp to reconnoitre the coasts and inlets, perhaps travelling as far south as the Gulf of St. Lawrence. During the winter, the settlement concentrated on survival. Games, quarrels, boredom, chores and waiting for a change in the weather so they could send out hunting and fishing parties made up the daily routine. With the break-up of the ice, the settlers were once again free to explore more of the country, stock up with wood, repair boats and make the long voyage home to Greenland.

No grave sites were found at L'Anse aux Meadows, suggesting that either nobody died there or the acid soil has left no remains. There is also speculation that if the settlers were recent converts to Christianity, they may have sent the bones of their dead shipmates to be buried in the sacred ground of the churchyards in Greenland. On the other hand, we know from the sagas that when Lief's brother Thorvald was killed by skraelings, he was buried and not taken back to Greenland.

The smithy at L'Anse aux Meadows is very persuasive evidence of Norse inhabitation of this site, as none of the native peoples were smelting iron in 1000 AD. Over the centuries, of all the native peoples who have lived at the site, only the Norse had the technology and ability to produce iron from bog iron ore. The blacksmiths did not produce any fancy work at the small smithy, only serviceable hardware for the repair of their precious ships. Bog iron, a crude form of iron ore, was dug out from the banks of Black Duck Brook and smelted into sponge iron at the smithy. Impurities were beaten out and the purified metal was taken to the forge to be shaped. It was a difficult and complicated process, and for all the effort it is estimated that only about two kilos of refined iron were produced there.

Life in the settlement was not easy even though resources were plentiful. Groups of settlers came in the summer to stock their boats with wood and berries and returned to Greenland the following spring. According to the sagas, the last group to arrive included Eric the Red's daughter Freydis, who came with two Norwegian brothers, Helgi and Finnbogi. The relationship between the three was not very amiable from the start, and constant frictions culminated in Freydis and her husband slaying the others. Little is known about the Norse expeditions to Vinland after Freydis, apart from one effort in the 12th century and another in the 14th century. The reason for the abandonment of such voyages and settlement is a matter for speculation, but there are indications that the Norse found the skraelings, or native peoples, inhospitable and hostile, and perhaps they decided to leave America to those who had been there before they came.

The scholars continue to discuss and argue whether the site at L'Anse aux Meadows is Vinland, but perhaps the details don't matter. The evidence speaks for itself. Norsemen did come to this northern tip of the island of Newfoundland and they did settle in this, the earliest known European settlement in the Western Hemisphere.

On August 2, 1991, in commemoration of the millenary of the first Norse visit to North America, a lone square sail appeared, on the horizon of Medee Bay. As it approached, there was no fear in the hearts of the onlooking inhabitants of the island. Skippered by a modern-day Norseman, Norwegian Ragnar Thorseth, the *Gaia* slowly edged her way towards the beach. Just as 1,000 years earlier the men on board had strained to see the turf roofs of the longhouses that marked the site of the tiny settlement, so too did this modern-day crew look out in anticipation. Unlike their distant ancestors, they were assured of a warm welcome.

The replica Norse ship took two and a half months to cross the Atlantic. Leaving Bergen in Norway, she followed the original route described in the sagas via the Orkneys, Shetlands, Faroes, Iceland and Greenland before arriving in L'Anse aux Meadows. She is living proof that the Norse had the technology and ability to cross the Atlantic in small, open wooden ships powered by sails and oars. The *Gaia* stayed only a short while before continuing on her journey southwards, but on this beautiful, sunny day her arrival in Vinland was welcomed and applauded by the present-day inhabitants of the island. This time she left of her own volition, and not because of the lack of hospitality.

How to Get There:

- Take Route 430 (the Viking Trail) north from the Trans-Canada at Deer Lake.
- After 403 km (242 mi) turn left onto Route 436 (St. Anthony straight 10 km [6 mi]).
- After 29 km (17 mi) enter the L'Anse aux Meadows National Historic Site.
- Continue for 1 km (.6 mi) then turn left for the Visitor Centre.
- Continue for 1.6 km (1 mi) to the parking lot.

Useful Information:

L'Anse aux Meadows National Historic Site: Tel: (709) 623-2608 or 623-2601

The Visitor Centre is open daily from mid-June to Labour Day, 09:00-20:00 (it may stay open until October, but check with the park)

VIKING VILLAGE
(map 30)

Time: 30 min
Distance: 1.8 km (1.1 mi) loop
Difficulty: easy; good for children

Condition: maintained; boardwalk; gravel and grass

Summary of Trail:

The trail is a short, flat walk from the Visitor Centre to the reconstructed houses and grass-covered mounds of the longhouse. The site looks natural enough, and although the trail and lawns are clipped, feels quite wild and desolate. This place truly is at the edge of the world. In June and July, icebergs drift

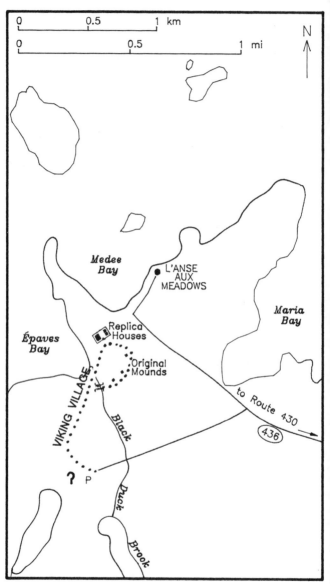

**Map 30: L'ANSE AUX MEADOWS
NATIONAL HISTORIC SITE**

in from the Strait of Belle Isle and mists roll in and out across the treeless tundra and grey sea.

How to Get There:
- See page 305 for directions to the site.

Trail Directions:
After examining the exhibits inside the Visitor Centre and seeing the short film about the excavations, go out through the back door to see the Norse site and the replica sod buildings. Take a look through the telescope before walking down the steps to the wide boardwalk. Plants that grow in this exposed spot are smaller and several weeks behind those further south. Sheep laurel is still not in flower at the end of July whereas the earlier flowering Labrador tea is still in bloom. Bakeapples, whose cousins further south are already producing fruit, are weeks away from fruiting. Spruce grows in low horizontal clumps like the tuckamore on the plateaus of Gros Morne. The path meanders towards the enclosure around the reconstructed village of large turf roofs.

5 min The plaque was unveiled August 2, 1991, in recognition of the achievements of Helge Ingstad and Anne Stine Ingstad in the discovery and excavation of the Norse settlement. The boardwalk ends and a gravel path continues to a fork. Turn right down the steps. The small mound on the right is a smithy or furnace building. Continue to the boardwalk across Black Duck Brook where more grassy mounds define the shapes of the original buildings. Each is marked by a granite marker (in the Visitor Centre pick up a small brochure with a site map and description of the buildings). They include three larger dwellings, one smaller dwelling, two workshops, an outbuilding and the smithy/furnace. Boardwalks and gravel paths are excluded from the area directly around the original site, and modern-day intrusions are kept to a minimum.

10 min After passing all the mounds, turn right at the fork and walk into the fenced enclosure of the replica village with the sloping roof of the longhouse and two smaller buildings like haystacks of fresh grass (left returns to the Visitor Centre). Proceed into the enclosure where a small *faering* or rowboat stands outside the longhouse. Inside, staff answer questions about the Norse as visitors huddle around a central fireplace. Even when the winds blow and the rains lash outside, behind the six-foot-thick walls and under the foot-thick roof it is comfortable and dry.

20 min Leaving the enclosure, take the right fork and return to the Visitor Centre. If it is a nice day, you may want to take the unofficial path around the back of the reconstructed buildings and walk along the coastline to the present-day community of L'Anse aux Meadows — approximately 15 min/ 750 m/yd.

25 min Back at the first fork by the smithy/furnace.
30 min Back at the Visitor Centre.

ODE TO NEWFOUNDLAND

The walking has been done and the writing is finished, and it is time to close the last page. But before doing so I would like to end on a few marvellous quotes about Newfoundland. Each time I read them they bring a smile to my face or a glow to my heart, and on a wintry night when the storm is blowing and the chimney pots rattling, perhaps they will remind you of what this wonderful island is all about.

"In Newfoundland it seems like the rest of Canada is a million miles away."
— Mary Lou Collins, Newfoundland singer

"The purity of the air in Newfoundland is without doubt due to the fact that the people of the outports never open their windows."
— J.G. Millais, observer, *Newfoundland and Its Untrodden Ways*, 1907

"What a charming folk these Newfoundlanders are! In all these dreary days, I have not heard a word of wrath or seen a sign of fear. . . . They are the best-tempered, best-mannered people walking . . . gay, good-hearted and generous; tolerant, temperate, tough, God-fearing."
— A.P. Herbert, a British humorist and MP, *Independent Member*, 1950

"Your average Newfoundlander is water-proof, dust-proof, shock resistant and anti-magnetic. Just as racehorses have been bred — over three or four hundred years — for durability. Your Newfoundlander will come out on top of it all. Endurance is his secret."

— Ray Guy, humorist, *You May Know Them as Sea Urchins, Ma'am*, 1975

"When sun rays crown thy pine-clad hills,
And summer spreads her hand,
When silvern voices tune thy rills,
We love thee smiling land.
We love thee, we love thee,
We love thee smiling land."

— Sir Cavendish Boyle, governor of Newfoundland, written between 1901 and 1904, now used as the first verse of Newfoundland's provincial anthem

BM 1994

BIBLIOGRAPHY

Anon. *Signal Hill - An Illustrated History*. n.p. Newfoundland Historic Trust Co-Operative Association. n.y.

Anon. *Decks Awash*. Vol. 6, no 5. (1977). n.p.

Anon. *Encyclopaedia Britannica*. Toronto. Encyclopaedia Britannica Inc. 1966.

Anon. *Terra Nova National Park Resource Description and Evaluation*. Glovertown, Nfld. Parks Canada. 1984.

Anon. *Tuckamore*. n.p. Environment Canada, Parks Service. 1989, 1990, 1991, 1992.

Anon. *Resource Description and Analysis: Gros Morne National Park, Newfoundland*. Rocky Harbour, Nfld. Canadian Parks Service. 1990.

Anon. *Rocks Adrift: The Geology of Gros Morne National Park*. Ottawa. Ministry of Environment. 1990.

Anon. *Port aux Choix National Historic Park — Management Plan*. Environment Canada, Canadian Parks Service. 1991.

Anon. *Terra Nova Sounds — A Visitor's Guide to Terra Nova National Park*. n.p. Heritage Foundation for Terra Nova National Park (Canadian Parks Service). 1992.

Anon. *Terra Nova Sounds — A Visitor's Guide to Terra Nova National Park*. n.p. Heritage Foundation for Terra Nova National Park (Canadian Parks Service). 1993.

Bangs R. and Roberson P. *Island Gods — Exploring the World's Most Exotic Islands*. Dallas. Taylor. 1991.

Barrett W. MacKay A. and Griffin D. *Atlantic Wildflowers*. Toronto. Oxford University Press. 1984.

Campbell A. *Daily Life at Plaisance*. n.p. (park literature). 1983.

Candow J.E. *Short Story of Signal Hill*. n.p. Canadian Parks Service Atlantic Regional Office. 1989.

Candow J.E. *The Signal Hill Noonday Gun*. n.p. Canadian Parks Service Atlantic Regional Office. 1989.

Candow J.E. "Deadman's Pond. Tradition based on a Legend." *The Evening Telegram* (St. John's). August 28, 1982.

Forsyth A. *Mammals of the Canadian Wild*. Camden East, Ont. Camden House. 1985.

Harris M. *Rare Ambition: The Crosbies of Newfoundland*. Toronto. Viking. 1992.

Ingstad H. *Westward to Vinland: The Discovery of pre-Columbian Norse House-sites in North America*. Toronto. Macmillan. 1969. Trans. Erik J. Friis.

Linderoth W.B. *L'Anse aux Meadows — Get away to Vinland*. Halifax. Canadian Parks Service. n.d.

Lothian W.F. *Terra Nova National Park*. Ottawa. Parks Canada. 1976.

Major K. *Terra Nova National Park, Human History Study*. Ottawa. Parks Canada. 1983.

McGhee R. "The Vikings — They Got Here First But Why Didn't They Stay?" *Canadian Geographic*. Vol.108, no.4. Aug./Sept. 1988. pp.12-21.

McLean S. *Welcome Home*. Toronto. Viking. 1992.

McLeod P. *Gros Morne: A Living Landscape*. St. John's. Breakwater. 1988.

Momatiuk Y. and Eastcott J. *This Marvellous Terrible Place: Images of Newfoundland and Labrador*. Camden East, Ont. Camden House. 1988.

Morgan B. *Random Passage*. St. John's. Breakwater. 1992.

Morris J. *City to City*. Toronto. Macfarlane, Walter & Ross. 1990.

Mowat C. *Outport People*. Toronto. McLelland and Stewart. 1983.

Mowat F. *The Boat Who Wouldn't Float*. Toronto. McLelland and Stewart. 1974.

Mowat F. *The New Founde Lande*. Toronto. McLelland and Stewart. 1989.

Mowat F. *Westviking: The Ancient Norse in Greenland and America*. Boston. Little, Brown. 1965.

Nicol K. *Best Hiking Trails in Western Newfoundland*. St. John's. Breakwater. 1987.

O'Flaherty P. *Come Near At Your Peril: A Visitor's Guide to the Island of Newfoundland*. St. John's. Breakwater. 1992.

Porter H. *Below the Bridge: A Memoir of Growing Up on the Southside*. St. John's. Breakwater. 1979.

Proulx E.A. *The Shipping News*. Don Mills, Ont. Maxwell Macmillan. 1993.

Proulx J. "The Struggle for Newfoundland." n.p., n.v., n.d., n.p.

Rosen M. *Bread Cove Story Area Document*. n.p., n.p. 1978.

Rowe F.W. *A History of Newfoundland and Labrador*. n.p. McGraw-Hill Ryerson. 1980.

Sackett M.M. *"Cape Spear."* Vol. Sept/Oct. 1982. n.p.

Scammell A.R. *My Newfoundland: Stories/Poems/Songs*. Montreal. Harvest House. 1966.

Stephenson M. *Canada's National Parks: A Visitor's Guide*. Scarborough. Prentice-Hall. 1983.

Stevens B. *Parks Canada Publication IAND QS-0323-000-BB-A-1*. n.p. Parks Canada, National and Historic Branch. 1973.

Stevens B. *Parks Canada Publication IAND QS-0325-000-BB-A-1*. n.p. Parks Canada, National and Historic Branch. 1973.

Such P. *Vanished Peoples: The Archaic Dorset & Beothuk People of Newfoundland*. Toronto. NC Press. 1978.

Tuck J.A. *An Archaeological Survey of Terra Nova National Park*. n.p. Parks Canada. 1980.

Tulloch J. "Lighthouse life in the 1830s — Cape Spear." n.p., n.v., n.d.

Tulloch J. "Daily life of the lightkeeper — Cape Spear Lighthouse." *Historic Resources Research Parks Canada*. Vol. July. 1984.

Walsh D. *Terra Nova National Park Trail Guide (The Hiking Trails of Terra Nova National Park)*. n.p. The Heritage Foundation for Terra Nova National Park. 1991.

INDEX

Bold page numbers refer to the trail references.
Map locations as indicated.